VISUAL ALLUSIONS
PICTURES OF PERCEPTION

Nicholas Wade

Department of Psychology
University of Dundee

LAWRENCE ERLBAUM ASSOCIATES, PUBLISHERS
Hove and London (UK)   Hillsdale (USA)

Reprinted 1992

Lawrence Erlbaum Associates Ltd., Publishers
27 Palmeira Mansions
Church Road
Hove
East Sussex, BN3 2FA
U.K.

British Library Cataloguing in Publication Data

Wade, Nicholas
Visual allusions: pictures of perception
1. Visual perception
I. Title
152.14

ISBN 0-86377-130-0 (Hbk)

Typeset by The Laverham Press, Salisbury
Printed by Page Bros, Norwich

CONTENTS

DEDICATED TO

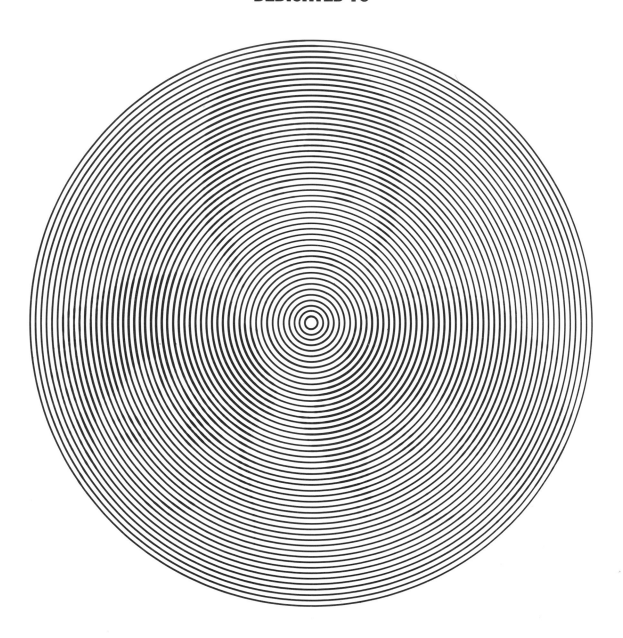

PREFACE

The process of perception unites the visual arts and visual sciences, but this process is examined in radically different ways by each discipline. Artists display their vision while scientists dissect it. Artists use their eyes to look at the world and to look at their work; even if they are representing what is in the mind's eye they need to look at the surface upon which the marks are being made; individuality of vision is encouraged. Scientists tend to use the eyes of others – of the subjects in their experiments – in order to gain some insights into the working of the visual system; they search for consensus and are concerned with universal rather than with idiosyncratic vision.

With these differences of approach it is not surprising that the language used to describe perception in visual art is quite different to that used in visual science. Unfortunately, this encourages the belief that they are independent rather than related endeavours. Artists and scientists often examine the same perceptual phenomena; the one by successive pictorial experiments and the other by formal laboratory procedures. This phenomenal commonality has been particularly apparent in a recent offshoot of geometrical abstraction that is called op art, and I tried in an earlier book (*The art and science of visual illusions*) to bridge the gulf of jargon that separates a common enterprise of furthering our understanding of seeing. In order to do this I used the verbal language of the scientist and the graphic language of the artist. That is, the phenomena manipulated in op art were dissected conceptually and illustrated graphically.

This book is not about visual illusions but about visual allusions. The distinction between them is more fundamental than a single letter. A visual illusion occurs when a genuine misjudgement is made: the moon appears to move when clouds pass by it; lines that are straight appear curved because of others intersecting them; shapes that are the same size appear unequal because of the patterns surrounding them. In all these examples the perception is unitary and compelling, but it does not correspond to the way the world would be described physically. If we have to *behave* with respect to our illusory perception our behaviour would be inappropriate. A visual allusion, on the other hand, involves the perception of at least two aspects of the world simultaneously. Pictures are the most common

visual allusions that we are exposed to: they are seen simultaneously as flat surfaces and as representations of other things. However, we rarely behave inappropriately to pictures; we treat them as what they are, marks on a surface; we do not try to reach for the pictured objects, although we do respond internally to what they represent. There is yet another type of visual allusion in which the marks can be interpreted in more than one way; this aspect is most closely akin to literary allusion. Like literary allusions, the alternative interpretations can be made difficult to discern. My initial interest was confined to such visual allusions – pictures in which an indistinct photographic image is embedded in a clearly defined graphic design – and illustrations displaying them are to be found in Chapter Four.

As with the earlier book, this one was largely illustrated before it was written, and I have tried to develop parallel arguments in the pictures and in the text. To this end, the book can be read through the pictures and their captions as well as the text. When writing the text to accompany the illustrations I had to confront broader issues that are implicit both in photography and in other pictorial representations of space. How does the represented space relate to the three-dimensional environment? Why have styles of representing space gone through abrupt changes in the history of picture-making? How does the process of perceptual representation in the picture-maker interact with that of graphical representation? What happens when we look at pictures representing objects in space? These questions are addressed in Chapters One and Two. In the course of thinking about these issues I found that I was re-examining my ideas about perception as well as those about pictures. Visual art is concerned with representing on a flat surface states that exist within the artist – what they see or think. Visual science is trying to plumb these internal states. Moreover, the subject matter of visual science shares with visual art an overriding concern with the two-dimensional: the science of perception is essentially a science of pictures, and theories about pictorial space in art have had many subtle influences on theories of vision. To be sure, the pictures presented in visual science are simple rather than sophisticated and they are usually displayed on a screen or a computer monitor, but the stimuli used for experiments in vision are overwhelmingly two-dimensional. It is my belief that visual science is setting itself an unnecessarily difficult task in trying to understand picture perception, because it is likely to be a more complex problem than understanding the perception of objects in three-dimensional space.

Seeing and thinking are themselves representational processes, but they are bound by the characteristics of the world in which they occur. We all live in a three-dimensional world and we perceive it accurately enough to move around in it successfully, and to carry out the other activities essential for survival. One of these other activities is picture-making, and this seems to satisfy a universal human appetite: we all make pictures, but some people make more acceptable ones than others. The pictures we make can be either spatialised, as in representations of objects, or stylised, as in written script. These descriptive terms are used for convenience as the contrast between them is not exact: representational pictures follow some stylised conventions, and written script is, obviously, spatially extended.

This book is not restricted to fine art (although it will make constant references to movements that have occurred within it). Rather, it is about the processes that are involved in the production and perception of a wider range of pictorial images. The illustrations are of both spatialised and stylised pictures, and one of my concerns is with the relationship between them. When I started drawing the book, there were only examples of the former – of graphic designs and their combination with photographic images. I became increasingly interested in letter and word shapes, and now Chapter Three is devoted specifically to them. Moreover, I have taken as my graphical starting point in Chapter One a manifesto painting by René Magritte in which the relationship between pictorial images of objects and words describing them are set in conflict: Magritte painted a curved briar pipe and wrote beneath it "This is not a pipe". I have not reproduced Magritte's painting, but I have produced a similar picture of my own. I even took a print of Magritte's painting into a tobacconists in order to purchase a curved briar pipe that matched its shape! Having an object rather than a picture of one allowed me to ask some simple graphical questions about representations of objects: the object can be photographed from different viewpoints, and the resulting photographic images can themselves be manipulated.

The illustrations in this book are drawings, photo-

graphs and combinations of the two, and the relationship between photography and vision is discussed in some detail in Chapter Two. At the outset my interest was with extending to photography the earlier approach adopted with op art, particularly to some of the darkroom manipulations that can be made of photographic images. There is almost as much latitude for making pictures with light as there is with paint, and descriptions of high-contrast photographic techniques are given in the book. Some readers might wish to experiment with these techniques in order to create their own photographic images, and so the methods used to produce the illustrations are described. There are a few references to photographic procedures in the body of the text, but the detailed coverage is given in two Appendices. Appendix 1 deals with photographic darkroom techniques generally and concentrates on the use of high-contrast film to reduce continuous-tone photographic images to two-tone black and white. The ways in which such simplified photographic images can be mixed and manipulated are described. Appendix 2 is concerned with the combination of graphic and photographic images. The graphic images can be created by drawing, by using texture screens or by photographing suitable textures that occur in the environment. Their combination with photographic images is mediated by high-contrast film, and an example of the stages through which the components pass in order to create a photo–graphic image is shown.

The term *image* is used extensively in visual art and visual science, although its application has often been so catholic as to be counter-productive. Images proliferate in our environment and in our language. One of the attractions of the term is its appeal to the spatial dimension both in pictures and in their internal representations, as well as in describing them verbally. However, there is no consensus concerning the definition of an image; in fact, it is rarely accorded this lofty status – its meaning is treated as self-evident. Scientists use it in quite different ways to artists. Indeed, there is a rapidly expanding area in visual science that is variously called image interpretation, image analysis, image processing or image understanding. These are all concerned with investigating ways in which machines can be designed to do something similar to seeing in humans; they are usually computers programmed to extract information about the world derived from the patterns of light captured by a camera. Two-dimensional representations of three-dimensional objects are analysed in order to retrieve the three-dimensional features of the objects. Such image analysis is often related to the initial stage in vision where a *retinal* image is formed in the eye. Thus, vision in humans and image processing in machines is considered to proceed from the analysis of two-dimensional images formed either on the retina or in a camera. I do not think that human vision (or that in other species) starts from a single time-frozen projection of the world.

This preoccupation with the retinal image reflects a confusion between the optical projection on to a surface and the biological processes that are initiated by light. In order to make these distinctions more explicit, a model of perception that involves a sequence of imaging stages is developed in Chapter One; the term *image* is used repeatedly, but always with some qualification, as in *retinal* image, *visual* image and *mental* image. *Images* in art refer, in the first instance, to the marks made on a surface. I call this the *pictorial* image. The term *image* is also used to convey the impact that the pictorial image has on the viewer: this impact can refer to its allusory three-dimensionality (which I refer to as the *graphical* image) or to more complex symbolic allusions to the human condition. I will say quite a lot about the former and virtually nothing about the latter.

The model involves only a few levels and it was developed to assist in thinking about the perception of space and the objects in it, including pictures. The more I thought about these imaging levels in perception, their links with artistic styles of representing space became more closely forged. It seemed reasonable to argue that picture-making has drawn differentially upon these imaging levels, with some of its earliest manifestations (like cave painting) reflecting the representation of the mental image stage in perception, and later ones (like linear perspective) reflecting a preoccupation with the optical image. Pre-Renaissance painting can be related to the visual image, whereas much of 20th century abstraction displays a concern with the surface on which marks themselves are made – with the processes at the graphical image level. The survey of styles in art is necessarily cursory because the concern is with representations of space rather than symbols. The reader who is particularly interested in these ideas can start at Chapter Five and then return to the earlier chapters.

I have tried to write the text using as little jargon as possible. When novel terms have been introduced I have tried to define them. I have also avoided citing any references in the text. This will make the book more accessible to the general reader, but it might irritate the specialist. Originally, I included a single list of references for the whole book. Alan Costall, Dennis Parker and Helen Ross all read the complete manuscript, and all suggested that some fuller form of referencing would be helpful to the reader. Accordingly, I decided to provide an annotated bibliography for each chapter, with extended annotations for a small number of central references and briefer ones for books and articles more specifically related to the chapter sections. These readers expressed some scepticism regarding my distinction between illusion and allusion, and so I have tried to make this more explicit in the text. None the less, their encouraging comments were most appreciated and their views were of assistance in many other ways. Peter Mayer read Chapter Three and made some radical remarks about its introduction which I might later wish I had followed. Michiaki Kondo read the final manuscript with great care, and picked up a number of inconsistencies in the use of terms, for which I am very grateful.

At an earlier stage, the embryonic first chapter was read by Alan Kennedy, Mike Swanston and Alan Wilkes. Their penetrating comments exposed many points that required elaboration and resulted in my expanding the material in it to three chapters! My greatest debt is to my research colleague, Mike Swanston, with whom I have had numerous discussions on many aspects of vision. Our research is concerned with motion and space perception and while the language in which our experimental work is described conforms to the demands of science, the sentiments are much the same as those described in this book. Mike also read drafts of the other chapters and made many constructive suggestions for improving them. Of course, all the errors that remain are my own.

Most of the spatialised pictures we see are photographic images, and most of the photographs we take are of family members. It is to my family that this book is dedicated, and visual allusions to them can be found throughout it.

Nicholas Wade
Newport-on-Tay
February, 1990

1   IMAGES OF VISION

An allusion is defined as a symbolic or covert reference. In everyday literary usage it is the covertness that is typically emphasised; something that is not stated directly is implied by the form of words chosen. For example, if I state that I do not intend to survey the whole area of literary allusion, there is the supposition that I will survey some of it. Likewise, to say of someone: "she is not the best actress in the world", does not carry the conviction that she is a challenger for that position. Allusions are used extensively in language because of their subtlety and potential ambiguity: they can make reference to intentions that are difficult to present directly, or they can be made in a manner that leaves their interpretation open to the reader. It is through this indirectness of intent and interpretation that allusions can be such powerful linguistic tools. When the intent or interpretation is appreciated the force of the message can linger in memory for much longer than a simple direct statement.

Similarly, visual allusions convey multiple meanings in graphical form, some of which are more directly expressed than others. As with literary allusions, the covert graphical message can be more alluring and memorable than the overt one. For example, Figure 1.1 appears, on first inspection, to be little more than a pattern of wavy, radiating lines at the centre of which is a clearly defined left eye. The pattern itself might be a little disturbing if you stare at it for long, because the lines will appear to move about. The left eye is, in fact, partnered by a right one, although the latter is not so distinct, graphically. However, when the pattern is viewed from a metre or so, rather than from reading distance, a full face will probably be visible. The radiating lines near the centre accentuate the contours around the eyes and on the side of the nose; the lips and hair also become visible. This is one form of visual allusion; the portrait is carried covertly by the geometrical design. There is another form of visual

allusion present in this picture, too – a spatial one. The wavy radiating lines probably appear to describe a solid surface, rather than a flat plane; there seem to be humps and hollows in it, especially near the edges. Here we are dealing with one of the most pervasive forms of covert reference in pictures – the allusion to the third dimension. Figure 1.1 also plays a trick with respect to this form of visual allusion: the solid surface that is implied by the wavy lines is not one that could occur naturally, rather it is like an impossible object. The contours that describe a hump on the left side make a hollow on the right! If you follow a hollow from one side around to the vertical midline it will seem to turn in on itself so that the perceived depth can reverse. Clearly, there is almost as much scope for visual allusions as for literary ones.

In both their literal (linguistic) and graphical forms allusions can only be conveyed if the message itself can be interpreted, that is, if the language in which it is conveyed can be understood by those involved in the communication. This statement seems trite with respect to written language, since we are well aware of its complexities and ambiguities, and of the difficulties involved in learning them. With respect to graphical forms the rules are not so clearly defined, but they are there, none the less. The letters that are combined to form written text are a good example of this: we are either ignorant of, or ignore, the relationship between the letters we use and earlier forms of visual communication from which they were derived. Letters and words are very special pictures. Some of the rules for interpreting pictures are a consequence of our cultural past – the conventions that have been employed throughout centuries of illustration. Others can be traced more fundamentally to the ways in which we see – or how our visual systems are organised. In this regard, the written form of language and graphics have rather more in common than is often supposed. That is, the processes in the visual system that recognise the objects in the environment and pictorial images operate in a similar manner to recognise the diverse written symbols we produce, both by hand and machine. The problem of how we can recognise hand-written text so easily is equally as perplexing as understanding our facility at recognising pictorial images.

The alternative definition of allusion, as a symbo-

1.1 *Chrys*. The radiating lines create the impression of a surface in depth, but the curves that appear on one side to protrude seem to recede on the other. The central eye is paired with another to its left, and a whole face will emerge with viewing from a distance – or if the picture is moved about.

lic reference, is clearly addressed to the points raised above, also. For example, in what sense does the word "pipe" provide a representation of a familiar object in which a dried leaf is burned and inhaled, consisting of a wooden bowl and a stem with a mouthpiece, etc.? Moreover, how does the graphical form of the lower-case letters "pipe" relate to those of the upper-case "PIPE"? In each instance we have no difficulty in making these equivalences – but understanding how we do so has not proved an easy task. Yet these are simple examples. Consider instead what is represented by the word "justice", and in what sense is it related to a figure with arms outstretched holding scales in one hand and a sword in the other?

Symbols such as this, and those that are replete in paintings of mythological scenes, are a matter of learning complex and subtle conventions: they provide the basis for semiotics, and as such are beyond the scope of this book. Before the allegorical nature of a history painting can be resolved, the figures, objects and scenes represented need to be recognised. In this book we will be dealing with the issue of spatial representation; that is, with the ways in which objects that are solid can be depicted, and how objects in different directions and at different distances can be incorporated in the picture. To be sure, there are also conventions involved in representing space, but they seem to me to be more fundamental than those involved in interpreting symbols. Moreover, I am a student of perception rather than linguistics or semiotics, and so the approach to studying pictures and written text is from the standpoint of spatial perception. I realise that there is no clear divide between the perception of space and the perception of symbols – as is evident in the consideration of pipes above. However, I believe that the discussion can be clarified by a more detailed analysis of the levels of representation involved, and this will be attempted in the next section.

The relationship between linguistic and pictorial representation is a fascinating one. Indeed, it is remarkable how many books on art are linguistically lavish but pictorially impoverished: some have no pictures at all, and so the word has replaced the image. I would like to think that in this book the language is graphical as well as linguistic. Text will be provided to describe and elaborate upon the illustrations – but many of the questions will be asked perceptually. Thus, the reader will be requested to apply as much perceptual analysis in reading the pictures as conceptual analysis in interpreting the words. The arguments presented in words will, I hope, be both supported and extended by the illustrations. I realise that this strategy of switching between text and illustrations can be tiresome at times, especially when it is not possible for the appropriate figure to be adjacent to the relevant text. For this reason, the legends to the figures generally repeat some of the ideas presented more fully in the text. With progression through the book the illustrations will tend to become increasingly complex and subtle, and may require longer looks. It is my general intention to make these later figures as aesthetically pleasing as I can, so that they can be enjoyed for their own sake.

Many of the pictures we see in newspapers and magazines serve the function of augmenting some verbal commentary. Illustrations in books often elucidate the spatial relationships between parts that are difficult to verbalise, as in medical or engineering texts: the same structure can be shown from different viewpoints, or parts that would normally obscure others can be pictorially dissected. The exceptions to this are the pictures that stand alone, and are displayed in art galleries. The spectator can contemplate these pictures in isolation, although a written commentary is usually on hand in the form of a catalogue. We generally feel more secure when we are told who painted the picture, what its title is and how other people think it should be interpreted. I will try to overcome some of these viewing habits by providing, initially, pictures of mundane everyday objects. None the less, they should not be taken for granted, because some searching questions about representation can be asked with such simple shapes.

The general areas of representation and allusion will be outlined in this introductory chapter. Chapter Two is concerned with pictorial allusions, from the representation of space in painting and photography, to the manipulations of spatial ambiguities in pictures. Chapter Three is entitled "Literal Pictures", and it examines and illustrates the many uses that have been made of the word as an image in its own write. The fourth chapter addresses the underpinning of visual allusions in the abstraction processes of vision itself. Finally, the relationship between pictorial images and perception will be reexamined in the light of the illustrations presented. The two Appendices describe some of the graphical and photographic techniques that have been employed in producing the illustrations.

Representations

The definition of allusion as a symbolic reference is, potentially, a very broad one. It could be given as the definition of representation, and it is in this sense that it is used here. A representation is a likeness or a reproduction of an object or idea – in the context of pictures it is an image. An image is a very useful concept, because of its inherent spatiality: we think of images in pictorial or spatial terms. It is a concept that thrives on its vagueness. Because the term is used in so many ways it will be useful to dissect it. In fact, it is misleading to refer to it in the singular. I will argue that there are a number of levels at which images are formed and that the discussions of representations may be clarified by making such distinctions.

The point of departure is the three-dimensional environment in which we perceive and behave. This environment contains objects, most of which are in contact with the ground, of different sizes, shapes and textures. With respect to the observer they have locations – they lie in specific directions at particular distances – and these will change as a consequence of object and/or observer movement. Many of the objects (such as people) have parts that move with respect to one another. Under normal circumstances our perception is concerned with the appropriate responses to objects in space, like approaching or avoiding them, hunting or gathering them, grasping and manipulating them. Amongst the objects in our environment are many that we do not gather or grasp because their function is symbolic: they represent something other than what they are as objects. Pictures constitute one such set of objects. They can be perceived like any other objects in the environment – they have a size, shape, texture and location – but, in addition, they can be perceived as representing something else, some other space than the ones they occupy. It is for this reason that pictures are special sorts of objects. Written words serve the same function in that they stand for something other than the ink marks on the paper. However, in the case of written language it is not the words that are objects in space but the pages on which they are printed.

We will refer to the marks made on a surface as the *pictorial image*, and the discussion will be confined initially to representations of objects in space. It need not be confined to figurative pictures, as opposed to "abstract" ones, but it is less cumbersome to do so initially. The pictorial image is made by a picture-maker who can see, and it is made for others to see. That is, the picture-maker is involved in selecting certain objects or scenes from the environment to observe, and then makes marks on a surface that, when viewed by the artist, correspond in some way to the scene as perceived. The picture-maker will probably expect other observers, when presented with these marks, to recognise their relationship to the original scene.

The process of seeing itself involves stages, and it is useful to outline them so that the distinction between perceiving objects and pictorial representations of them can be clarified. Light is reflected from objects in all directions; some of the reflected light enters the eye and is bent by the various transparent surfaces within it. The light then falls upon receptors at the back of the eye, thereby modifying their electro-chemical state. Therefore, the first stage of visual processing is usually referred to as the *retinal image*, which is the pattern of electro-chemical activity occurring over the surface (the retina) containing the light-sensitive receptors. The pattern of light projected onto the retina is often thought of, for conceptual convenience, as an *optical image* – that is, as though the retina was a screen on which a picture of the scene was projected. Many problems arise from equating the retinal and optical images and these problems have had a pervasive, even pernicious, effect on our theories of vision, both in the past and the present, and they will be returned to in more detail later.

The optical image bears a geometrical relationship to the scene in three-dimensional space and to the pictorial image. That is, at a given moment the location of points on the retina can be described geometrically, because the optical characteristics of the eye are known. Since light travels in straight lines the projections from a scene or picture to the stationary retina can be described. Under contrived conditions, like viewing through a single pinhole, it is impossible to discriminate between a scene and an exact pictorial image of it. However, under normal viewing conditions, using both eyes with a moving head and body, the scene is readily distinguished from a picture of it.

We have evolved to perceive objects and scenes, rather than pictures of them, and so it is reasonable to assume that the next stage, which will be called the *visual image*, is concerned with a representation of objects in three-dimensional space. The objects do not need to be labelled or categorised as such – that is, they do not need to be named. Rather, it is their perception as surfaces with particular orientations, dimensions and locations that is available at the level of the visual image. To say that the visual image represents objects is shorthand for describing their three-dimensional properties like length, breadth, height, direction and location. To categorise those properties as representing an instance of a class of objects requires a higher level of representation. The visual image representations serve the function of determining our behaviour towards objects in space. It is this level that is common to all seeing organisms, although the particular representation will be reflected in the optical quality of the eyes, the complexity of the nervous system and the environmental pressures for survival. In short, all animals with eyes form visual images in so far as they respond appropriately to significant objects in their environment. Again, this is shorthand for describing properties of objects. Indeed, for many animals it has been shown that they respond to a very circumscribed range of object properties. For example, the male stickleback distinguishes between females and males largely on the basis of the red underbelly of the latter. Males that intrude into the territory of another are attacked. However, males will also attack models that bear little resemblance to a stickleback, as long as there is a red area on their lower parts. Thus, their visual images are quite different to ours, but they have clearly served the stickleback well in evolutionary terms.

In the case of humans the significant objects have become exceedingly diverse, and they are not restricted to the primary demands of survival and reproduction. Human survival depends upon intellectual as well as nutritional sustenance, and amongst the former, pictures have proved to satisfy a universal appetite, as has language. Pictures are both objects (e.g. painted canvas with a wooden frame or paper with a matrix of ink dots of varying size) as well as representations of objects. As objects they form visual images, but as representations of other objects they will be called *graphical images*. Thus, when we are discussing pictorial images (the contents of the picture) we need to progress through the levels of retinal and visual images to the graphical image. It is at this level that we "go beyond the information given", that is, we treat the pictorial image in terms of what it represents rather than what it is. Written words present us with a particular kind of graphical image because they are inherently two-dimensional. However, they are not representations of objects but representations of categories of objects.

Categories are concepts at the next level of representation, which is called the *mental image*. Mental images are dependent upon the earlier forms of images, but they are not so constrained by processes in the eye. At the level of the visual image the dimensions and locations of three-dimensional surfaces are represented from a particular vantage point. This is often called a viewer-centred description, because it is constrained by the location of the observer. As a consequence of movements of surfaces and movements of the observer, many successive viewer-centred visual images can be integrated to yield a description of the object that is independent of any particular viewpoint. This is called an object-centred description, and it is available at the mental image level. Thus, the mental image consists of a description of the generalised properties of the object. It is also at this level that objects or pictorial images acquire their significance as symbols: linguistic labels can be applied to the object and to its constituent properties.

Access to the mental image is possible via the visual image directly (as with objects in space), or indirectly mediated by the graphical image (as with pictorial images). Written words form graphical images that are rarely acknowledged as such because their significance is defined almost entirely at the mental image level.

Mental images are not so constrained by processes in the environment, either. It is possible to imagine – to form mental images of – objects or events that have never been experienced. It is also possible to form mental images of events long since past, or to plan for events that have not yet occurred or may never occur. The mental images we form of familiar objects can be manipulated in unfamiliar, or even impossible, ways. For example, imagine a unicorn smoking a pipe with its bowl directed downwards and where the ensuing smoke descends rather than rises. Alternatively, the whole image could be inverted, so that the smoke ascends but the unicorn is upside-down.

The levels of representation outlined above are displayed schematically in Figure 1.2. The arrows denote the influence that one level has on others. So, for instance, the visual image is influenced by the retinal image, and can in turn influence the graphical and mental images. The dashed lines from visual and mental images to pictorial images signify that the influence is mediated indirectly – that is, the marks in the pictorial image will be made via the hand, or some other device, on the basis of signals

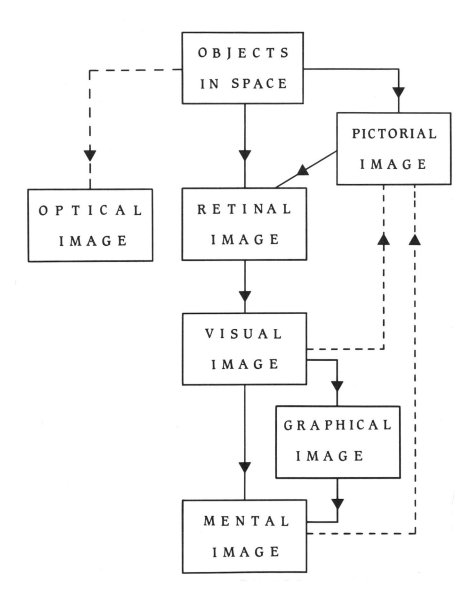

1.2 Image processes in vision. A retinal image can be formed either from objects in space or from a pictorial image (the marks on the picture surface). The visual image corresponds to the perception of surface properties, like orientation, texture and location; it is a three-dimensional representation of surfaces, and it guides behaviour to objects in space. Object names are provided at the mental image level, which also contains the stored (learned) significances of objects. The allusory aspects of pictorial images – their allusion to a space they do not occupy – is due to processing at the graphical image level. The contents of the pictorial image can be influenced from the visual and mental images. The optical image is a convenient fiction that has been used in analyses of vision.

from the visual or mental image levels. The optical image is shown as a cul-de-sac, because it is an abstraction that does not correspond to any stage in vision.

The dissection of the term "images" into its pictorial, optical, retinal, visual, graphical and mental components is only a first step towards understanding representations. None the less, I think that it can be of assistance in discussing visual allusions. Some of these terms are already in general use, but they are not applied consistently. The confusion between retinal and optical images has been outlined already. The term visual image has been taken to refer both to the perception of objects and to the

manipulation of internal (mental) images. I will attempt to apply these terms consistently in the manner they are defined above. I believe that the names given to the various image levels adequately reflect the processes taking place. For example, the visual image concerns the perception of surfaces in the environment; it requires light for its operation, and it does not function as a consequence of mental activity initiated in the absence of external stimulation of the retinal receptors.

This book is concerned mainly about the relationship between pictures and perception – about the manner in which three-dimensional space is alluded to in pictures, and about those pictures that convey

1.3 A photograph of a curved briar pipe.

multiple meanings, some of which are more directly expressed than others. While the discussion will often refer to objects in three-dimensional space, only their representations as two-dimensional pictures can be displayed. The only three-dimensional object with which I can assume you have some immediate experience is this book itself. Thus, I find myself in the dilemma that has plagued perceptual psychology: while trying to consider issues of object perception, of the visual image, I will present pictorial images that access the higher level of graphical images. The danger is that theories derived from presenting two-dimensional pictures are assumed to apply to the perception of three-dimensional space, rather than the reverse. When we understand the visual image, the perception of objects in space, we will be in a better position to interpret the graphical image, the perception of that special class of objects called pictures.

We will now commence with a more detailed (and illustrated) consideration of pictorial, retinal, visual, graphical and mental images. Because the illustrations are necessarily two-dimensional we will be dealing mainly with pictorial and graphical images. We will return to the issue of retinal and visual images in Chapter Two.

A pictorial image can be said to represent some

1.4 This is not a pipe – after Magritte's painting entitled *The Perfidy of Images*.

Ceci n'est pas une pipe.

object when it contains some of the essential features of the object. Thus, for example, a picture of a curved object, with a thick cylindrical-shaped wooden bowl at one end and a black tapering stem at the other might be said to represent a pipe (see Figure 1.3). Indeed, if it is drawn with all the artifice of a painter like René Magritte few would describe it as other than a pipe. Magritte has made several paintings of curved briar pipes. His most celebrated is called *The Perfidy of Images*, because below the hovering image are the words *"Ceci n'est pas une pipe."* Magritte's image and words have been applied to my own pipe in Figure 1.4. When this picture is seen for the first time there is an air of disbelief in the spectator – of course it's a pipe, what else could it be? It could be what it is, a painting in oil on canvas or, as here, a printed image in ink on paper. The pipe can't be smoked, or even handled. The viewer is being confronted with the paradox that although it is the shape of a pipe it is actually marks on a surface.

There are a number of fundamental issues raised by Magritte's painting and by Figure 1.4. Firstly, what are the essential features that the image shares with the object? Magritte has in part answered this question himself. In some of his other paintings he presents a pictorial image of a common object, for example a jug, and gives it a name that would not normally be associated with it, like "bird". Here the spectator realises immediately that some trick is being played. However, we see the trickery in the unusual assignment of labels, not in the fact that the pictorial image is pigment on canvas, rather than being a jug. In the case of the pipe the labels seem appropriate, but the written message conflicts with the pictorial image. Clearly the pictorial image of the pipe shares something with actual pipes that the pictorial image of the jug doesn't share with actual birds. That something is, of course, its shape. More precisely, it is its optical image qualities. The shadow cast by a real curved briar pipe on a screen (see Figure 1.5) would have a similar outline to the shape of the painted pipe. We can go further and note that the tones and textures in the pictorial image can be manipulated systematically to suggest a similar depth or solidity to that found in a pipe (see Figure 1.6). (Many more techniques can be employed to create the allusion to depth in a flat image, but a discussion of these will be deferred until the next chapter.) Thus, when a pictorial image has the optical image qualities of the object we are likely to consider it as a representation of the object: that is,

1.5 Silhouette of a pipe.

1.6 A full-tone photograph of a pipe.

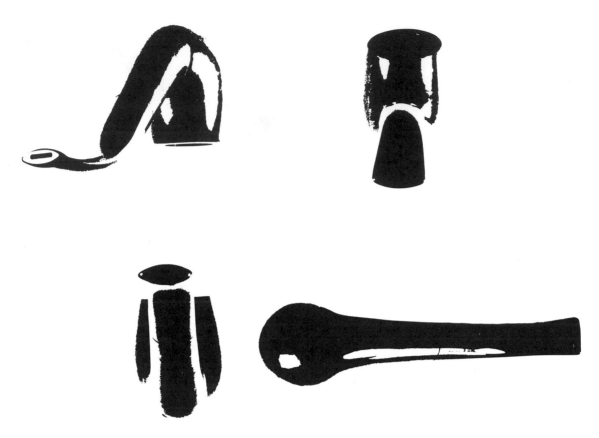

1.7 Four views of the same pipe.

the pictorial image will be recognised as representing the object.

That this is an oversimplification is obvious when we consider that the pipes represented pictorially thus far have all been imaged from a particular vantage point. All the pictorial images are of a pipe viewed from the side. This will be called the stereotypical view. This is not *the* shape of the pipe, but *a* shape – one of many alternatives, some of which are shown in Figure 1.7. The pipe has not changed in its three-dimensional physical characteristics, but the viewpoint has altered. Pictorial shape presents a problem because it is a consequence of projecting three dimensions onto two, and this is a characteristic of both optical and pictorial images. In so far as we are dealing with perception of pictures then the question of shape must be addressed.

In the present context we can ask, what are the characteristics that correspond to our recognising certain shapes as representing a pipe? Is it the silhouette? Figure 1.8 shows the silhouette of the stereotypical view of the pipe. Here the object can be recognised in an unambiguous manner. However, if the viewpoint is changed to that of Figure 1.9 then some ambiguity is introduced: while it is recognised as a pipe, its bearing is not defined. The stem could be pointing towards, or away from, the viewer.

Shape is often described in terms of the boundaries between the object and its background – that is, its outline, as in Figure 1.10. Here we have the outline of the silhouette. Only the regions in which the contrast changes from black to white are registered. With such simple outlines there will be the same problems of ambiguity as are found with silhouettes. None the less, outlines can be more informative (and less ambiguous) when a wider range of boundaries are signalled – that is, when more boundaries between light and shade are given, as in Figure 1.11. These extra boundaries provide a stronger impression of the solidity of the pipe. If the regions of light and shade within the object are so important, are the outlines of the silhouette necessary at all? They have been removed in Figure 1.12, and the minimal marks remaining would probably be recognised as a pipe, even though the physical boundaries that separate it from other objects or the background are not given.

Even more radical dissections of the pictorial pipe can be carried out – dissections that could not be conducted on the pipe itself. Figure 1.13 consists of a sectioned and reversed pictorial image of my pipe. It will probably be recognised as being like the other pipes pictured before, particularly if it is viewed from farther than the normal reading distance or if the eyes are somewhat defocused. That is, the bowl is on the left with the upward curve of the stem towards the right. However, the local regions, the vertical sections, are all in the reverse direction to the global impression. This effect was produced by taking a photograph of the pipe, with its bowl on the right side, slicing it into vertical strips and then reassembling it with the rightmost sections being placed on the left and vice versa. Thus, the individual sections correspond to a rightward facing pipe, but the overall impression transcends these local features. Clearly, our recognition of pictorial images can survive all manner of graphical insults!

It is obviously very difficult to specify the pictorial features that represent a pipe. It is equally difficult to specify the perceptual processes that result in recognising an actual pipe. Recognising a pictorial image as a representation of an object combines these two representational problems. A pipe has to contain essential features or properties, some of which are relational – a bowl, a stem, a mouthpiece; the stem is attached to the bowl, which is greater in size than the mouthpiece, etc. Some of the relational features can themselves be modified. If the stem is rotated, as in Figure 1.14, the pipe would still function, though the smoker might not find its use so congenial. But what if the normal relationship is disrupted? Is Figure 1.15 a picture of a pipe? All the parts are there in stereotypical view, although it could not perform its function.

Thus, the specification of the pictorial features that represent a pipe, or the perceptual process that enables its recognition as a picture of a pipe, seem to depend on some process of inference. The pictorial image needs to capture certain essential features of the object, whereas the graphical image needs to extract certain essential features from the visual image. Magritte was side-stepping some of these issues by painting his pipe from a stereotyped viewpoint: the recognition of the pictorial image was

1.8 A silhouette of a pipe in stereotypical view.

1.9 A non-stereotypical silhouette of a pipe. The orientation of the stem to the bowl is ambiguous – it could be interpreted as directed towards or away from the viewer.

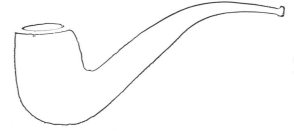

1.10 Outline of a pipe.

1.11 A line image of all the boundaries between light and shade in the original photograph (Figure 1.3).

1.12 Highlights of a pipe, with the outlines removed.

1.13 A pictorially dissected pipe. A photograph of a pipe, with the bowl on the right, was sliced into vertical sections, and reassembled in left–right reversal.

1.14 Photograph of a curved briar pipe, with the stem rotated.

necessary in order to contrast it with the representation of the word. However, we are now in a better position to suggest what defines the stereotypical view. The pipe can be thought of as having three major axes – one in the direction of the stem, the second along the bowl and the third across it. There is no vantage point from which none of these is foreshortened but there are some vantage points from which a single axis alone is foreshortened. Note, however, that in Figure 1.4 (and in Magritte's painting) the pipe was tilted slightly towards the viewing point, so that some part of the circumference of the bowl could be represented. That is, the axis across the bowl was present but foreshortened, rather than being absent altogether (as in the case of the silhouette in Figure 1.5). Note, also, that there are other pictorial representations that do not foreshorten two of the three dimensions of the pipe, and two such are shown in Figure 1.7 (the lower pair). These are far more difficult to recognise as pictorial images of a pipe. Therefore, it is not simply a matter of adopting a vantage point that foreshortens only one axis of the object, because certain axes are more salient than others. The axis across the bowl is symmetrical (circular) and that along the bowl approximates symmetry (being nearly cylindrical), but the axis along the stem is asymmetrical. Thus, it would appear that the definition of the stereotypical view (for a pipe, at least) is that which involves the minimum foreshortening of an asymmetrical axis. Rotation of the pipe in any direction away from the stereotypical view will result in a foreshortening of the asymmetrical axis, and will render the pictorial image of the pipe more difficult to recognise. To make the same point graphically, the stereotypical view corresponds to the least ambiguous silhouette. The graphical image of Figure 1.8 has an unambiguous orientation, but the same does not apply to that of Figure 1.9. The stereotypical view, therefore, is not an arbitrary convention but it reduces the potential for ambiguity in pictorial images of three-dimensional objects.

The second issue raised by Magritte's painting concerns our readiness to accept the equivalence of pictorial image and object. What is it about the optical equivalence of shapes that makes them so compelling? Could it be that in terms of their projection onto the retina they are equivalent? While this might apply under contrived viewing conditions when only one eye is used, in the case of the painting we have plenty of visual evidence that painting and object are not the same: the painting is flat, the pictured pipe is not supported on anything, and so on. We recognise the pictorial image as a representation of a pipe *in spite of* these factors. It would seem, then, that we have learned certain pictorial conventions. We have learned that objects projecting a certain shape onto a flat surface can be represented by that shape.

The third fundamental issue implicit in *The Perfidy of Images* is the manner in which the message "Ceci n'est pas une pipe" is conveyed. The words were painted on the canvas, too. They represent another set of shapes that are defined by convention. Here the cultural basis for the convention is plain to see: there are many different scripts – e.g. Roman, Greek, Cyrillic, Chinese. That is, the shapes of the basic units are often radically different. In the case of most European languages the basic shapes, the letters, are the same but their arrangements can be radically different, as in English and French. In general, there are rules relating the sounds made in speaking the language with the letters or letter groupings that represent them. In this book it is the written form of language that is of primary importance. Magritte, in addressing a French speaking audience, assumed that the words in his message would be understood. That is, they would be able to recognise the shapes he painted as letters that could be assembled to make words which would convey a message. In the message the shape of the letters "une pipe" are taken to represent the category of objects that can be used to draw air into the mouth through some burning herbal mixture. Therefore, Magritte was using one form of pictorial representation (the written word) to say that another form of representation (the shape of the pipe) was not the object represented. It could equally well be argued that the shape of the pipe was being used to say that the word "pipe" does not represent the object. More will be said about this issue in Chapter Three.

Pictorial images are themselves spatial – they involve marks made in two dimensions – but the things they represent need not be. For simplicity I have used as examples the representations of objects, like pipes, which are themselves spatially extended. It is when dealing with such objects that we can draw some relationship between the form of the object and the shape of the pictorial image. My pipe has fixed boundaries, it is solid, and so has a relatively constant form. This constancy of form ceases to apply as soon as we consider living matter. The same arguments about form and shape are inappropriate when considering people and their

1.15 Photograph of a pipe, with the bowl and stem separated.

1.16 Photograph of a pipe with the stem twisted.

1.17 Another photograph of a pipe with the stem twisted.

portraits. To be sure, stereotypical views are employed, but views of what? A face has no fixed form because it is dynamic, it is constantly changing. There are, however, limits to the changes in form that can occur, and the visual detection of these must lie at the heart of our remarkable facility at recognising faces. It is, therefore, much more demanding of the artist, or photographer, to render a picture of a person – a portrait – because the frozen representation has an even more tenuous link with the dynamic form. In spite of this we are remarkably good at recognising pictures of people. This is due in part to the skill of the artist but mostly to the sophistication of our visual processing.

The visual image is not prone to all the vagaries of the graphical image, described above. Three-dimensional objects are seen three-dimensionally, and their changes in location over time, their motions, are also seen. The visual image corresponds to our perceptual activity – to the perception that guides our behaviour. To be sure, we can reflect upon this visual image but such reflection is not necessary for its operation. The visual image operates without language, although its operation can be described by language; it is the level which is common to all seeing species. However, all species do not see in the same way, because of the gross differences in eye structures and in the neural machinery for processing the retinal images. They respond to those visual images that increase the chances of survival.

Humans have rather basic eyes. The optical quality is inferior to that of almost every commercial camera available today. Despite this, human vision is so intricate because of the sophisticated neural machinery that processes the images from the retina. The visual image is not synonymous with the retinal image, even though the latter is used as its source. The visual image can call upon signals from two retinal images simultaneously in order to derive information regarding the solid form of the object imaged optically. The visual image can also call upon a sequence of such images so that the motion of the object, or the motion of the observer, can be derived. These dynamic and three-dimensional aspects of the visual image have evolved as a consequence of constraints in the environment: motion and three-dimensional form are significant properties of objects and their arrangements in space. Neither of these are characteristics of the pictorial image, nor do objects exhibit the fragmentations and manipulations like those shown in Figures 1.5–1.13.

It is possible to allude to both motion and three-dimensionality in pictorial images, but we will see in the next chapter how this has drawn more on optical image properties than visual ones, particularly for representing three-dimensional space.

To recapitulate, light travels from objects to the two eyes, forming two slightly different retinal images that change with movements of the observer; these furnish the basis for the visual image. The prime function of the visual image is to guide behaviour. Amongst the behaviours guided by the visual image are increasingly intricate manipulative skills, which in turn can be used to create a novel type of object – a picture. That is, the marks made by a skilful manipulator can represent something other than the marks themselves. It is suggested that the processes involved in interpreting pictorial images – the graphical image – occur after those for the visual image. The visual image runs off virtually automatically, if the visual apparatus is in order, whereas the graphical image involves processes of inference. The picture is seen as an object and the pictorial image is treated as if it was an arrangement of objects in space. The visual image should not be considered in static terms: it is changing constantly as a consequence either of the motion of objects or the observer (or both). Accordingly, the visual images of objects are not restricted to particular viewpoints. The solid form of objects is derived both from stereoscopic vision and observer motion. This information regarding the form of objects, independent of viewpoint, is represented at the level of the mental image. Pictorial images are dependent upon mental images for their production as are graphical images for the interpretation of pictorial images. Indeed, it is possible to demonstrate the manner in which mental images can be manipulated on the basis of pictorial images. Figure 1.16 presents a picture of a now familiar pipe with an unfamiliar arrangement of the bowl and stem. In spite of the fact that it is a pictorial image the graphical image is of a pipe in three dimensions, and the mental image of it can be changed to represent it from different viewpoints. For example, could Figure 1.17 represent the same pipe viewed from a different position? Put another way, could the pipe represented in Figure 1.16 be rotated to produce the one in Figure 1.17? In fact it could not, because the stem of the pipe in Figure 1.17 is twisted in the opposite direction to that in Figure 1.16. What is of interest is that this task is possible at all: a pictorial image of an object is represented at the graphical image level as if it was the object, and its viewpoint is manipulable at the level of the mental image. Of course, mental images can be generated independently of pictorial images. If asked to form a mental image of a chair we can do so with ease and it is also possible to imagine an elephant sitting on it. Does it have tusks? In these instances the mental images are generated on the basis of verbal labels rather than pictorial images. There has been much debate concerning the manner in which the mental image is represented and manipulated. Some believe that it is analogous to the visual image, so that the manipulations would be rather like rotating the object itself. An alternative view is that the mental representation is more like a descriptive list of the properties of the object.

It might have been noted that virtually nothing has been said of colour. I doubt if anyone has seen a purely black-and-white pipe, like that in Figure 1.3, or even a grey one as in Figure 1.6, and yet they were, most probably, recognised immediately. Similarly, we have little difficulty in recognising the images in pencil or charcoal drawings, newspaper photographs or on black-and-white television. It is as though the perception of space can operate independently of the perception of colour. Indeed, it must be able to because many species of animal have no colour discrimination whereas they can make luminance discriminations. This distinction is often emphasised in the research on vision by scientists – space perception does not often intrude on studies of colour vision, and vice versa. I will be guilty of perpetuating this distinction, since I will be presenting achromatic rather than chromatic pictorial images. My concern is with images, and their inherent spatiality, rather than in the subtleties of colour.

Written words are special types of pictorial images that do not represent specific objects but classes of object. Written words do not have an existence as objects, only as pictorial images. Unlike pictorial images of solid objects, words do not need to be placed in special frames, but appear with many other words on a flat paper surface. The combination of words, according to the rules of language, provides a message. However, I am dealing with the much simpler case of the word as a label, which stands for a class of objects. Considered as a pictorial image the word is processed at the level of the graphical image, but it must have ready access to the mental image level in order for its categorial nature to be available. The pictorial image of the word is rarely considered in terms of its particular pattern properties. It was not always so, since written symbols derive from stylised pictograms.

Allusions

Allusions as covert references are frequently used in literary work. Not only can additional interpretations be given to the text, but it is also possible to use allusion as a vehicle for ideas that would otherwise be unacceptable. Taken to its extreme, allusion can engulf the whole of the message, so that nothing is as it seems on the surface, as in allegories. The essential aspect of an allusion is that a certain degree of ambiguity is embedded within the message.

The same applies to visual or pictorial allusions: the marks made on the picture plane are capable of multiple meanings, some of which are more probable than others. There are many methods of intro-

1.18 *The arrow in the eye.* The arrow and all the letters (apart from the "e") subtend the same visual angle at the represented eye.

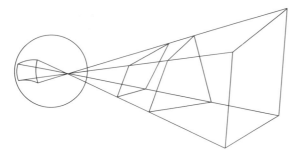

1.19 The visual pyramid. The three shapes enclosed within the visual pyramid project the same shape to the eye.

ducing this ambiguity in pictorial images, and they will be mentioned in increasing detail throughout the book.

Any two-dimensional image of a three-dimensional object is spatially ambiguous. This statement is often examined in the context of the putative optical image cast in the stationary eye: an optical image of a given size can be produced by an infinite number of objects that subtend the same angle at the eye. Thus, the arrow in Figure 1.18 subtends the same angle as all the letters, with the exception of the "e" which doubles up as an eye. The *size* of the optical image is equal in all cases, but its form would be different. However, the same argument can be applied to the shape of the optical image. A square optical image of a given size could be produced by an infinite number of objects that subtend the same shape and angle at the eye (see Figure 1.19). The same applies to the orientation of the optical image, too.

Despite this ambiguity of the optical projection to the eye, we do not have many problems with seeing a particular object of a given size and shape at some specific distance. That is, our visual image is not prone to the equivocalities of the stationary optical image: we tend to see things the way they are rather than as they are projected onto the eye. This is called perceptual constancy by psychologists, and it provides one of the oldest theoretical issues in the study of perception. It is often asked "how is it possible for our perception of objects to be accurate when the optical image formed by the object is ambiguous?" The usual answer is that we compensate in some way for the ambiguity by utilising other sources of information in the optical image. For example, only one image of a given size can produce an optical image if we have information about its distance from the eye. Therefore distance information can be used to compensate for the potential ambiguity of the projected size. In the case of Figure 1.18, if we have information that the arrow is further away than the letter "V", and they both subtend the same angle at the eye, then the arrow must be larger than the "V"

This theoretical position can be criticised because it takes as its starting point a single optical

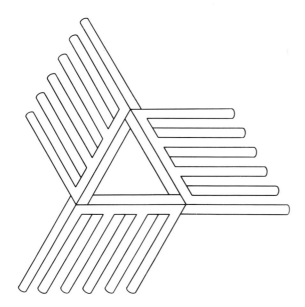

1.20 An impossible figure (that is, a representation of an object that would be impossible to construct). It is actually a double impossibility, with the impossible triangle in the centre, flanked by a series of "devil's pitchforks".

1.21 (Facing page) *Eternal triangles.* Two portraits of M. C. Escher.

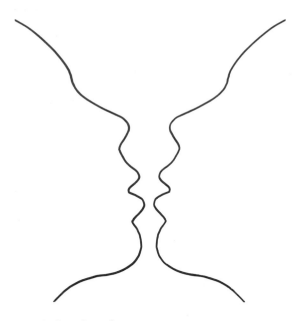

1.22 Outline of vase/faces motif.

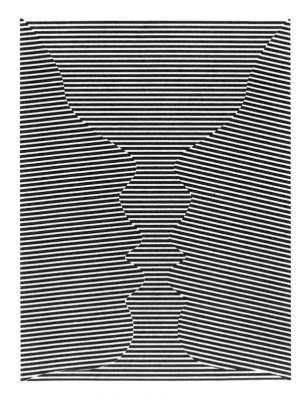

1.23 Striped variation of the vase/faces motif.

image frozen in time. As was argued in the previous section, the visual image derives from information supplied by paired retinal images which are themselves constantly changing as a consequence of movements of the observer. The theoretical concern with projective ambiguity of the type shown in Figure 1.19 displays the pervasive influence that pictorial images have had on theories of vision: the ambiguity implicit in static pictorial images is assumed to be a feature of three-dimensional scenes, too. The pictorial image has replaced reality in much of our perceptual theorising.

The pictorial rules (to be described in Chapter Two) that have been applied in reducing three dimensions to two can also be manipulated to create startling or impossible environments. A simple example is shown in Figure 1.20. In this regard, one of the greatest exponents has been M. C. Escher who is represented in Figure 1.21. The fascination here is that the drawings are interpreted as representing objects, but the objects represented could not be constructed because the spatial constraints of the environment have been contravened. These pictures work so well because they obey the pictorial rules in local regions but defy them globally. That is, the connections between regions that are represented in appropriate perspective are manipulated, and this creates the impossibility when an interpretation of the whole figure is attempted.

The two-dimensional pictorial image can also contain some intentional ambiguity, such that a given shape can be interpreted in a number of ways. In the psychological literature the most common example of this is the vase/face motif, like that shown in Figure 1.22. Here the same lines can be seen as two profiles or as a vase. Although both can be visible, only one is seen at a time, and there is a tendency to oscillate between the two. Psychologists usually attribute this motif to the Dane, Edgar Rubin, who used it early in this century. Its pedigree is much older, however, and fine examples of it can be found in 18th century French prints, in which the profiles not only define a vase, usually in a naturalistic setting, but the profiles themselves differ, each representing a particular person. Often the naturalistic setting itself is used to carry other profiles: the foliage of trees is particularly suited to this purpose. Examples of such interpretative ambiguity that appear in textbooks on perception are pictorially impoverished by comparison to the early artistic prints. None the less, even with such simplified figures the extent of allusion can be manipulated by making one interpretation more probable than the other. In Figure 1.23 the usual symmetry between the two profiles is broken down. The profiles themselves are symmetrical, but the inclined lines defining them make the backgrounds appear different on the left and right, and this makes the vase more immediately visible than the profiles.

There is an even more basic ambiguity that occurs in simple spatial representations of three-dimensional geometrical figures, like crystals. In the last century, the crystallographer, Louis Necker, noticed that drawings of symmetrical crystals, as in Figure 1.24, appeared to oscillate in depth – first one face would appear nearer than the other and then they would reverse. Many more examples of such reversing figures have been described since Necker's report. Silhouettes (as, for example, in Figure 1.25) also display a similar tendency to fluctuate in depth. In these cases of spatial fluctuation in depth the optical image does not contain sufficient information to define a stable state, and so the graphical images switch between the equally likely alternatives. For Figure 1.25 the sails of the windmill could be directed either in front or behind the milling tower. This is very much like the ambiguity of the pipe silhouette shown earlier (Figure 1.9). The windmill shape like that shown here has a longer history, though, having been described over 200 years ago.

In a photograph or a figurative painting, the sizes of the marks in the pictorial image relate to the visual angles subtended by the objects they represent. Thus one of the most fundamental forms of visual allusion is the implied depth or distance in a pictorial image. The depth seen in pictorial images is frequently described as an illusion. In one sense it is an illusion because the depth does not exist. However, the depth is simultaneously seen not to exist – the picture as an object is seen as flat. It is precisely this perceptual duality that led to the distinction between visual and graphical images described above: the processes can occur separately so that the flatness of the picture is analysed at the visual

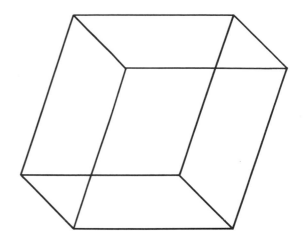

1.24 Necker's rhomboid: Louis Necker described the fluctuations in depth that occurred when viewing a crystal of this shape down a microscope. It is now usually represented as a skeleton cube, and is referred to as the Necker cube.

1.25 An example of a reversing figure. Silhouette of a windmill. The sails fluctuate in apparent orientation, so the oblique ones seem to be in front of the mill for some of the time, and behind at others. Robert Smith presented a similar illustration in an 18th century book on optics.

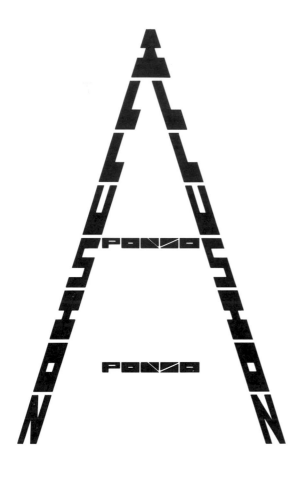

1.26 *Size distortion.* The Ponzo illusion refers to the apparent inequality of two equal extents when they are enclosed by converging lines. The upper horizontal extent looks longer than the lower one.

image level and the pictorial cues are analysed at the graphical image level. The use of the term illusion in the context of pictorial depth can create theoretical confusions because it contradicts the definition of illusions typically applied in perceptual psychology. An illusion involves the misjudgement of some specific feature of a figure; that is, some dimension in a display, such as size or orientation, is misjudged. There is no duality involved – the size or orientation are unambiguously perceived, but the perception does not correspond to the physically measured size or orientation, and our behaviour is guided by the misjudged dimensions. The same does not apply to pictorial representations of scenes: the depth is not misjudged in terms of our behaviour with respect to the pictorial image. We do not try to reach through the picture plane to pick up the represented apple!

In perceptual psychology the term illusion is applied to certain spatial distortions produced by particular line configurations. They are called geometrical optical illusions, and most of them were initially described in the second half of the 19th century. For example, the name Ponzo in Figure 1.26 is written twice at the same size. The upper one, however, appears longer horizontally than the lower one. This effect is due to the converging lines bracketing the names. This is an illusion of size or extent. Another major class of spatial illusions involves distortions of orientation. Thus, the central lines in Figure 1.27 appear tilted counter-clockwise, whereas they are actually parallel to the sides of the page. This tilt illusion is produced by the clockwise inclination of the lines surrounding the centre. Classifying visual illusions in terms of distortions of size and orientation does not encompass all instances of them, but it remains a useful working model.

1.27 *Orientation distortion.* The vertical lines in the centre appear to be tilted counter-clockwise because of the clockwise inclination of the lines surrounding them.

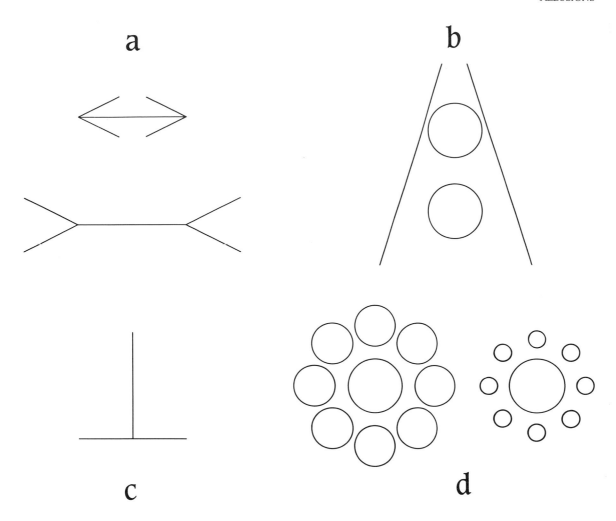

1.28 Four illusions of extent: (a) Müller-Lyer illusion: the inward and outward pointing arrow heads lead to the apparent inequality of the horizontal lines. (b) Ponzo illusion: the upper circle appears larger than the lower one. (c) Horizontal–vertical illusion: the vertical line appears longer than the horizontal, even though they are physically equal. (d) Titchener illusion: the circle surrounded by smaller circles looks larger than that surrounded by larger ones.

Many monographs have been written about visual illusions, and there is little need to rehearse the arguments for and against the various theories that have been proposed to account for their occurrence. However, there is one type of theory that does warrant brief mention because of its relevance to issues raised in the next chapter. This theory applies mainly to the subclass of illusions of extent, and it proposes that the configurations, though two-dimensional, are interpreted as three-dimensional because of cues, like converging lines, contained within them. It is as though these visual illusions contain parts that are presenting us with allusions to the third dimension. Examples of such illusions, given in simple line form, are shown in Figure 1.28. In general, whenever lines converge or diverge the impression of distance created will distort the perception of any other lines contained within them. This type of theory cannot account so readily for orientation illusions, like those shown in Figure 1.29,

19

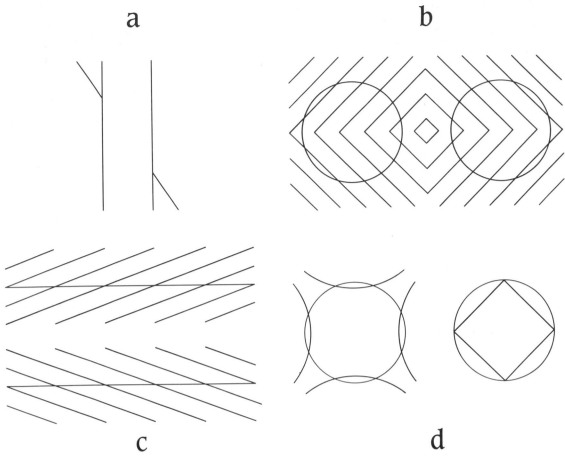

1.29 Four orientation illusions: (a) Poggendorff illusion: the oblique lines are in alignment although it appears that the upper one, if extended, would pass above the lower one. (b) Orbison variant: the circles look squashed when making acute angles with the chevrons. (c) Zöllner illusion: the cross-hatched lines distort the apparent orientation of the horizontal lines. (d) Lipps variant: the circles appear distorted by the lines intersecting or meeting them.

even though many of them are dependent on converging or diverging lines.

This book is not concerned with visual illusions like those above, involving relatively small spatial distortions, but with visual allusions. As was argued earlier, this distinction is not a trivial one. Visual illusions occur when an observer misjudges some spatial aspect in a figure; this can apply even with knowledge of the physical measurements of the figure. For example, the Ponzo illusion (Figure 1.26) involves a distortion of size, so the relevant dimension (horizontal extent) is itself misjudged. So, an illusion corresponds to a unitary perception. Visual

allusions, on the other hand, occur when both features of a figure – direct and indirect – are perceived. For instance, the pictorial allusions to pipes in the first section of this chapter involved the perception of the printed surfaces as well as a recognition of the objects represented on them. This distinction is crucial to the discussion in the next chapter, because pictorial depth has often been referred to as an illusion of depth. According to my definitions, they are allusions to depth because the observer perceives the direct and indirect aspects of the picture – the flatness of the picture surface as well as the allusion to depth in the pictorial image. If they

1.30 *Allusion.*

were examples of depth illusions then the dimension of depth – the surface of the picture plane itself – would be misperceived. A picture provides an illusion of depth only when the represented depth is perceived as real depth. As will be mentioned in the next chapter, this only occurs under the most contrived of conditions.

The illustrations to be presented most profusely later in the book (Chapter Four) are those that carry at least two pictorial messages, one of which will be carried covertly by the other. Thus, the geometrical design in Figure 1.30 carries within it a dimly defined (self-)portrait. Here we have a clearly visible geometrical pattern bearing an almost-hidden image – one that is near the threshold of visibility. As parts become visible, and recognisable, the remaining parts can be organised perceptually so that the allusion is bared. Once the covert image has been seen it is difficult to return to the state of perceptual naivety that existed on initial inspection, although the portrait will be much more difficult to see when the lines of the geometrical pattern are sharply focused in near vision. In the illustrations that follow some will be more difficult to disentangle than Figure 1.30, and may remain unseen: when this happens I am guilty of alluding to an allusion!

Bibliography
General

Gibson, J. J. (1966). *The senses considered as perceptual systems.* Boston: Houghton Mifflin. James J. Gibson has written three major books on vision and this is his second. In it he argues that traditional distinctions between low level processes like sensation and higher level processes like perception are spurious. Instead he proposes that the senses pick up the rich sources of environmental information that are available. In the context of vision he suggests that there are many invariants in the pattern of light projected to the eye (the optic array). An invariant is some aspect of the optic array that remains unchanged with movements of the observer through the environment. Gibson has been especially critical of experiments conducted under the reduced and controlled conditions of the laboratory because they remove invariants that are present in the real world. Gibson has also been concerned with the analysis of pictorial information, which he describes in Chapter XI entitled "The structuring of light by artifice".

Gombrich, E. H. (1960). *Art and illusion. A study in the psychology of pictorial representation.* London: Phaidon. This is the best known of Ernst Gombrich's many books combining an extensive knowledge of the history of art with an interest in perceptual psychology. He addresses the problem of style in representational art and argues against the view that artists paint what they see because seeing itself is considered to be dependent upon past experience. Therefore, artists represent a mixture of immediate perception with mediated knowledge. Gombrich takes the traditional empiricist position that perception involves resolving an initially ambiguous input by an "effort after meaning", and that there is no "innocent eye" which can be free from such efforts.

Gordon, I. E. (1989). *Theories of visual perception.* Chichester: Wiley. Ian Gordon has provided a very accessible survey of contemporary theories of perception. They are presented under the headings of Gestalt theory, functionalism, neurophysiology, empiricism, Gibson's direct perception and Marr's computational approach. The contrast between Gibson's direct theory of perception and the indirect or mediated approaches of empiricist theories is clearly stated, and Gibson's views on picture perception are evaluated.

Gregory, R. L. (1970). *The intelligent eye.* London: Weidenfeld & Nicolson. Richard Gregory is one of the foremost advocates of a cognitive approach to perception. He proposes that sensory information provides a basis from which to select perceptual hypotheses built up by experience. This, he argues, is the nearest we come to reality. His position is entertainingly presented in this book, which is based on a series of lectures delivered at the Royal Institution. The book is concerned almost entirely with analyses of pictorial stimuli, but the chapters on "The peculiarities of pictures" and on "Pictures, symbols, thought and language" are particularly recommended.

Hagen, M. A. (1986). *Varieties of realism. Geometries of representational art.* New York: Cambridge University Press. Margaret Hagen has extended Gibson's approach to pictorial representation by providing a more detailed geometrical analysis of spatial mapping. Three-dimensional space can be mapped on to a two-dimensional surface in many ways. Hagen describes how different geometrical transformations can be ordered hierarchically. She identifies the aspects of the scene that change during the various mapping procedures and those which do not. She then relates the different geometrical transformations to styles of representational art, and argues that they are all varieties of realism.

Marr, D. (1982). *Vision. A computational investigation into the human representation and processing of visual information.* New York: W. H. Freeman. David Marr's computational theory of vision has been enormously influential in recent years, and it is clearly described in this book. Vision is analysed as a series of representations, starting from some camera-derived image of a scene and ending with a description of the objects that would have created that image. The representations are initially very crude, like averaging the intensity of light falling in a small area of the image, but they become increasingly refined. One of the early processes involves determining where edges and boundaries fall in the image; these are then grouped to form a primal sketch, which in turn uses information from successive frames or simultaneous views to deliver a 2½-D sketch. This is like a drawing from a defined viewpoint with the orientations of the surfaces to the picture plane made explicit in some way. The processing up to this level has taken place without any information regarding the likely objects in the scene. However, the final stages, in which an object-centred description is derived, do draw upon stored knowledge of objects in the environment. In addition to defining the computational goals that need to be achieved for successful vision, Marr suggests some of the mathematical procedures (algorithms) that could be involved in transforming one representation into another; he also implemented some of these procedures in programs for a computer.

Reed, E. & Jones, R. (Eds.) (1982). *Reasons for realism. Selected essays of James J. Gibson.* Hillsdale, N.J.: Lawrence Erlbaum Associates Inc. Gibson's changing approach to both perception and pictures is charted in this selection of his writing. The essays are skilfully grouped under the following headings: foundations of ecological optics, movement and motion, the perception of action and events, the perception of pictures, and implications of ecological realism. In the third section the development of Gibson's ideas about picture perception can be clearly followed. He started from a position in which he equated successful pictures with those that acted as accurate optical substitutes for the scenes they represented. That is, the optic arrays from the picture and the scene were similar. As a consequence of considering caricatures and other nonveridical but recognisable pictures his position changed to one of stressing the invariants in pictures. The perception of pictures involved the pick-up of information, of invariants, in the picture that are like invariants in the environment. Gibson also made the distinction between direct perception of objects in the environment, which occurs without any process of representation, and indirect perception (as in viewing pictures) which is mediated by other processes.

Representations

Bryson, N. (1983). *Vision and painting. The logic of the gaze.* London: Macmillan. A closely reasoned essay opposing the view that art represents visual experience. The social and political function of art is stressed at the expense of "realism".

Costall, A. (1986). The "psychologist's fallacy" in ecological realism. *Teorie & Modelli, 1*, 37–46. A critical examination of Gibson's ecological approach to perception, especially his concept of the mutuality of organisms and environments.

Cutting, J. E. (1986). *Perception with an eye to motion.* Cambridge, Mass.: MIT Press. Gibson's proposal of invariants is developed to analyse motion perception. Of particular interest is the discussion of experiments on viewing pictures from positions other than the station point.

Foucault, M. (1982). *This is not a pipe.* Translated and edited by J. Hawkness. Berkeley: University of California Press. Magritte's pipe paintings are analysed in this translation from the original French. It is addressed to the relationship between language and the world (that is, between words and objects), and it presents other pictures by Magritte to support a distinction between resemblance and similitude.

Furbank, P. N. (1970). *Reflections on the word "image".* London: Secker & Warburg. A literary and philosophical discourse on the use of the term "image" to signify metaphor or simulacrum.

Gablik, S. (1977). *Magritte.* Boston, Mass.: New York Graphic Society. A standard biography and appraisal of Magritte's life and work. The chapter on "The use of words" examines Magritte's pipe pictures and his many other graphical enquiries into our use of language.

Gibson, J. J. (1950). *The perception of the visual world.* Boston: Houghton Mifflin. Gibson's first book on vision in which he outlines his ideas on the richness of stimulation in providing veridical information about the layout of space.

Gombrich, E. H., Hochberg, J., & Black, M. (1972). *Art, perception and reality.* Baltimore: The Johns Hopkins University Press. A collection of essays on the nature of representation by each of the three authors. Gombrich addresses the issue of caricature and portraiture, Hochberg relates eye movements to the way a picture is processed, and Black carries out a logical analysis of resemblance.

Henle, M. (Ed.) (1976). *Vision and artifact.* New York: Springer. Contributions from authorities on vision or art are grouped into sections concerned with visual perception, visual thinking, and artifact. Those most pertinent to issues of representation are to be found in the first section, most particularly by Metelli, on transparency, by Kanizsa and Gerbino, on convexity and symmetry in figure-ground organisation, by Kennedy, on attention, brightness and the constructive eye, and by Wallach on the apparent rotation of pictorial scenes.

Kanizsa, G. (1985). Seeing and thinking. *Acta Psychologica, 59*, 23–33. An insightful paper that attacks the notion of unconscious inference in perception. Kanizsa argues that seeing follows a different logic to thinking: seeing is considered to operate according to autonomous principles of organisation that do not involve reasoning.

Polanyi, M. (1970). What is a painting? *British Journal of Aesthetics, 10*, 225–236. The problem of why perspective pictures do not appear distorted when viewed away from the station point is addressed. Polanyi restates his distinction between the subsidiary awareness of the flat picture plane and the focal awareness of the represented depth in paintings.

Rogers, D. & Sloboda, J. A. (Eds.) (1983). *The acquisition of symbolic skills.* New York: Plenum Press. The selected and edited proceedings from a conference. Of most interest are the chapters by Pratt on intellectual realism in drawings and by van Sommers on children's drawings.

van Sommers, P. (1984). *Drawing and cognition. Descriptive and experimental studies of graphic production processes.* Cambridge: Cambridge University Press. The production of everyday graphical works, especially by children, is analysed in stages and compared with language production.

Allusions

Committee of Friends of Palazzo Grassi (1987). *The Arcimboldo effect. Transformations of the face from the sixteenth to the twentieth century.* London: Thames & Hudson. This copiously illustrated exhibition catalogue reprints many of the fantastic faces painted by Giuseppe Arcimboldo, a 16th century Milanese artist. His paintings consist of collections of related elements – vegetables, flowers, books or beasts – that are arranged to be immediately recognisable as faces. The book also presents earlier illustrations, like Leonardo's anamorphic faces, as well as modern manipulations of facial features by artists like Dali, Duchamp and Magritte.

Coren, S. & Girgus, J. (1978). *Seeing is deceiving: The psychology of visual illusions.* Hillsdale: N.J.: Lawrence Erlbaum Associates Inc. A comprehensive review of the history, research and theories of visual spatial illusions, like the Müller-Lyer. The authors propose a component theory in which factors like optical blur, neural inhibition and cognitive processes interact in the generation of illusions.

Day, R. H. (1984). The nature of perceptual illusions. *Interdisciplinary Science Reviews, 9,* 47–58. Perceptual illusions are said to occur when processes normally serving veridical perception in the natural world are activated under artificial conditions.

Del-Prete, S. (1981). *Illusorismen.* Bern: Benteli. Sandro Del-Prete is an artist with an eye for the unreal. He presents many of his ingenious, and often amusing, illustrations based principally on figure-ground alternation and impossible figures.

Ernst, B. (1986). *Het begoochelde oog. Onmogelijke en meerzinnige figuren.* Utrecht: Meulenhoff/Landshoff. The author presents a wide variety of impossible and ambiguous figures, including photographs of many constructed "impossibilities". The graphical procedures for their design are described together with some theoretical background regarding interpretations of their occurrence.

Gillam, B. (1980). Geometrical illusions. *Scientific American, 242,* 86–95. A clear account of the main classes of theory addressed to visual spatial illusions, with their advantages and shortcomings. Illusion configurations are related to the patterns that occur in the natural environment.

Goldsmith, E. (1984). *Research into illustration. An approach and a review.* Cambridge: Cambridge University Press. An analysis of the uses of illustration in education. Summaries of many studies in visual communication are presented, particularly those concerned with conveying ideas graphically to children and across cultures.

Hofstadter, D. R. (1980). *Gödel, Escher, Bach: an eternal gold braid.* Harmondsworth, Middlesex: Penguin Books. This book is a continuation of Hofstadter's intriguing and unconventional commentary on problems of reference and representation. It conflates his interests in mathematics, perception and music, making passing reference to some of Magritte's pictures, and developing some of his own linguistic pipe dreams.

Lanners, E. (Ed.) (1977). *Illusions.* Translated by H. Norden. London: Thames & Hudson. A light-hearted, well-illustrated survey of illusions, broadly defined. The reader can start at either end of the book and finish in the middle!

Necker, L. A. (1832). Observations on some remarkable phenomena seen in Switzerland: and on an optical phenomenon which occurs when viewing a figure of a crystal or geometrical solid. *London and Edinburgh Philosophical Magazine and Journal of Science, 1,* 329–337. This is the first formal report of apparent depth reversals in outline figures. Necker remarked that engravings of crystalline forms frequently displayed "a sudden and involuntary change in the apparent position of a solid or crystal represented in an engraved figure".

Robinson, J. O. (1972). *The psychology of visual illusion.* London: Hutchinson. Geometrical optical illusions are classified into those of extent, orientation, depth and movement, and theories of illusions are appraised. Figural after-effects and geometrically repetitive patterns that can disturb are also considered. There is an excellent bibliography of works on illusions.

Sakane, I. (Ed.) (1979). *The expanding visual world. A museum of fun.* Tokyo: The Asahi Shimbun. The author is editor of the Arts and Sciences department of the Japanese newspaper Asahi Shimbun. He has a regular column devoted to visual puzzles and paradoxes, and this book derives from the column. It is superbly illustrated, and the pictures are grouped under the following headings: anamorphic art, impossibilities, visual games, topological art, visual illusions, and technological art.

Sakane, I. (Ed.) (1984). *The expanding perceptual world. A museum of fun. Part II.* Tokyo: The Asahi Shimbun. This is an exhibition catalogue of art works that pose pictorial puzzles. The quality of the illustrations match those of the 1979 book, and they are classified under: invitation to humor, the world of illusion, visual games, light magic, the paradox, science fantasy, topological art, and the alphabet room.

Smith, R. (1738). *A compleat system of opticks in four books.* Cambridge. Surveys Newtonian optics together with some thoughtful descriptions of visual phenomena, particularly relating to binocular vision. The line illustrations (on fold-out pages) are very clear, and these include a distant view of a windmill which presents perceptual uncertainty regarding the orientation of the sails.

2 PICTURES AS ALLUSIONS

Pictorial images consist of marks made on a two-dimensional surface. The marks themselves can be produced by a multitude of means – by pencil, paint, dyes, silver crystals or electronically activated phosphors – and the surfaces on which they can be made are equally varied. Picture production has a history that is almost as long as that for humankind. No early records remain of any marks made on decomposable surfaces, like skin or bark, but there is ample evidence of the pictures and designs that were made on stone implements and on cave walls. Thus, it seems as though pictures serve some fundamental function in human societies, although what that function might be remains a topic for speculation and debate.

The development of pictorial skills paved the way for the representation of sounds and objects as written symbols. Before the invention of script, however, it was visual space rather than sound that was depicted. Pictorial images were about the objects, animals, people, events, stories and myths that were experienced by the picture-maker. The pictorial images were resemblances of these experiences that could be communicated to other members of the society. Thus, from the very beginning of artistic expression the picture-makers faced the problem of distilling aspects of their internal images into simpler two-dimensional shapes (pictorial images) so that the pictures could be recognised by themselves and others. When representing objects in space the artist must compare the pictorial image with the scene and both these processes involve access to the visual image. The goal of the artist might not be a match between the perception of the pictorial image and the perception of the scene, but there are likely to be some areas of correspondence. However, the history of picture-making is often presented in terms of the refinements in representing external objects or events: the goal is seen as matching the pictorial image with the scene as closely as possible. Such approaches tend to neglect the part played by perception, particularly by the perception of pictures, both on the part of the artist and the observer. The visual image intervenes between all the processes of picturing. Since the formation of the visual image is itself a representational process, its interaction with pictorial images is unlikely to be simple.

This chapter will examine some of the issues involved in the allusion to three-dimensional space in a two-dimensional image, and parallels will be made between aspects of the pictorial image and the optical, retinal, visual, graphical and mental images. For many styles of painting this level of allusion – the recognition of pictorial images as spatially extended – would be taken for granted, and the artist would have more subtle and complex goals to achieve. For example, in 15th and 16th century history painting the figures represented can be readily recognised as human, but their allegorical roles can only be appreciated by those who have learned the conventions for their interpretation. Such works of art stir the imagination by going beyond perception, and interacting in intricate ways with mental imagery. The interpretation of such symbols in pictures is a matter for semiotics, to which I have little to add. My aims are much humbler, namely to consider the relationship between perceptual and pictorial representations of space, rather than the interpretation of pictorial symbols.

This close association between picture-making and perception will be kept to the forefront in the present chapter. The first section is concerned with pictorial representations of space, and the various cues that can be used to allude more strongly to the third dimension. The second section explores the similarity between photography and perception, and introduces methods for manipulating images photographically. The final section returns to pictorial representation and examines the facility provided by simplified representational techniques for manipulating our perception, and provides some more complex examples of pictorial allusions.

Pictorial Representations of Space

Pictures are by their very nature spatial, albeit flat and two-dimensional. If the pictorial image is intended to represent some object seen by the artist, then both the object itself, and its perception by the artist, will be three-dimensional. One of the reasons why the visual image has been neglected by many commentators on art is that it corresponds quite closely to Euclidean space. In general, we see things the way they would be described by a traditional physicist – objects have specified solid dimensions and they are located with respect to other objects at a given time, and if the observer or the object moves then some of these relations will change. In psychological parlance these effects are called the perceptual constancies. Therefore, space and its perception are in close correspondence. The artist then is faced with the fundamental problem of making the pictorial image in two dimensions represent a scene that is, and is seen as, three-dimensional. How can the marks be made so that they convey to the artist and to other observers the impression of the third dimension that is absent in the picture itself? The answer that is often accepted is: by making the pictorial image mimic features that are present in the retinal image, or in some equivalent optical image-forming device. We have seen, in Figure 1.18, how the static optical image bears a fixed, projective relationship to objects in space. Therefore, all that seems to be required is to transfer the optically projected dimensions onto the picture surface, so that the pictorial image mimics the conceptual optical image in the eye. Although this might seem straightforward, it is not so, because it assumes that we have some direct access to a static optical image and the dimensions projected onto it. It has been said of the eye that it is the only optical instrument that forms an image which is not intended to be seen. This statement is particularly apposite in two ways. First, it is a conceptual convenience to think of the retinal image in optical terms. The projections of light rays onto the retina follow the laws of optics, but the processes at the retinal level are electro-chemical. The retina is not a passive screen, and the abstract and static optical image needs to be distinguished from the electro-chemical and dynamic retinal image. Secondly, it is an error to consider that the eye sees. The eye and the retina are necessary for seeing, but their presence is not sufficient for vision. The optical image-forming properties of the eye could be functioning perfectly, but there would be no vision if the optic nerve was cut. The eye and retina require the neural machinery of the brain to furnish us with vision, and that is why visual and graphical image levels are so important in the scheme presented in the "Representations" section in Chapter One (see Figure 1.2).

Pictorial representation proceeded apace without any knowledge of retinal images, and many artistic styles, including linear perspective, were developed before the optical workings of the eye were even dimly understood. The source that picture-makers did, and do continually, draw upon was their own perceptual experience – their own visual and mental images of objects and events in space. The development of styles for representing space in pictorial images can be thought of as reflecting the significances attached to optical, visual, graphical and mental images at different periods. I suggest that styles can be differentiated according to the importance that they placed on one particular level. Of course, they do not operate in isolation, but one may be emphasised at the expense of others. Paradoxically, the levels we tend to associate most specifically with pictorial images – optical and graphical images – are the most abstract in terms of picture making: the use of optical images requires a theory of image formation; the appreciation of the dual nature of pictures (as objects and as representations) requires a theory of sequential image processing. Visual images make no such demands. Perceptual experience of the objects in the environment is immediate, though reflecting on its nature requires mental imagery.

Returning, then, to the picture-maker faced with making marks on a flat surface that will be recognised as representing objects in space, what aspects of the visual image should the marks represent? These will include the texture and dimensions of the object, its relation to other objects in terms of distance and direction, and the surface upon which it is supported. (As stated in Chapter One, the colour characteristics of visual, graphical and pictorial images will be ignored here.) Some aspects of the visual image do correspond to projective features of the retinal image, and these are utilised for representing the relative distances of objects in similar directions. One such common feature is that nearer objects obscure more distant ones that are in the same line-of-sight. For example, the marks of Figure 2.1 would be interpreted as some curved object in front of another similarly shaped one, because the surfaces of the former are relatively uninterrupted whereas those of the latter are broken. In the jargon of perceptual psychology this is called interposition or occlusion or overlay. It is a rule that is rarely broken in representational art, and it is a simple consequence of light travelling in straight lines. The only conditions under which the nearer object does not occlude the farther one is when the former is transparent.

Occlusion does not occur only for objects in similar directions but at different distances. In the environment objects are generally supported by others or by the ground (unless they are lighter than air). Accordingly, the most basic aspect of occlusion is the removal from view of the ground that is immediately beneath and behind the object. The amount of ground that is obscured will depend upon the size of the object. The location of objects with respect to the background will, however, vary with distance from the observer. If we consider a horizontal ground plane, then similarly sized objects on it will appear higher the farther away they are. Again this is a feature that is common to both optical and visual images, and it is often referred to as height-in-the-field. The two outlines in Figure 2.2 are about the same size, but the upper one may appear more distant. The impression of distance is not very compelling because no background is represented. It would be much more effective if the ground surface upon which they were resting was also drawn. But how should the ground plane be represented? When we look at a textured surface, like grass or pebbles or a tiled floor, then the apparent size of the elements (like the single tiles) will remain relatively constant with increasing distance. If the apparent size does diminish, it is at a much slower rate than in the optical image. If the sizes are represented in the pictorial image as they are seen then there is a marked mismatch between the graphical image of the pictorial image and the visual image of the scene. That is, the picture will not look like the scene. The represented ground plane would appear to rise steeply upwards in the pictorial image. Perhaps, this was one of the reasons why the ground plane was often represented as receding obliquely across the surface of the picture in Chinese and Japanese art, as well as in pre-Renaissance paintings. An alternative strategy used in many Eastern prints was to leave the ground plane devoid of any texture. Oblique projection (in which the representation of distance is along oblique lines) also serves an additional function with respect to the representation of the dimensions of objects. When we look at a geometrically regular object, like a table-top, then the near and far sides appear to be the same size, even though they project different sizes to the eye. The representation of a table as a parallelogram, in oblique projection, is more acceptable at the graphical image level than is a rectangular, pictorial image (see Figure 2.3). More information regarding the object is available in oblique projection, too: each leg of the table is depicted, and the occlusion of part of one provides evidence for the solidity of the form.

The artistic styles of representation using oblique projection, like Eastern and pre-Renaissance, are often referred to in terms of the artist painting what is known about objects and space rather than what is

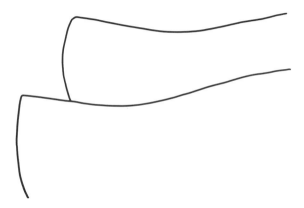

2.1 Interposition: a line drawing in which the lower curve appears to occlude part of the upper one.

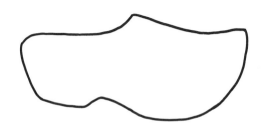

2.2 Height-in-the-field: two equivalent outline drawings, in which the upper one might appear to be more distant than the lower one.

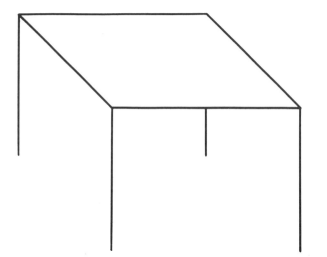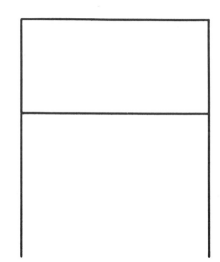

2.3 Two pictorial representations of a table. In both cases the parallel edges are drawn the same length, but the left one is in oblique projection. Note that the interpretation of these simple pictorial images as representations of a table probably results in the upper edges appearing to be longer than the lower ones.

seen. I believe that this analysis is inappropriate. It can be argued that the artists were painting what they saw, in terms of the constancies of the visual image, rather than their knowledge of the dimensions of objects. That is, they were trying to represent their visual images. The reason that their pictorial images appear strange to us, is that we look at them with a different pictorial history. It is interesting to speculate how they would have appeared to the artists, themselves. That is, they would have had no experience of pictorial images in linear perspective, and so their own perception of their art may well have lacked the strangeness that it holds for us. We cannot expunge our experience of previous pictorial images we have viewed, and the majority of these will have been in perspective (since they would be predominantly photographic images in newspapers, magazines and books). Perhaps the only way in which we can obtain any insight into this issue is by studying picture perception in present-day cultures with different histories of pictorial representation to our own. It has been argued earlier that the picture is both an object and a representation of other objects, and so the pictorial image is processed at the level of the graphical image (Figure 1.2); at this level the rescaling of the marks made in pre-Renaissance paintings does not correspond to objects that we would see in the environ-

ment, nor the pictorial images we have become accustomed to seeing. None the less, we can generally recognise the objects represented in them and also assess the relative distances depicted.

Pictorial images in linear perspective, on the other hand, do not create any such conflicts when they are rescaled at the level of the graphical image. They use some of the cues to the third dimension previously mentioned, like occlusion and height-in-the-field, together with many more. The principles of linear perspective were demonstrated by the Florentine genius Brunelleschi, early in the 15th century, and they were formalised by his contemporary Alberti. Linear perspective provided a theory of image formation based upon the fact that light travels in straight lines and will converge to a point in the observer's eye. This much was known to Euclid (around 300 BC), and these principles were employed in Graeco-Roman art. They are basically statements regarding the visual angles subtended by objects at different distances, i.e., statements about the projection characteristics of the optical image. What Alberti added was a systematic method for transferring the optical image to the picture plane. In order to achieve this he defined the fixed station point (the observer's eye) and the horizon line which was parallel to the ground plane, but intersected it in the picture plane at the central

2.4 Alberti's window: the eye defines the station point (SP), and the distance that it is separated from the picture plane (PP) will determine how much of the scene is contained within the pictorial image. The line parallel to the ground plane (GP) is called the horizon line (HL). A frontal view of the picture plane is shown on the right. The intersection of the ground plane (which is the vertical line) and the horizon line defines the vanishing point (VP).

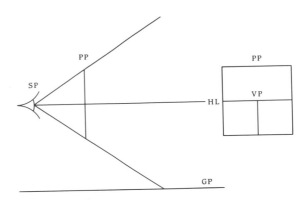

2.5 The projection of equally separated dimensions (like tiles) on the ground plane onto the picture plane.

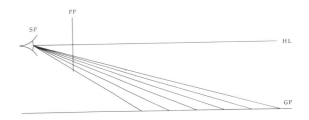

2.6 Parallel lines on the horizontal ground plane that are at right angles (orthogonal) to the picture plane converge to meet at the central vanishing point.

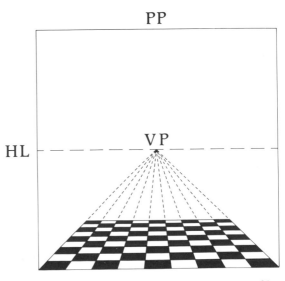

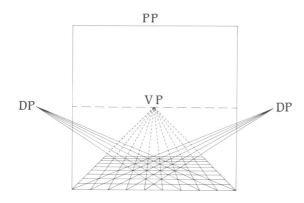

2.7 The two lateral distance points (DP) are determined by extending the lines through the corners of the tiles.

Conversely, the distance points can be used to scale the dimensions of tiles in the picture plane.

2.8 A texture gradient. A photograph of a stony riverside.

vanishing point (see Figure 2.4). The entire array of light that passed through the picture plane to converge at the station point (of the eye) was called the visual pyramid. The amount of the scene included in the visual pyramid was dependent upon the dimensions of the picture plane and the separation of the station point from it. With a small separation a wide-angle view is obtained, but with a long separation a narrow angle would be enclosed in the visual pyramid and picture plane. The system described the rules for representing the ground plane. Take, for example, a tiled checkerboard floor: the regular spacings between the tiles parallel to the picture plane are represented as systematically decreasing dimensions (Figure 2.5), and the lines at right angles (or orthogonal) to the picture plane converge to meet at the central vanishing point (Figure 2.6). Furthermore, the lines extended through the diagonals of the tiles in the picture plane converge to two lateral distance points at the height of the horizon line (Figure 2.7).

In contrast to the earlier forms of representing space, linear perspective required that the artist should disregard the perceived dimensions of objects in a scene and represent instead the visual angles subtended at the eye, which was located at a specified station point. This enabled the artist to incorporate a far wider range of cues to distance in a consistent manner over the picture plane. That is, in addition to occlusion and height-in-the-field, the projective features of the ground plane could be represented, irrespective of its composition. The checkerboard floor provided the yardstick for examining the artist's mastery of the perspective method, but not all ground planes are tiled and horizontal! Natural ground planes, like grass, stones, paths and so on are textured, but not as regularly as the tiled surface favoured by Alberti. Indeed, texture gradients – the variation in the density of the projected texture with distance from the station point – provide one of the most pervasive sources of information for distance in the environment. Figure 2.8 illustrates the texture gradient on a stony surface: the number of stones within a given area of the picture is much greater in the upper parts, and this provides a powerful cue to receding distance. It is worth noticing that the texture gradients do not require that the elements are the same physical size, but the cue works better pictorially if the variation is not too large. Many of the classes of objects in the environment are of similar size. For instance, people differ in height, but not by very much. Thus, the variation in the projected sizes of people in a crowd can give the impression of distance in a pictorial image. Moreover, if we accept that people are about the same size, then when grossly different sizes are represented in the pictorial image it is likely that the smaller one is farther away. Thus, familiar size is another cue that can be used in creating the impression of distance in the pictorial image. Familiar size is likely to be a more complex cue to distance than the others mentioned above because it can only operate after the familiarity has been established. That is, the objects must first be recognised as familiar, and this involves access to the mental image level; thereafter, the information from the mental image can be brought to bear at the graphical image level when interpreting represented distance in the pictorial image.

In the natural environment the light source is the sun and, if it is not occluded by clouds, shadows will be formed by objects. Shadows can be informative about both shape and depth. In the case of Figure 2.9 the picture is of a shallow footprint in sand. Depressions in low relief, like this, can usually be recognised from their shadow properties, when the surround is even. Shadows cast by objects onto other surfaces indicate their relative distances. In Figure 2.10 the shadow of a man reading a book falls on both the ground and the wall of the turret providing some information of the distance separating the man from the wall. If we were to see the shadow alone we might be able to hazard a guess at the object that formed it, although it would probably not be very accurate in this case, unlike Figure 2.11, which is easier to reconstruct from shadows alone. A further service that shadows can provide concerns the shape of the surface upon which they are cast. Thus, in Figure 2.12 the shadows from the headlight and the wires deviate markedly from their own shapes; these deviations are consistent with the interpretation that the surface onto which the shadows are cast is corrugated, and this is reinforced by the vertical shadows cast by the corrugations themselves. In order to abstract this information about surfaces it is necessary to have some knowledge about the shape of the illuminated object; if this is not available then the shape of the surface may be judged erroneously. This is similar to the problem of interpreting silhouettes that was mentioned in Chapter One. Shadows also share with

2.9 (Facing page) Photograph of a footprint in sand.

2.10 Shadow cast by a figure onto a horizontal and vertical surface.

2.11 Long evening shadows of two people leaning on one another.

2.12 Wavy shadows formed by wires and a headlight falling on a corrugated surface.

2.13 Aerial perspective: the contrasts of the mountains in the photograph decrease with distance.

2.14 Linear perspective: a photograph of Dundee taken from the observation deck of the Tay Road Bridge. The lamp standards display interposition and height-in-the-field; their equal separations in space subtend diminishing separations in the photographic image, as do the projected sizes of the lamps, themselves. The details of the buildings are not readily visible due to their reduced contrast. The water presents a powerful texture gradient.

transparent objects the property of not occluding the surfaces on which they fall. For example, the bricks in the wall of the turret in Figure 2.10 that are in the shadow of the man can still be clearly discerned, but they differ in tone.

Another cue to distance that depends upon tone is called aerial perspective. Typically, distant objects are not as distinct as nearer ones and they are often tinged with blue. Only the former aspect can be illustrated in black and white, as with the alpine scene in Figure 2.13. Here, like the shadow examples, the cue is not operating in isolation, but others like occlusion are also present.

When all these projective cues are incorporated in the pictorial image a compelling allusion to three-dimensional space is produced, as is shown in Figure 2.14. From the 15th century onwards linear perspective became the dominant system for representing space. Pictorial images in linear perspective were considered to provide a more convincing allusion to the third dimension because they followed more closely the manner in which light passes through the eye. This was not appreciated at the time of its inception, and the relationship between perspective and perception was intuitive rather than formal. Perspective pictures must have been as amazing to 15th century observers as apparently moving pictures were to those in the 19th century: it seemed as magical to create the allusion to depth on a flat picture as it was to craft motion from a se-

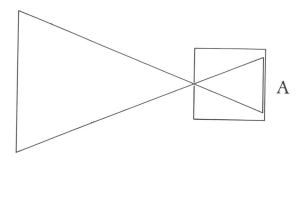

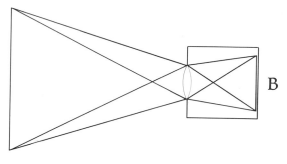

2.15 Cameras. A a pinhole camera. The dark chamber (camera obscura) admits light only through a small aperture, resulting in a reversed and inverted optical image of the scene on the surface opposite the aperture. Ideally, the pinhole camera has infinite depth-of-field, i.e., all imaged edges will be sharp, no matter what their distance from the aperture. The optical image is of very low contrast, and if a light sensitive film is placed opposite the aperture long time exposures would be required. B: a lensed camera. The enlarged aperture admits more light and so shorter exposures are possible for film. The lens brings light rays to a focus at the rear surface; without the lens a very blurred image would be formed. However, the lens can only focus light from certain distances, and so the depth-of-field is more restricted with a lensed than a pinhole camera.

quence of still pictures. However, the painting of pictures in accurate linear perspective according to Alberti's method was both painstaking and tedious. In the following decades a variety of devices were either enlisted or invented, notably by Leonardo da Vinci and Albrecht Dürer, to reduce the tedium. One of the methods Leonardo proposed was an extension of Alberti's conception of the picture plane as a window, and it is often called Leonardo's window. If a scene is observed through a glass window with one eye and a stationary head, then tracing on the window all the contours aligned with objects in the scene will yield a picture in accurate linear perspective. Dürer proposed additional methods using grids, gnomons or sighting vanes, and sighting lines that were more direct than Alberti's method.

It was the properties of one of the devices used by Leonardo, the camera obscura, that eventually led to the realisation that the images represented in perspective pictures shared many features with the optical projections to the stationary eye. The camera obscura, or dark chamber (now often called a pinhole camera), had a small aperture on one side through which light could pass, forming an inverted and reversed image on the opposite side (see Figure 2.15A). If the image was cast on a glass or paper screen then it could be traced, so that an accurate central perspective drawing of the external scene was obtained without any complicated grids or measurements.

In the late 16th century the similarity between the working of the camera obscura and the eye was remarked upon, and lenses were even placed in larger apertures to focus the optical images (see Figure 2.15B). By the early 17th century the astronomer Johannes Kepler confirmed this similarity by showing how an optical image was brought to a focus in the plane of the retina, following refraction of light at the cornea and the surfaces of the crystalline lens. The optical image is also inverted and reversed. Once the similarity between image formation in the eye and camera had been proposed there was an overwhelming temptation to equate the characteristics of perception to those of the optical image. In other words the properties of the visual image were reduced to those of the optical image. This speculation was fuelled by the success of perspective representation: if the pictorial image creates an allusion to three-dimensional space, and its geometry is similar to that of the optical image then the allusion to space must be in the eye, too. The

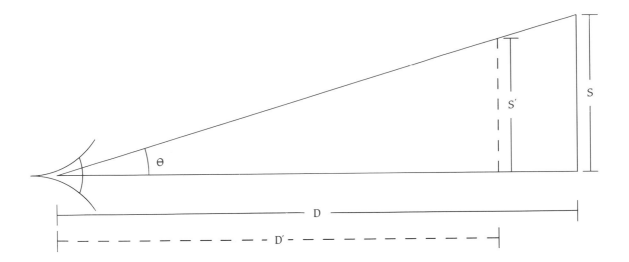

speculation was further fuelled by the desire, within the scientific community of the 17th century, to reduce all phenomena to mathematics. The geometry of images could be calculated with precision and they followed laws of projection. Perception could then be measured mathematically. Ironically, it was the foremost geometer of the time, René Descartes, who laid bare the shortcomings of this equation, by providing evidence that visual perception did not always correspond to the dimensions of the retinal projection. If it did, then our perception would follow the law of the visual angle: objects of constant size would appear to get smaller as they receded from us, because their size on the retina would decline. This would be so irrespective of the ground upon which the object was seen. As we have already stated, we see objects as remaining much the same size, despite their varying distance from us, and this is called size constancy. Descartes argued that our perception of size is based upon retinal image size, but it is not equated with it; the perceived distance of the object is also taken into account. That is, there is a relationship between perceived size and distance, and if we perceive distance appropriately this can be used to rescale the information from retinal size (Figure 2.16). The visual image uses the retinal image but it should not be identified with the dimensions of the image in the eye.

This might seem to raise a problem for pictorial images. Why is the allusion to the third dimension successful in perspective pictures if they mirror the optical image rather than the visual image? The reason is that we have to look at the pictures. The

2.16 Size-distance invariance. An object of size S units and at a distance of D units subtends an angle θ at the eye (where $\tan \theta = S/D$). If the apparent distance (D′) is less than the physical distance, then the apparent size (S′) will be correspondingly smaller. The size-distance invariance relationship is described by the following equation: $S/D = S'/D'$.

perspective picture produces an optical image similar to that produced by viewing the scene itself from the station point adopted for the pictorial image; the rescaling process can then proceed in the brain so that the projective cues to perceived distance can be used to modify perceived size. As was suggested earlier, our visual images of external space are generally veridical – that is, they correspond closely to the physical dimensions of external space, like extent and time. This veridicality of the visual image is a consequence of using as many sources of information as possible: objects are not perceived in isolation, but in the rich context of their surroundings. It is the projective features of the surroundings that makes possible the judgement of the distance and the rescaling of projected size. This applies both to the perception of objects in three-dimensional space or of the same scene painted in accurate linear perspective and viewed from the station point. The richness of the context, of all the cues to distance that are in correspondence rather than conflict, enables the perspective painting to provide such a compelling allusion to its missing dimension.

If a distant object in space was pictured in isola-

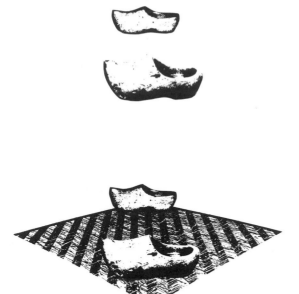

2.17 Photographs of cloggs at different distances, without and with a textured ground.

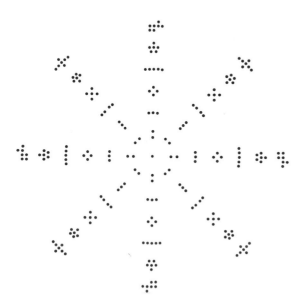

2.18 Radiating dots: when the single central dot is fixated it becomes increasingly difficult to see the number of dots drawn at increasing eccentricities.

tion, but at its accurate visual angle, then it would look far smaller on the canvas than in the scene (see Figure 2.17). This is because the pictorial image would be devoid of any context whereas the scene is replete with context. There is a similar tendency when an object is viewed in isolation, say a patch of light in an otherwise totally dark room, then the judgement of its size is determined principally by its projected dimensions on the retina, because the context for rescaling it has been removed. Thus, the perception of objects or of pictures can be reduced to the dimensions of the optical image, if no other projective features are available. Such conditions are rarely present in our perception of scenes. These reduced conditions are, however, a prerequisite of painting: the canvas is initially blank, and marks need to be made on it. It is for this reason that the painters in linear perspective had to work so hard and estimate visual angles with outstretched thumbs, or use gnomons and grids, or Leonardo's window, or the camera obscura. If objects were painted the size they looked then they would not match with the projected sizes of other painted objects in the scene. Thus, they had to follow strict regimes to maintain the projective characteristics of the pictorial image. The completed picture will look like the scene because the contextual cues will be used similarly for both of them to rescale projected size.

The pictorial image, in accurate linear perspective, has therefore many features in common with the optical image. There are, however, many shortcomings in the representation of a scene in a picture when compared with the perception of that same scene. The projective features are in accord for one position only – the station point defined by the artist. It is only when the eye is at that particular point that the pictorial image would correspond to the spatial dimensions of the static optical image. Any lateral movement of the eye to a different position would destroy the equivalence. This is one of the reasons why the most successful attempts at fooling-the-eye (*trompe-l'oeil*) place strict demands upon the viewer. Perspective peep-shows, like van Hoogstratten's in the National Gallery, London, consist of scenes painted inside a cabinet which can only be seen through a small peep-hole, with one eye. Similarly, Pozzo's ceiling, in the Church of St. Ignazio in Rome, is to be viewed from a central star marked on the floor beneath it. From that position the painted ceiling, which is hemi-cylindrical, appears to be dome-shaped. These are illusions of

2.19 Two photographs of the same scene, focusing either on the foreground or background.

depth, because the depth in the pictorial image is misjudged, and treated as real depth.

In normal perception the eyes never remain stationary for many moments – they either rotate in the socket or the head itself moves as well. It is noteworthy that viewers of perspective pictures rarely seek the appropriate station point, and yet they still experience the allusion to depth in the pictures. Precise alignment of viewing and station points might not always be essential because the

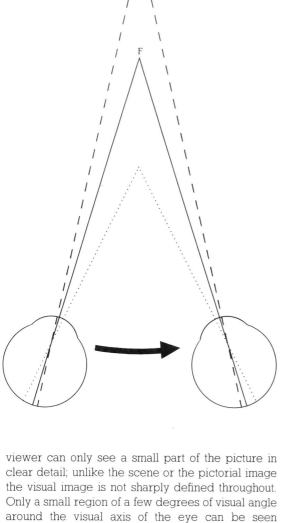

2.20 Motion parallax: if one eye fixates on a point (F) at a given distance and then the head moves to the right, while maintaining fixation (as shown on the left), then near objects will appear to move in the opposite direction and more distant ones will be seen to move in the same direction. This is shown on the right, with the optical image motions represented with respect to the stationary eye.

viewer can only see a small part of the picture in clear detail; unlike the scene or the pictorial image the visual image is not sharply defined throughout. Only a small region of a few degrees of visual angle around the visual axis of the eye can be seen sharply, the rest becomes increasingly blurred and indistinct (see Figure 2.18). Most detailed spatial processing occurs within the small central region of the retina. In order to see the detail elsewhere the eye must move to place that region centrally on the retina. It is only when the picture is either very small or viewed from a great distance that the pictorial image falls in its entirety within the region of clear vision. Under these conditions the frame of the picture would then be visible. When three-dimensional scenes have frames, as when looking out of a window, there is plenty of information concerning the closeness of the frame with respect to the distant

scene. This is not the case for pictures: the plane of the frame is the same as that of the pictorial image.

The pictorial image in linear perspective generally depicts objects at different distances with similar clarity, apart from those represented at great distances which will be a little hazy and bluish due to aerial perspective. Again this would not match our perception of the scene: only those objects at and around the optical focus of the eye will be seen clearly, others that are nearer or farther will be out of focus (see Figure 2.19). In order to see objects clearly at different distances the focusing power of the eye must change. This process, which is called accommodation, occurs quickly because of changes in the curvature of the crystalline lens. Thus, we can change our accommodation rapidly from near to far objects, but when we are focusing on one the other will be indistinct.

2.21 The differences between approaching a picture and an object can be illustrated with these photographs of a statue. The upper photograph was enlarged to produce that on the lower left. This is essentially like approaching a pictorial image, so that some detail in it subtends a larger visual angle. The photograph on the lower right was taken with the camera much closer to the statue. Note that the pictorial dimensions of the statue are about the same, but those of the background differ considerably: approaching the object (which is essentially like the lower right photograph) results in the occlusion of more of the background.

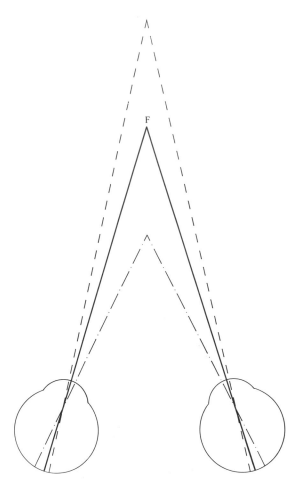

2.22 Retinal disparities in binocular vision. If the eyes fixate point F then objects farther away will form uncrossed disparities and nearer ones will have crossed disparities. These can easily be demonstrated by holding up the two index fingers at different distances in the straight-ahead direction. Fixate on the nearer finger with both eyes, then close the left and right eyes in turn. The far finger will appear to the right when using the right eye, and to the left with the left eye – uncrossed disparity. The opposite, called crossed disparity, occurs when the far finger is fixated.

Pictorial images are static and stable. They represent a scene from a particular position at a particular time. Perception is, by contrast, dynamic: it changes over time, not only as a consequence of eye movements and accommodation, but also because the whole body moves through space. When we look at a scene and move sideways then the relative positions of objects in the scene will change slightly: some will become occluded and others will be disclosed. These projective changes are referred to as motion parallax, and this gives useful information regarding the relative distances of objects from us. For example, Figure 2.20 represents an eye fixating upon an object at a given distance: when the head moves to the side (while maintaining fixation) objects that are farther away move over the retina in the opposite direction to the head whereas those that are nearer move in the same direction. The extent of the motion depends upon the relative distance from the fixated object – the shorter the separation the smaller the movement. Clearly motion parallax cannot be incorporated into static pictures. Therefore, as soon as the observer moves there is a conflict between the cues to distance in the pictorial image and those that would be produced by the three-dimensional scene. This applies to any motion of the observer, not just to lateral movement. Suppose that the observer walks towards the picture, then all visual angles increase equally, whereas walking towards objects results in the greatest angular increases for near objects (see Figure 2.21).

Despite all these mismatches between pictorial images and visual images we continue to see pictures as providing compelling allusions to three-dimensional space. However, the paradox is even more perplexing. Let us assume that all the projective features in the pictorial image correspond to those in the optical image. The eye is perfectly still, has clear vision throughout the picture plane, and the picture is viewed from the appropriate station point. This remains inadequate because it assumes that there is only one eye! The projective cues to distance that are enlisted in linear perspective presume a single station point and therefore a single eye. In psychology these are often called the *monocular* cues to distance. The visual image is based upon two retinal images, not one, and each receives a slightly different projection of the external space (see Figure 2.22). The differences or disparities are due to the lateral separation (by 65mm or so) of the eyes. Even though the projections

2.23 Stereoscopic photographs of a stereoscope. The left eye sees more of the left side of near objects and vice versa for the right eye. This has been simulated with these two photographs of the stereoscope, which were taken from slightly different positions. If the photographs are mounted in an instrument, like that portrayed, it would appear to be three-dimensional. It is possible to combine the two photographs without the aid of a stereoscope, and the lower pair are provided for this purpose. While holding the head symmetrically above the two photographs bring the index finger close to the eyes; by opening and closing each eye in turn find the position in which the finger points to the same part of each photograph; keep fixating on the tip of your finger and you will probably see three stereoscopes, then move your finger away. The one in the middle is projected to each eye, and if you combine them successfully (it takes some time for most people), it will appear much more solid than the flanking pictures. The lower stereopair is a left–right reversal of the upper pair, because free fusion involves combining the left photograph in the right eye with the right photograph in the left eye. If you try to combine the upper pair you might see a reverse stereo effect, called pseudoscopic, in which the disparities are reversed and the stereoscope appears to be behind the plane of the paper.

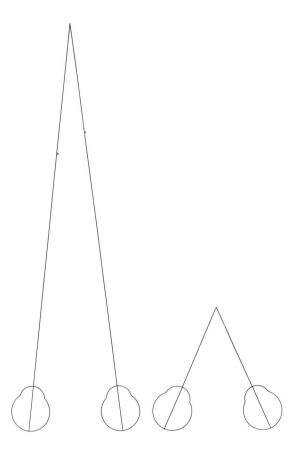

2.24 Convergence of the eyes varies with the distance of the object fixated.

differ only slightly, these differences are systematic and they furnish us with stereoscopic vision. When two flat pictures (like those in Figure 2.23) are viewed separately, one to each eye, then they are combined in the brain to give a solid visual image. The instrument shown in Figure 2.23 is a stereoscope; with this device it is possible to manipulate the differences in the retinal disparities produced by the two pictorial images, and it has been found that we can detect minute disparities. The depth that is seen in a pair of stereoscopic pictures also depends upon the relative angle between the eyes, which is called convergence (see Figure 2.24). For the same retinal disparities the perceived depth is greater the smaller the degree of convergence.

These binocular cues to distance of retinal disparity and of convergence provide strong evidence that the picture plane is flat even though the projective cues within it are appropriate for a three-dimensional scene. The only ways in which two identical images could be projected onto the eyes are for distant or flat objects. This shortcoming of projective pictures was known to Leonardo da Vinci. He wrote: "a painting, though conducted with the greatest art and finished to the last perfection, both with regard to its contours, its lights, its shadows and its colours, can never show a relievo equal to that of the natural objects, unless they be viewed at a distance and with a single eye". This conclusion was reached on the basis of his perception rather than on a formal knowledge of retinal disparity. The link between retinal disparity and stereoscopic vision was not forged for another three centuries.

It is clear from perspective cabinets and the like that perspective representations work best when they are viewed monocularly and also when the frame of the picture cannot be seen. This does not account for the fact that perspective pictures still provide a compelling allusion to solid space even when they are viewed by a moving, binocular observer, often from locations far removed from the ideal station point. How can the projective cues in a picture function if it is not viewed appropriately? As was suggested in the "Representations" section in Chapter One, we need to distinguish between the visual image of the picture as an object and the graphical image of the pictorial image within it. As an object, a rectangular, framed picture will be subject to shape constancy. If the picture is viewed from one side then, despite the projection of the frame onto the eye as a trapezium, it will appear more nearly rectangular. Thus, shape constancy

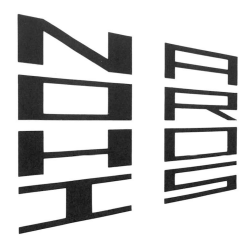

2.25 *Shifted perspective.* The letters are arranged in a grid which will appear rectangular if viewed from the extreme right side, then the word ANAMORPHOSIS will be recognised. This was drawn using the same principles as were employed in the 16th and 17th centuries to produce anamorphoses: a pictorial image in central perspective was initially drawn within a regular rectangular grid. The grid was then transformed with regard to some eccentric station point and the contents of the original grid cells were transposed to them.

initially rescales the projected dimensions of the picture, to make it more nearly rectangular. Following this process the projective features within the picture then operate as though the picture was viewed from a more frontal position. That is, there are two processes in operation, one for the picture as an object, and the other for the pictorial image; they need to function in that sequence if the perspective cues to depth and distance are to provide a convincing allusion to the third dimension. It is for this reason that a distinction has been made between the visual image and the graphical image.

Linear perspective provides a system of compressing the three dimensions of space down to the two dimensions of the pictorial image, so that an allusion to the former is provided. When one dimension is systematically compressed in this way it can equally systematically be distorted. Such per-spective distortions soon appeared on the pictorial scene. Leonardo himself experimented with the first anamorphoses, and these were developed into a precise art form in the 17th century. An anamorphic representation generally requires two stages; the first involves producing a pictorial image in central perspective and this is then transferred to another surface at an angle to the initial picture plane. For example, the letters in Figure 2.25 form a wedge-shaped block when looked at normally on the page, but when viewed with one eye from the extreme right-hand side they can be seen in a square block. More complex anamorphoses have been produced with radiating pictorial images that can be seen in appropriate perspective when reflected from a cylindrical mirror.

It was stated at the outset of this section that representations of objects-in-space in pictorial images are never dependent solely on optical, retinal, visual, graphical or mental images. They all interact, but one may be emphasised at the cost of others. For example, the importance placed on optical image formation in the Renaissance was not divorced from the content of the pictorial images. Alberti's prime concern was to provide artists with a method for defining a realistic pictorial space in which the traditional symbolic allusions could be treated. Mental images played a central role in determining the objects and personages included in the pictorial images. Indeed, many of the pictorial spaces represented were themselves imaginary. This remained the case for several centuries, until an increased concern for representing naturalistic scenes was evident in the pictorial images produced. The realistic scenes could be painted or drawn with recourse to the rules of perspective.

The hallmark of post-Renaissance painting was the considered selection of the station point, so that the contents of the pictorial image could be appropriately composed. However, in the late 19th century a movement, subsequently called Impressionism, arose in which such careful consideration over the selection of a station point was eschewed. Rather, the Impressionists sought to capture on canvas the snatched glimpses of their surroundings from arbitrary station points. These were often upwards, downwards or sideways views that would not have been entertained as suitable station points for earlier representational styles. Such fleeting, and usually unexpected, glances needed to be captured with celerity, and so the Impressionists tended to paint quickly, thereby abandoning the tonal subtleties of former styles.

It has often been argued that the Impressionists were influenced by photography, particularly by the existence of faster films that enabled snapshots to be taken. This view is tempting to embrace, but it does not seem to have very convincing evidence to support it. It can be argued, perhaps with greater conviction, that the photographic snapshot – the unusual viewpoint – developed as a response to Impressionist paintings: the painted vision was the precursor of the photographic view. None the less, once the vision was appreciated by photographers it was, and still is, applied with great effect.

Amongst the offshoots from this Impressionist movement were the neo-Impressionists, like Seurat. These artists explored the optical image in a novel way, and were especially concerned with understanding the manner in which colours can be combined in the vision of scenes and of pictorial images. They were influenced by the discoveries about shape and colour perception made earlier in the century by the likes of Helmholtz, and how they could be incorporated into their paintings. The pictorial image and its optical effects were not considered in terms of lines, instead they were comprised of dots that were too small to be seen at the appropriate viewing point for the pictorial image. With this technique the dots of different colours combined more like light than pigment mixed on a palette. Here we can see the interplay between the science and art of colour mixing, and the emergence of a new appreciation of the artists' material, pigment, and its relation to vision. Thus, the optical image was subjected to detailed dissection by the Impressionists and neo-Impressionists, although they continued to represent their vision of external space. With the benefit of hindsight, it might be thought inevitable that subsequent developments would emphasise the artificiality of representation rather than its reality.

Developments in the 20th century have been so multifarious that it would be folly to characterise them in a particular manner. However, as a broad generalisation it is suggested that the focus has shifted from the optical image to the graphical image: the picture has become an entity in itself, rather than a substitute for something else. The picture and the pictorial image become one and the same thing: the pictorial image does not represent space but it represents itself. More will be said about this in Chapters Four and Five.

Photography and Vision

It is a cliché that the eye is like a camera. Certainly, in terms of optical image formation there are many similarities between the eye and a camera. The images are inverted and reversed and they are in accurate central perspective. Indeed, in the previous section it was shown that the use of the camera obscura as an aid to art influenced its application to the science of the eye. However, when we say that the eye and the camera are alike we assume that the human eye is under consideration but we do not specify the type of camera. It probably would not be a pinhole camera, but rather a more modern one. That is, one with a lens and controls for the exposure duration (shutter speed) and the aperture setting (diaphragm diameter).

The pupil in the eye is rather like the aperture in a camera. When the light intensity is low the pupil/aperture increases in diameter to allow more light into the eye/camera, and the diameter decreases with increasing light intensity. The range of pupil diameters in the eye is quite small – from about 2mm to 8mm – and therefore the modulation of retinal illumination is around 1:16. Cameras generally have a wider range. For example, if the aperture settings range from $f2$ to $f16$ the modulation of film illumination would be 1:64. (The f number specifies the ratio of the focal length of the lens to the aperture diameter. Thus, a setting of $f2$ indicates that the focal length of the lens is twice the aperture diameter.)

The aperture setting on a camera influences the depth-of-field in the photographic image. Depth-of-field refers to the range of distances over which objects in the scene will be focused in the photographic image. The smaller the aperture the greater the depth-of-field, as is shown in Figure 2.26. A pinhole camera, with an aperture of about 1mm, will have an infinite depth-of-field; that is, all imaged objects will be in focus, no matter what distance they are from the camera. However, long exposures are required for such photographs because so little light enters the camera through the tiny aperture. It is for the same reason that short-sighted people can see clearly for much greater distances when they look through a small hole in a card or through a small opening made by crooking the index finger. In these cases the field of vision is also greatly reduced because the aperture is in front of the eye.

In cameras there is a close relationship between aperture setting and exposure duration, such that they vary reciprocally: as the aperture decreases in diameter the exposure duration increases. This is to ensure that, for each exposure of the film, the amount of light (aperture × duration) remains relatively constant. The exposure duration or shutter speed has no parallel in the eye. The camera captures a static image whereas the eye operates dynamically: there are no static images in the eye. Indeed, if the image cast on the retina is stabilised artificially (by some optical device worn on the eye) so that it moves exactly as the eye does, then the visual image disappears after a few seconds. The eye is under continual motion even when we try to fixate on something. The movements are usually very small

and of high frequency, and they are a consequence of slight instabilities in the muscles controlling the eye. Far from degrading the visual image the movements are essential for its continued functioning. If a camera moved in the way the eye does the photographic images it produced would be blurred, unless the exposures were exceedingly brief. There are, of course, regular interruptions to our normal vision when we blink, but we generally remain unaware of these because the process set in train by light striking the receptors persists for some time after the stimulation ceases.

Modern cameras are also able to focus on objects at different distances by adjustments of the lens position. Lenses are made in many forms, though, from fish-eye to telephoto: fish-eye lenses have a panoramic field-of-view whereas telephoto lenses have very narrow ones. The standard lenses that are fitted to most 35mm cameras have a field-of-view of around 47°; in other words, all objects within an angular subtense of 47° horizontally with respect to the camera will form an optical image within it. In the case of human vision the visual field for one eye subtends about 140° horizontally and 120° vertically. This raises the question: should the visual field of the eye be matched by that of the camera? The answer will depend upon the use for which the image in the camera is to be put. For the present let us pursue the eye-camera analogy, and assume that the optical images in the two systems are to be compared, and so their overall fields-of-view are comparable. Under these circumstances the optical image quality in the camera will be vastly superior to that in the eye. The crystalline lens in the eye is a simple one that produces a number of aberrations not found in the compound lenses of cameras.

The principal optical errors in the eye are spherical and chromatic aberrations. Spherical aberration refers to the fact that light passing through different parts of a single lens will be brought to focus at different distances from the lens (see Figure 2.27). The rays near the axis of the lens are focused farther from the lens than are those striking the lens peripherally. This means that a point source of light cannot be focused at a point; rather there is a range of positions where some of the rays are focused, and the best image is found at a position between the extreme focal planes. This image is a blur circle rather than a point. Spherical aberration can be reduced by preventing light from striking the more

a

b

c

d

peripheral parts of the lens – that is, by reducing the diameter of the aperture through which the light passes before striking the lens.

Chromatic aberration occurs when white light (made up from all the wavelengths in the visible spectrum) passes through a single lens. The short wavelength light (corresponding very roughly to blue) is refracted or bent to a greater degree than the longer wavelengths (Figure 2.28). Again, this results in blur circles being formed, but in the case of chromatic aberration these are coloured: the initial blur circle, at the focus for short wavelength light appears to have a blue centre and a red halo, whereas that for long wavelength light has a red centre and blue halo. The disc of least confusion, between these extremes, appears yellow. The compound lenses of cameras are called achromatic because they are made up from components with different optical characteristics, so that they do not display chromatic aberration. In the eye some of the optical effects of chromatic aberration are reduced because the lens itself is slightly yellowish, and so some of the short wavelength (bluish) light is absorbed before it strikes the retina.

The particular blur circles that are formed on the retina depend upon the state of optical focus that is in operation. The focusing mechanism of the eye differs from that employed in cameras. In fact, in the eye most of the refraction of light takes place at the cornea, the transparent surface of the eye; this is the boundary between the medium of air and that of the eye, which has a higher refractive index than air. The crystalline lens carries out the fine focusing, and this is achieved by varying the curvature of the lens (Figure 2.29). Therefore, in order to focus on objects close to the eye the front and rear surfaces of the lens take on a greater curvature. For the camera the lenses are of fixed curvature and focusing is achieved by moving the lens towards or away from the film. in order to focus on near objects the focal length is increased by moving the lens away from the film (Figure 2.30).

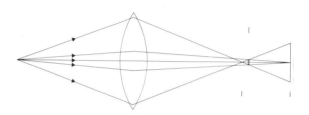

2.27 Spherical aberration: light rays striking the peripheral parts of the lens are brought to a focus closer to the lens than those near the axis. These foci are marked by the vertical lines at the bottom. The best focus is a blur circle, which is located at the position marked by the upper line; it is called the disc of least confusion.

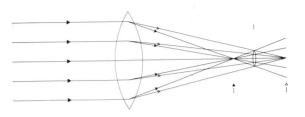

2.28 Chromatic aberration: white light striking a lens is broken down into its spectral components. Here the short and long wavelengths are represented by solid and outline triangles, respectively. The short wavelength light is refracted more than the long, and brought to a focus closer to the lens (shown by the lower lines). The disc of least confusion (shown by the upper line) is yellow.

2.26 (Facing page) Depth-of-field: four photographs of the same scene (in the grounds of St. Andrews Cathedral), with the same camera focus but different apertures (and shutter speeds). The depth-of-field (the range over which sharp focus is maintained) increases with decreasing aperture setting: (a) $f2.8$; (b) $f5.6$; (c) $f11$; (d) $f22$.

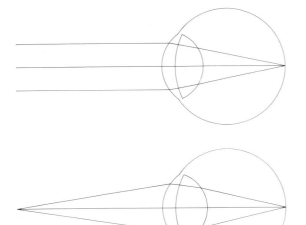

2.29 Accommodation: the crystalline lens of the emmetropic (normal) eye focuses light from optical infinity when in a relaxed state (upper illustration). Contraction of the ciliary muscles surrounding the lens results in its increase in curvature so that focus is appropriate for near objects (lower illustration). Note that the lens only carries out fine focusing; most of the refraction occurs at the cornea – the boundary between air and the eye.

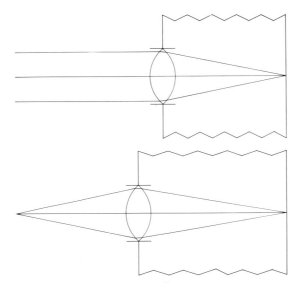

2.30 Focusing in a camera. The lens is of fixed focal length and objects closer than optical infinity (about six metres) can be focused by moving the lens further away from the film.

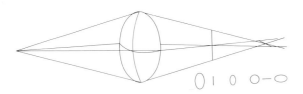

2.31 Representation of a toroidal cornea producing astigmatism. It is as though the cornea acted like two lenses with different focal lengths for different orientations. Therefore, a point source will be brought to two different line focuses, and the intervening locations produce the range of patterns shown at the bottom.

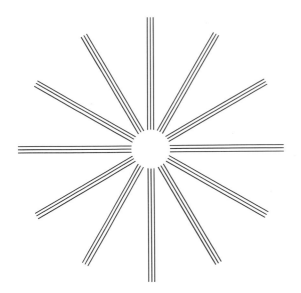

2.32 Astigmatic charts. Patterns like these can be used to determine the presence of astigmatism. If one set of lines on the left look darker and sharper than others this is probably due to astigmatism. To demonstrate that the apparent difference is not due to differences in printing, the book can be rotated: if the effect is due to astigmatism the sharper focused lines will remain tied to the orientation of the eyes, rather than to the page. Differences between orthogonal orientations might be seen in the pattern on the right, so that the verticals appear darker and sharper than the horizontals, or vice versa. It is often the case that the white spaces between the lines that appear blurred look pinkish or greenish. For some people the maximum difference occurs when the lines are oblique.

There is another aberration found in eyes that rarely occurs in cameras – astigmatism. In cameras all the optical surfaces of the compound lens are ground to be spherical, so that a point of light is brought to a point focus. In biological systems such symmetry is rarely encountered. It is unusual to find eyes that have optical surfaces that are parts of spheres: there is usually some deviation from this. Often the deviation is not great, but it is measurable. The most common form that the cornea takes is toroidal; that is, the curvature along one axis, say the vertical, is different to that along another, say the horizontal. It is as though the cornea was curved like part of a fat inner-tube tyre rather than a sphere: the radii of curvature differ in directions at right angles to one another (Figure 2.31). This has the effect of producing two focal points for the eye, corresponding to each of the curvatures. The differences in curvature mostly occur in the vertical and horizontal axes of the eye. Accordingly, lines at right angles in a scene cannot be brought to a focus simul-taneously in the astigmatic eye. If the vertical line is in focus the horizontal is blurred, and vice versa (Figure 2.32). Astigmatism also modifies the shape of the retinal image: it is elongated slightly in the axis of least corneal curvature.

It is for these reasons that a century ago the great authority on physiological optics, Hermann von Helmholtz, said of the eye: "if an optician wanted to sell me an instrument which had all these defects, I should think myself justified in blaming his care-lessness in the strongest terms, and giving him back his instrument. Of course, I shall not do this with my eyes, and shall be only too glad to keep them for as long as I can – defects and all. Still, the fact that, however bad they may be, I can get no others, does not at all diminish their defects, so long as I maintain the narrow but indisputable position of a critic on purely optical grounds!"

As Helmholtz realised, perhaps better than any of his contemporaries, vision is not determined solely by the optical properties of the eyes. Indeed, it is remarkable how little we are aware of the effects of these optical aberrations in our normal vision, and correcting for some (like chromatic aberration) optically before the light enters the eye makes relatively little improvement in our vision. Thus, although our optical images are inferior to those produced in a camera, this is not reflected at the level of the visual image. Before the visual image is formed, however, the retinal image needs to be processed. Similarly, before the optical image formed in the camera can be seen it, too, needs processing, for the image stored on the film is a latent one.

The latent image on film is rendered visible by means of chemical reactions in developers. The resulting photographic image will vary in its tone and contrast with the development time: however, most developers have clearly specified operating times and temperatures, so that an optimal tonal range will be achieved in the photographic image. These operating procedures will be dependent upon the type of film used. Moreover, there are often specific developers for particular films. Film generally consists of light-sensitive silver salts suspended in gelatin and coated on some stable and permanent base. The sensitivity of the film to light varies according to the size and density of the silver halide crystals: film emulsion with large crystals will be sensitive to light at lower intensities of illumination, or will be able to respond more quickly, than emulsion with smaller crystals. The factors of crystal size and their distribution in the emulsion determine the speed of the film: fast films (defined by high ISO, ASA or DIN ratings) have large crystals and slow films have small ones. This in turn influences the granularity or sharpness of the photographic image: slow films form sharper images. Thus, a photographer needs to select a film with a speed suitable for the light conditions prevailing.

No such choice is available to the retina. Its light-sensitive components – the photoreceptors – are fixed, and have to adapt to a vast range of illuminations. None the less, most photographers would welcome the use of such adaptable material. In film speed terms, the retina consists of two components – one fast and the other slow. The "fast" system corresponds to the rod receptors: these operate at low levels of illumination and are found mostly in the peripheral parts of the retina. The "slow" system consists of the cone receptors: these function at high levels of illumination, and provide better spatial resolution. They are found most densely packed in the central region of the retina. There are three different types of cones, which are selectively sensitive to short, medium and long wavelengths of light.

The eye, then, functions more like a battery of cameras rather than a single one. It has a wide visual field (like a wide-angle lens) but the spatial resolution is most precise only around a relatively narrow central region (like a telephoto lens). These central regions have properties like slow films, whereas the periphery acts more like a fast film. Moreover, the dynamic range over which the eye can operate is vast. The retina can detect light over a range of around $1:10^6$. That is, the lowest intensity that it can detect is about one-millionth the value of the highest it can respond to without damage. This remarkable versatility is not due to the photoreceptors alone, but also to the neural structures that process the information. Several of these neural structures are in the retina itself (Figure 2.33). The analogy between vision and photography usually stops at this level – at the optical image level – but it can be taken further. That is, there are processing analogies to the visual image and beyond that can be speculatively pursued. Whether these analogies are appropriate is another matter, but it is useful to have reference to photo-chemical analogies to provide a little counterbalance to the prevailing computer models of visual processing. We will start, however, with a brief outline of how information about shape is processed in the visual system.

We know quite a lot about the electrical activity that occurs in the retina, along the visual pathways to the brain, and in the brain itself, but we still do not understand the physiological basis for perceptual experience. Perhaps the most important discovery regarding the neural coding of light in the visual system is that the messages are not solely about the presence or absence of light striking the retina; rather it is the *patterning* of the light that is significant. For primates the significant patterns to which the visual system responds are contours (boundaries between lighter and darker regions in the scene), wavelength (colour), movement and whether one or both eyes have been stimulated. Moreover, the features are mapped on the visual cortex in a manner similar to the mapping on the retinal surface. Stimulation of adjacent areas in the retina results in activity in adjacent areas in the visual cortex. Thus the

2.33 *The structure of the retina.*

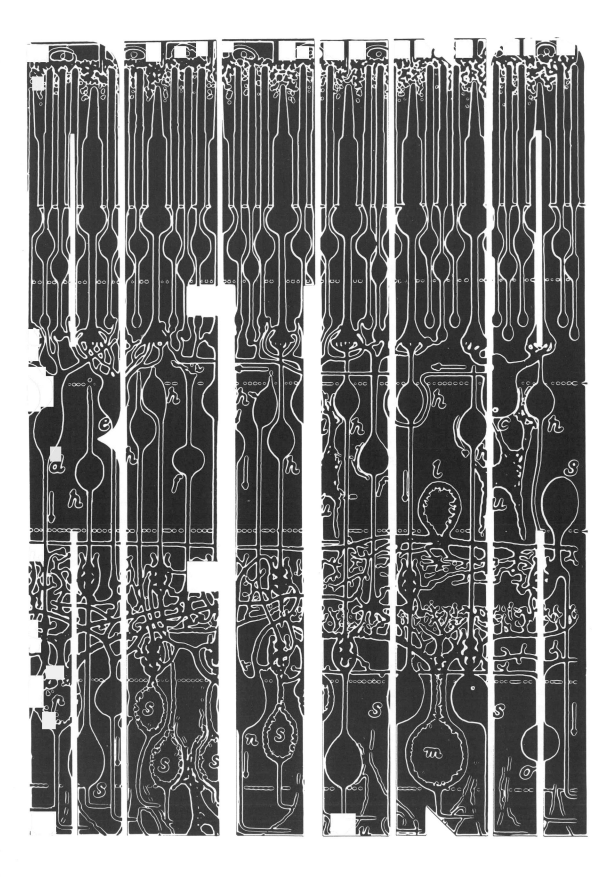

spatial relationships in the retinal image are retained in the activity of cells in the visual cortex. The fragments of information, furnished by the individual cells activated by a pattern on the retina, are eventually compiled to provide some description of the objects in space, that is, a mental image. The early symbolic description in the brain would appear to have many features in common with those aspects of shape explored in the "Representations" section of Chapter One, when trying to find some graphical definition of a pipe: boundaries between light and dark (contours) are extracted, as are more gradual changes in intensity; regions that have similar intensities or contour orientations are grouped together and areas are marked in which groupings are terminated. These are like finding the silhouette and highlight boundaries in Figures 1.8 and 1.11, matching areas of equal tone in Figure 1.6, and the islands of common intensity as in Figure 1.12.

Combining all these fragments can lead to a description of the projected shape of the object. It would not be a description of the object, because it would be about the surface properties of the object and it would be viewer-centred. That is, it is dependent upon the particular vantage point of the viewer. It is possible to use some aspects of the description, like the gradual changes in intensity (as in Figure 1.6) to provide a reasonable estimate of the object's three-dimensional properties, although additional information is required to confirm this. Under the normal conditions of vision the additional information is provided by using two eyes and moving them and the head. The two projections to the eyes are slightly different, and these slight differences furnish us with stereoscopic vision: we can see in solid form (or depth), and so the description that is extracted in the brain can utilise information about retinal disparities to restore the third dimension to our visual image. The other source of information regarding three-dimensionality concerns motion of our eyes in space, or motion of the objects themselves. If the head is moved from side to side, while fixating on a particular object, then other objects in space that are farther away will move with the head, and those closer will move in the opposite direction. This motion parallax was described in the first section of this chapter. Motion of an object itself can also provide vital information to assist in describing it three-dimensionally.

The three-dimensional viewer-centred visual image provides information appropriate for behaviour, for reaching, avoiding, moving or approaching the surfaces of the object. However, the viewer-centred visual images are continually changing as a consequence of motion of the perceiver or the object or both. Accordingly, a series of viewer-centred images can be integrated at the mental image stage to provide a description of the object that is independent of a given viewpoint – an object-centred description. Only when this stage has been attained is it possible to classify alternative views, like those shown in Figure 1.7 for a pipe, as exemplars of the same object. Therefore, the object-centred description is free from the vagaries of the vantage point. It is nearly the visual equivalent of the word in that it provides a definition of a specific object (e.g., the curved briar pipe) that is independent of the point from which it is viewed. As a conceptual category it is much narrower than the word "pipe", but it shares many of its properties.

This type of analysis of visual processing owes much to computer approaches to optical image processing of the type proposed by David Marr. Such approaches have been illuminating in a number of ways. First, trying to devise machines (computers and their programs) to recognise objects as we do has proved extraordinarily difficult. This has made us aware of the enormous complexity and sophistication of the processes going on in our brains when we recognise objects, people or events. Secondly, some recent approaches to computer vision have suggested a progressive series of increasingly elaborate descriptions of the optical image, and of the object that could have produced it.

The computational approaches to vision suggest that the optical image is initially fragmented into more primitive units, like contour segments, line terminators, small aggregations of points etc. These processes can be mimicked by photographic processes as well as via calculating rules for the computer, as was alluded to above. The computer processes might seem to be more like those occurring in our brains than are photo-chemical processes. It remains, however, a belief that the computational analogy will be more beneficial in enhancing our understanding of human vision. It can be argued that both analogies are false, because they start from an inappropriate origin. Both are concerned initially with a static optical image, typically imaged by a single device.

The computational models are directed to the graphical rather than the visual image. That is, they are addressing a more complex problem than that posed for biological systems. The problem is not how we recover three-dimensionality on the basis of two retinal images but, rather, how do we perceive two-dimensional (pictorial) images on the basis of visual images that are three-dimensional? The fact that the static retinal image has been conceived of as a two-dimensional optical image is irrelevant – we do not see our retinal images, but we perceive objects in space. The solution that is being proposed here is that pictures are a special class of objects, and the pictorial images are processed at the graphical image level – after the surface characteristics of the picture have been processed. If the perception of three-dimensional space precedes that for two-dimensional pictures then the adequacy of computational theories of vision can be questioned.

I have argued that the visual image concerns the perception of three-dimensional spatial properties of objects. This corresponds to aspects of our phenomenal experience, and it is a reasonable inference from the behaviour of others. I have not said how this three-dimensional representation is achieved, but its achievement is one of the most fundamental aspects of perception. It is likely to be dependent upon the processing of signals from two moving eyes in a moving body, but what the precise processes are remains to be determined. Despite this ignorance about processing I consider that it is an error to use a static picture as the basis for forming theories of vision. Indeed, it can be argued that pictorial images have played a perverse role in influencing our theories of vision. The analogy of the eye with the camera has resulted in a "picture-in-the-eye" approach to vision. That is, it is often implicitly assumed that there is a pictorial image in the eye, as though the retina was a screen. The problem of understanding vision is then presented as one of how the pictorial image on the retina can be processed. Sometimes this even leads to a "picture-in-the-head" approach. Even texts that argue explicitly against this idea often support it implicitly with illustrations of pictorial images "projected" on the surfaces of the two cortical hemispheres. Obviously, there is an important issue concerning how the visual image is derived. In the case of human vision it is not necessary to think of this in terms of recovering three-dimensional vision from two-dimensional images, because we do not have access to the two-dimensional images. A great many problems have arisen from considering the stages of vision in pictorial terms. Certainly we need to understand how pictorial images are processed as graphical

images, but that will derive from our knowledge about visual images. In this sense both photography and computational approaches (as they exist at present) are inappropriate models for human vision.

Pictorial Allusions

The photographer does not need to appreciate the rules of perspective in order to apply them to the photographic image. The optics of the camera usually ensure that the pictorial image will be in correct central perspective. However, the photographer, like any other representational artist, does need to select the scene to be imaged – that is, a subject from a particular viewpoint and at a specific time. The aids to pictorial imaging afforded to the photographer are not without their drawbacks. The photographer is, in the first instance, constrained by the physical objects in the scene. In other words, having selected a viewpoint, a camera, a lens, a particular film, and the relationship between aperture and shutter speed, whatever is in the visual pyramid for the camera will be imaged. Objects may be out of focus but they will not be out of image. The graphic artist, on the other hand, has far more freedom: the pictorial image can be formed from a selection of the objects in the scene, or others not physically present can be included, or the scene itself can be imaginary. When it was stated at the dawn of photography that "from today painting is dead", this aspect of painting was clearly overlooked. That prediction hardly proved to be an accurate one!

The selection of a subject and a viewpoint is the common demand upon the picture-maker, irrespective of the medium in which the pictorial image is to be presented. The viewpoint will be dependent in part upon picture-makers' aims, and the purpose to which the pictorial image is to be put. For example, if the intention is to draw attention to the allusory nature of the pictorial image, then the picture-maker could select a viewpoint which involved a scene framed within a frame. That is, the pictorial image may contain a window through which another scene is represented, in addition to the frame that surrounds the whole pictorial image. This device was used extensively by Magritte, and it can be considered as a parody on Leonardo's window. In his painting, *Euclidean Walks*, he represented a scene through a window, which was interrupted by a canvas on an easel; the scene painted in this area was a continuation of that represented in the area of the window. Thus, the picture (as an object in space)

2.34 *St. Andrews Cathedral.*

consisted of a pictorial image which included within it another pictorial image. The same technique has frequently been used in photography, when the viewpoints have been arranged to frame another scene, or to repeat the photographic image within itself. They are more complex compositions than those involved in the three examples here of photographs in which there is some degree of framing within the pictorial image (Figures 2.34–2.36).

The photographer does not, of course, have to accept the image that is captured on film in the camera. There are many techniques of image manipulation that can be enlisted – to remove unwanted parts of the image, to introduce new ones, or to

change the characteristics of imaged objects (like tone and texture) or their relative positions. More will be said of such techniques later in this section and in Appendix One. The photographer, too, can create imaginary worlds in the darkroom: that is, film

2.35 (Facing page) *The Picasso Museum, Barcelona.* The reflections in the large glass window render it difficult to discern the surfaces represented. The archways and the walled windows are reflections but the posters are seen through the glass. It may be noted that the position of the clown's face in the central poster is matched by that of the photographer!

2.36 *Forgan Cemetry, Fife.*

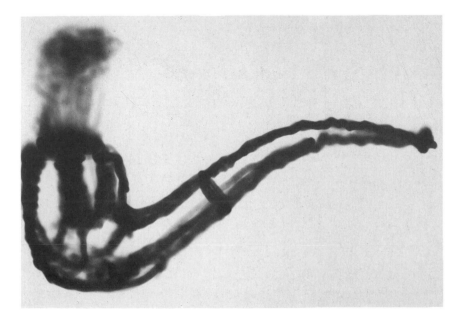

2.37 *Lighted pipe.* The photograph was produced by shining a small spot of light onto unexposed photographic paper and drawing the shape of a pipe. The lighted pipe does appear to smoke!

2.38 *Photo–graphics.* A photogram made from two rolls of film and a compass: they were placed directly in contact with unexposed film which was then fogged (exposed to unpatterned light). The shadows of the objects protect the underlying film from the fogging illumination, and it is the shadows that are visible in the printed negative.

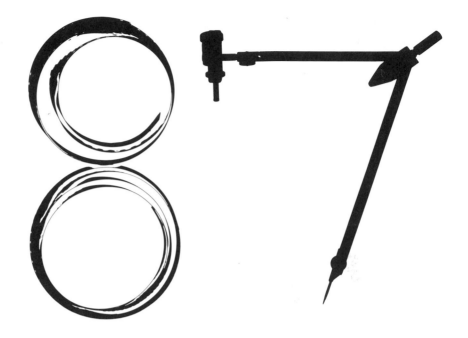

2.39 The pattern was produced by scraping the emulsion from film with a scalpel before it was fogged and developed: the scrapings themselves are also visible.

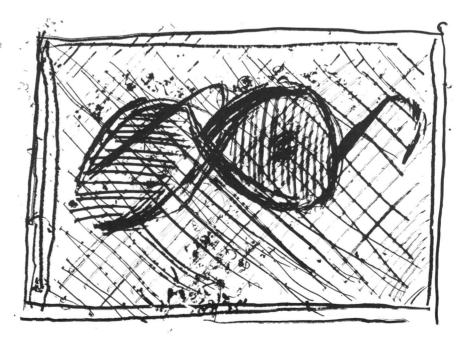

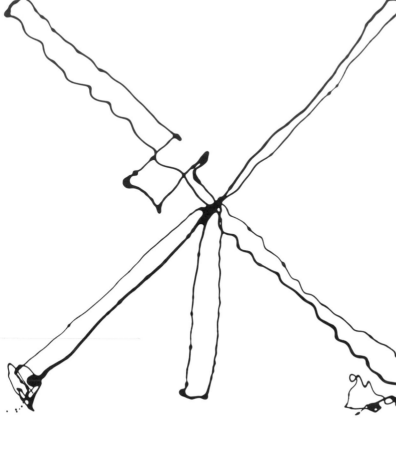

2.40 Dribbling photo-opaque onto unexposed film and then fogging it can produce patterns like this one.

can be used like a canvas, on which the marks are made (via light) in many ways (see Figures 2.37–2.40). These marks do not correspond to any scene in the environment. Neither do they correspond to any image in a camera. The action of light on film is being used as a medium similar to that of paint on canvas, or charcoal on paper. Whether this should be called photography or graphic art is a moot point. It depends how photography is defined: if it is the action of light on film or light-sensitive paper, then these are examples of photography. The equivalent definition of painting is the use of paint on a surface: a painter does not need to use a brush but can apply the paint in any manner. For example the painting shown in Figure 2.41 was produced by dribbling or splashing paint onto the surface with a stirrer, after the manner of Jackson Pollock and, in Figure 2.42, the paint was poured onto the surface which was tilted one way and then another. According to these definitions a camera is no more necessary to pro-

duce a photograph than is a brush necessary for a painting: as their names indicate, all they require are light and paint, respectively, and a surface upon which they can act.

None the less, most people would consider that photography involved the making of pictorial images that had, at some stage, been formed in a camera. We will deal with this case initially and present some pictorial images more or less as they were captured in the camera. There is, of course, no specific image that is captured on film in the camera: the manner in which the latent image is expressed in the photographic image will be dependent upon its processing, and there is no absolute standard for

2.41 (Facing page) Black-and-white photograph of detail from a tachiste painting.

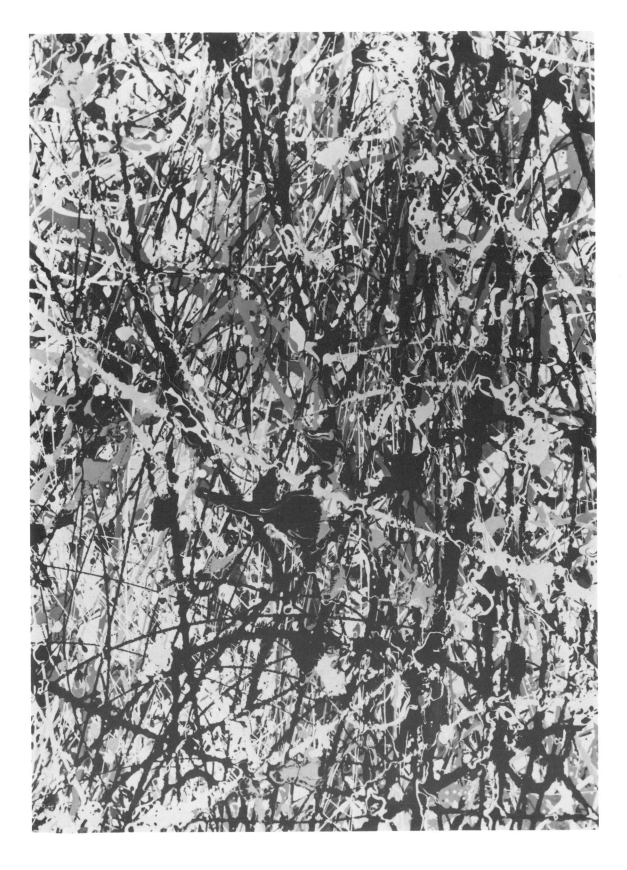

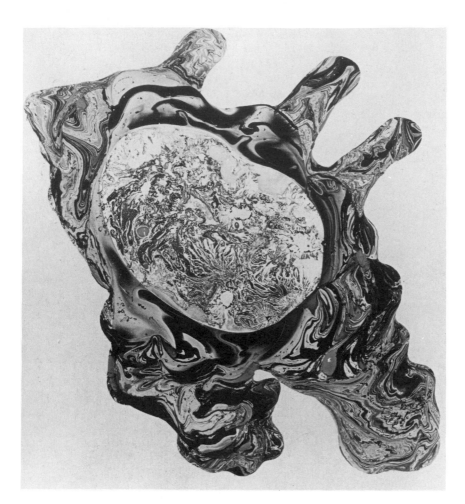

2.42 Photograph of a pattern produced by pouring oil-based paints gently onto water and tilting the surface on which they were suspended. The oil pattern on the water surface is transferred to the underlying board.

that. The closest approximation to a standard would correspond to development of the latent image under the precise conditions recommended by the manufacturers of the developer used. This will yield a negative image which will need to be printed in order to restore the contrast relations (the blacks, greys and whites) to approximate those in the original scene. There is much greater latitude for modifying the tonal qualities in printing the photographic image on paper than in the developing phase. For the former, the exposure duration and aperture setting for the enlarger will be dependent upon the type of paper and the characteristics of the developer used; the details of the photographic image can be modified by dodging and burning (under or overexposing local regions of the print, respectively). The final photographic print is likely to be in continuous tone (that is, with a continuous range of greys between the extremes of black and white), whereas the prints made from them that are presented in newspapers or magazines are just black and white, with no intermediate greys. By the same token, there are no photographs in this book, but only prints in black ink on white paper. The continuous-tone photograph is reproduced in half-tone by means of a special high-contrast film: the silver crystals are not distributed evenly throughout the emulsion of the film, but are in the form of minute, evenly-spaced dots. The dots themselves are too small to be seen, unless a magnifying lens is used,

2.43 (Facing page) *Skyscrapers, Melbourne, Australia.*

and so light areas in the original have virtually no black dots, and black areas have virtually no white spaces between the dots, with greys as intermediate. The appearance of continuous tone in such half-tone prints is yet another pictorial allusion: in many cases we are unable to discriminate between a photograph of a scene and a half-tone print of it!

Pictorial images are formed and presented on a picture plane. This applies to static pictorial images like paintings, drawings and photographs, as well as changing ones like cinematic and television pictures. In the graphic arts the rules of linear perspective can be applied most conveniently when the picture plane is vertical; other orientations of the picture plane can create practical problems. For example, painting a tall building from close to its base would be an arduous task because the picture

2.45 (Facing page) *Bavaria*. The statue overlooks the meadow in Munich on which the Oktoberfest is held.

plane would need to be almost horizontal and facing downwards, or the painter would need to transfer the projected dimensions from one station point to another picture plane. Taking a photograph under those conditions, on the other hand, is straightforward (Figure 2.43) – simply point and press. The orientation of the picture plane is much more fluid in photography. This enables the photographer to produce pictorial images of scenes from unusual viewpoints – often ones that would not be entertained by a graphic artist (Figures 2.44–2.47). The artist can, of course, take and use photographs as aids to memory, when composing or completing some graphic work in the studio, and there have been many examples of this practice.

2.44 *Spanish coastline.*

2.46 (Facing page) *Pit tip.*

The prints of the photographic images referred to in the previous paragraph were originally in continuous tone. Quite different photographic images of objects can be obtained by using different film. For example, Figures 2.48 and 2.49 are photographic images of the same scene under approximately the same conditions, with the same camera, aperture, shutter speed etc; the former was imaged on standard continuous-tone black-and-white film whereas the latter was on film that was sensitive mainly to infra-red light. Yet a different image results from using high-contrast film that provides only blacks and whites with no intermediate tones (Figure 2.50).

2.47 *High wire.*

2.48 Photograph of an apple tree in autumnal sunshine. The film was Ilford FP4, rated at ASA 80, taken at *f*32, ⅛sec.

2.49 The same scene as in Figure 2.48, taken with the same camera at the same settings, on Kodak high-speed infra-red film (4143). Both films were developed and printed in the same way. Note how the leaves and grass are lighter, and the wall is darker.

2.50 The same scene as in the previous two figures, converted to high-contrast film (Kodalith ortho film type 3, 2556). Only the highlights and dark shadows are retained.

2.51 *Black cockatoos.* The original photograph was on colour negative film. It was enlarged onto lith film and contact printed on film before printing onto paper.

2.52 It is often difficult to recognise the objects represented in photographic negatives, as is the case with this reclining nude.

This last type is called lith or litho film, because of its widespread use in lithography. It is the film type I use most extensively, and the majority of the pictorial images that are presented from this point onwards are likely to have been processed on lith film. Some more details concerning the properties and processing of lith film are included in Appendix One.

Rendering a pictorial image in black and white, devoid of any intermediate tones, has relatively little adverse effect on the recognition of the object as a member of a given category, like dogs or flowers. In other words, the subjects in the scene can be recognised, but there is often difficulty in identifying them. For example, in Figure 2.51 the birds and the branches are immediately recognised, but the fact that the birds are black cockatoos is not so readily discernible. Where any impression of tone does appear in the photographic image it is a consequence of finely stippled black dots. This is the attraction of lith images for printing, because continuous tone can be reduced to small black dots varying in size and density. However, negatives – in continuous tone or black and white – can be very difficult to recognise: without the shading to provide clues to the solidity of the form in Figure 2.52, it can take a long time to discern the form from which it was derived. Even when a positive and a negative are juxtaposed, as in Figure 2.53, it can be difficult to recognise the form that was photographed. The wispy hair and the protuberances suggest a face, with a side view of the bony orbit and the nose. There is some deliberate obfuscation in this photographic image: it is derived from a side view of a face, but the near symmetry around the horizontal axis has been exploited and the image is presented inverted. Viewing it with the page upside-down will yield a more recognisable photographic image.

When positive and negative lith images are placed in register then no light will be transmitted through them – the blacks of the positive will match precisely the whites of the negative. However, each lith image is formed on an emulsion that is suspended on an acetate backing. Because the backing has a defined thickness the two images will be separated slightly from one another, unless they are placed emulsion to emulsion. The separation can be utilised to make a line image – that is, one in which only the boundaries between black and white areas are reproduced. If the positive and negative are registered as closely as possible and then taped together, the separation between them can be seen

2.53 A positive and negative photographic image of a face, viewed obliquely from the side. The combined images are ambiguous because of their near-horizontal symmetry, but the nose and the bony orbit can be distinguished, as can the eyelashes. They will be recognised more readily as representations of a face if the page is inverted, because the contours of the cheek which occlude part of the nose are more easily seen.

2.54 Photographic line image produced by sandwiching a high-contrast positive and a negative, and contact printing them onto film; light exposure should be from all sides to ensure that it passes through all boundaries between the positive and negative.

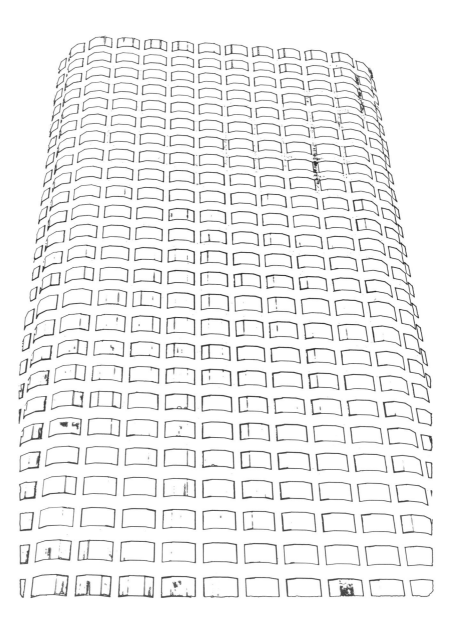

by viewing from the side. Similarly, if they are illuminated from the side (or better still from all sides) then a line image will be formed on any underlying, unexposed film (see Figure 2.54). The photographic images that are best suited to this manipulation are those with well-defined areas of light and shade, rather than those with too much spatial detail. The precise registration of the positive and negative images is essential for producing continuous lines. Alternatively, the positive and negative can be displaced intentionally out of register, so that a shadow effect is produced. This technique works particularly well with printed words, as they can appear as though they are in relief (see Figure 2.55).

There is another technique that can be employed for producing photographic line images. It was discovered over a century ago by Armand Sabatier, and is now called the Sabattier effect (with an additional "t"), pseudo-solarisation, or just solarisation. The details of the process are described in Appen-

ILLUSORY CONTOURS

2.55 A line image of letters: the positive and negative are deliberately displaced to give an impression of shadows cast by solid letters.

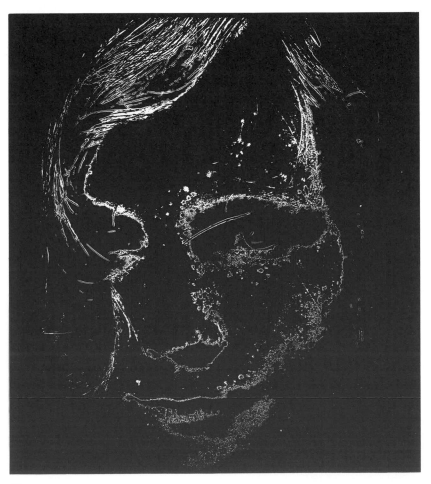

2.56 *Hairlines.* The Sabattier effect, often called solarisation, derived from a photograph of a face.

dix One. These line images are generally subtler than those produced by sandwiching positives and negatives, and the Sabattier effect can be applied to photographic images that are more detailed than would be suitable for line separation (see Figure 2.56). The Sabattier image is initially white on black: the borders between light and dark areas are protected from development whereas all other areas blacken. The white-on-black image can readily be reversed by a further printing, as is shown in Figure 2.57. Moreover, it is possible to apply the Sabattier effect differentially to the photographic image: in Figure 2.58 the reflection of the boat in the water has been rendered in line form using this technique, and the boat itself is rendered in high contrast. The Sabattier process can be repeated several times, yielding strange but still identifiable photographic images (Figure 2.59). Here we have a multiple solarisation of a portrait of Man Ray, who made so many fascinating solarised photographs earlier this century.

One of the great advantages of using lith film is the ease with which photographic images can be combined. This can consist of using the same image several times, the components having been processed to different stages of contrast as in Figure 2.60. This is usually called posterisation. However, more interesting allusions can be generated by using different photographic images and then combining them. For example, the two components of

Figure 2.61 are photographs of the Royal and Ancient Golf Club in St. Andrews and of a golf ball; both were solarised (treated to the Sabattier process) and then combined. This pictorial image is black on white, whereas Figure 2.62 is mainly white on black: the stark whiteness of the spaceman emphasises the silver of the space suit, and the black surround alludes to the vast emptiness that engulfed him.

The photographic image, more or less as it was produced in the camera, can be manipulated by a variety of means. For example, once printed it can be physically modified by cutting it up and re-assembling it (Figure 2.63), or by combining several photographic images of the same or similar subject matter (Figure 2.64). Returning to the pipe imagery discussed in Chapter One, it can be seen from Figure 2.65 that it is even possible to light my (pictured) pipe, and it smokes! Pictorial experiments like these can be performed with ease because of the characteristics of the medium: they would not be entertained lightly with paintings! The photographic image is both disposable and indestructible. Unsuccessful experiments can be overlooked and new ones embarked upon. The lost photographic image components can be replaced, as long as the negative from which they were made remains intact. It is this indestructibility of the photographic image that is at the same time its strength and its weakness.

The range of image manipulation techniques that

2.57 *Opera Bridge.* The photograph, from which this solarised image was derived, was taken from inside the Sydney Opera House. The internal girders of the building complement the lattice work of the Sydney Harbour Bridge, which is visible from inside the Opera House.

2.58 *Crail harbour.* The upper half of the photographic image is rendered in high contrast, whereas the lower half, the reflection, is solarised.

2.59 *Man Ray.* Multiple solarisations of a portrait of Man Ray, who experimented extensively with this technique, though generally with paper prints rather than with film. The film was solarised successively, each time producing new, but fainter Mackie lines (the fine white lines formed at the contrast boundaries in the original image).

2.60 Posterisation: the original black-and-white photograph was converted to three different lith images – extracting different light intensities. The lith positives were converted to negatives, and then printed (in precise registration) in succession on the same paper. The resulting photograph has a range of discrete tones (greys) rather than being only black and white.

2.61 *R & A.*
A combination derived from solarised photographs of a golf ball and the Royal and Ancient Golf Club, St. Andrews.

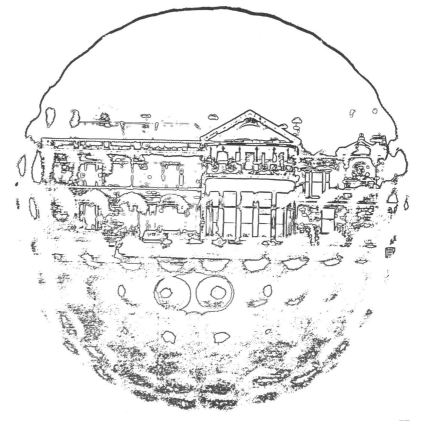

2.62 *Man in the moon.* A combination derived from two Apollo 11 pictures – one of Aldrin placing the American flag and the other of the moon.

2.63 (Below) *Pit head.* The original continuous-tone photograph was cut up into squares, as was a high-contrast conversion of it. They were then reassembled so that adjacent squares were of the two types: continuous-tone or black-and-white. Therefore, a given cell on the left is in one of these tones and its correspondent on the right is the converse. In one sense, the two photographic images are quite different, although they are derived from the same scene and probably look very similar.

2.64 (Previous page)
Pipeface. Composite
photograph.

are available in photography makes it an ideal
medium for creating pictorial allusions. Some of
these can be allusions to space in much the same
way as a painter might select a viewpoint. For
example, in Figure 2.66 the converging lines on the
left and right are at approximately the same angle
with respect to the picture plane, but they represent
quite different objects – the near wall on the left and
the distant bridge on the right. This allusion is similar
to one in Magritte's painting *Euclidean Walks*, mentioned earlier: one set of converging contours in
his painting-within-a-painting represents a conical

tower; the other equivalently converging lines represent a receding road. The pictorial cues to distance in Figure 2.66 are sufficient to specify the
represented distances of the wall and the bridge
piers, and so there is relatively little confusion produced by the converging lines. The tonal changes in
Figure 2.66 provide pictorial cues to distance that
are not present in high-contrast photographic
images, like Figure 2.67. The viewpoint is unusual,
being directed upwards, and the familiar aspect of
the building imaged, its commanding tower, is not
visible from the station point adopted. Despite this
the building can be recognised, if only by the name
inscribed on its surface. In this picture the convergence of the vertical parallel lines is a function of
the near-horizontal picture plane adopted. However,
even when the picture plane is near-vertical the
sides of high buildings converge in the pictorial
image. When this convergence is removed or
reversed the pictorial image has a strange character
to it (see Figure 2.68).

2.65 *Smoking pipe.*

2.66 *Euclidean drives.*

2.67 *Empire State Building.*

2.68 *Nathan Philips Square, Toronto.* The converging verticals on the left have been made parallel on the right.

It is unlikely that there is much confusion initially when looking at Figure 2.69, but some might develop with more protracted observation. In this instance the orientation of the various imaged parts are not in correspondence: either the main lines of the cathedral and baptistry are not vertical, or the pillars through which they are seen are awry. It is, of course, the latter, as the photograph was taken from within the inclined campanile at Pisa. The mismatch in orientations is quite small here, about 7°, unlike that in Figure 2.70. This strangely appearing struc-

2.69 *Pisan pillars.* The Baptistry and Cathedral spires at Pisa were photographed through the tilted pillars of the campanile.

2.70 (Facing page) *Antipodean vision.* The shape appears rather anthropomorphic, with an ornate head-dress, central eyes and outstretched arms. When rotated 90° clockwise it will take on a different construction!

ture will probably be recognised if the page is rotated 90° clockwise: it is a high-contrast image of the Sydney Opera House reflected on itself. When it is viewed with the page vertical the bilateral symmetry makes it difficult to dissociate the two parts. It appears like a single coherent structure, as does Figure 2.71, which could be a snowflake pattern, with its three-fold symmetry. In fact, it can prove extremely difficult to dissociate the component elements from which it was made, even though it has been presented earlier in this book. The radiating lines represent the carriageway of the Tay Road Bridge, and the concentric lines are the piers. The bridge forms a 30° sector with respect to the centre, and so it is represented twelve times in the composite photographic image. If a horizontal line is taken from the centre to the right, then the 30° sector

counter-clockwise to this represents the single image of the bridge: it might be easier to discriminate if such a sector is compared with the right half of Figure 2.66.

We are notoriously poor at discriminating between pictorial images when they are reversed from left to right. Even though the human face is rarely perfectly symmetrical about a vertical axis we often have difficulty in recognising a left-right reversal of a familiar portrait. Thus, the two views of the face shown in Figure 2.72 will not appear appreciably different, even though each is reversed relative to its neighbours. We also have considerable difficulty in identifying pictorial images when they are upside-down. The inverted faces in Figure 2.72 look quite different to the upright ones, and, were it not for the symmetry of the whole design, they would

2.71 *Three-fold symmetry.* Rotations and reflections of the Tay Road Bridge.

not be recognised as the same. Even familiar pictorial images (i.e., familiar from other pictures of a person rather than from the actual individual) are often difficult to recognise when they are presented upside-down (see Figure 2.73).

The pictorial allusions presented so far have been spatial – allusions to aspects of representing the texture or dimensions of objects. Many of the objects in our environment are not static, but change their position over time. This dynamic aspect of representation has not, as yet, been examined here. How can motion be expressed? Motion is the change of position over time. The dimension of time is excluded from the static pictorial image, as in painting or photography. Therefore, motion is reduced to the change in position over the space of the pictorial plane. In the graphic arts there are several ways in which the impression of motion can be so represented, and some of the best examples can be found in comics. Some of these devices for depicting motion are shown in Figure 2.74. Painters

generally use other methods for introducing dynamic elements into their pictorial images. For example, a subject (an animal or person) can be represented in a posture that would only be encountered in life in a dynamic context: a deer in mid-spring, a person in mid-gesture (see Figure 2.75). Photographically, the allusion to motion can be rendered in an equivalent manner (Figure 2.76), by using a very short exposure, so that the posture is frozen in mid-action, or the exposure time can be extended, so that the image of the moving object or person is blurred (Figure 2.77). Alternatively, the moving object can be imaged sharply but the background can be blurred – by rotating the camera in the same direction as the object (Figure 2.78).

Even when we take an implicitly two-dimensional pictorial image, like a written word, then its motion can be alluded to (Figure 2.79). Here, essentially the

2.73 (Overleaf) *Lenin.*

2.72 *David Brewster.* A kaleidoscopic portrait of the inventor of the kaleidoscope.

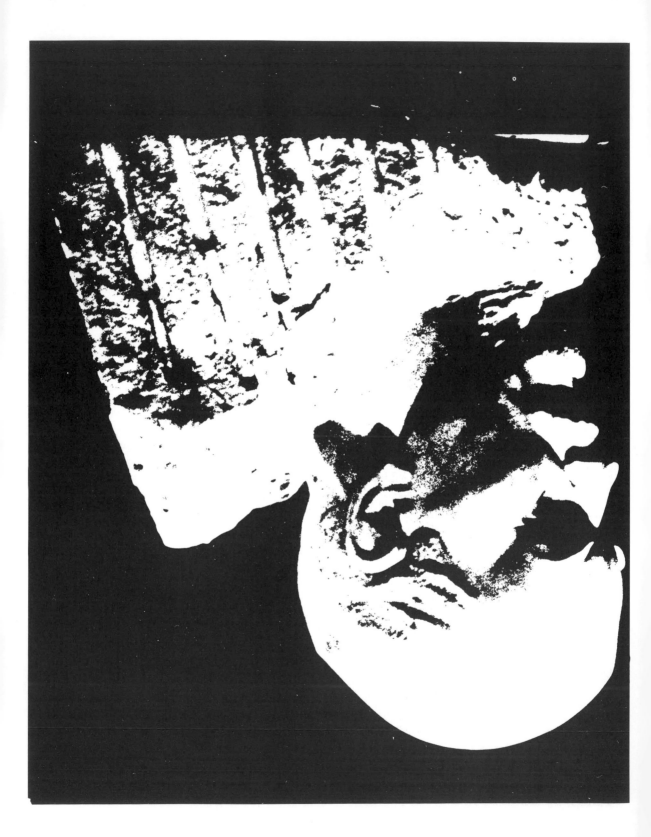

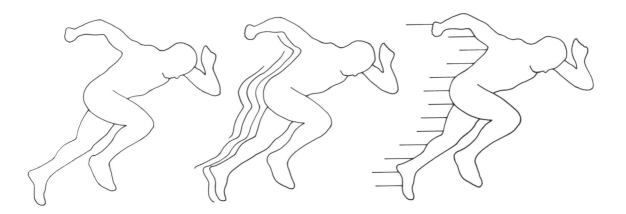

2.74 (Above) Drawings representing movement. The single outline suggests movement

because of the posture. The addition of lines or tracers enhance this impression of running.

2.75 (Below) *Stone me.* A variety of expressions and gestures are captured in this scene.

2.76 Photograph of a cyclist in motion. The motion was frozen with an exposure of ⅟₅₀₀sec.

2.77 Photograph of the same cyclist with an exposure of ⅟₆₀sec, during which time she moved with respect to the film creating a blurred image.

2.78 Photograph taken at ⅟₆₀sec exposure, panning the camera to follow the motion of the cyclist, making the background blurred.

2.79 *Movement.*

same techniques can be applied to script as those applied to graphical images generally. It was suggested in Chapter One, that written words are pictorial images that refer to classes of objects or concepts, rather than specific instances of objects. When the words are referring to motion or space there are not the same pictorial demands made of them as is the case for representational images of

the type mentioned in this chapter. To present a spatial example, there is no demand that the letter and word shape for "square" should comply to the spatial aspects that it represents. It could readily be made in this shape, however, as is shown in Figure 2.80. In this case, the letters and word are becoming pictorial images that refer to classes of objects or concepts, rather than specific instances of objects. as linguistically. It is this relationship between written words and pictorial images that will be examined in the next chapter.

2.80 *Square-shaped.*

Bibliography

General

Gibson, J. J. (1979). *The ecological approach to visual perception.* Boston: Houghton Mifflin. Gibson's third and final book develops his concept of ecological optics. In contrast to traditional optics, ecological optics is concerned with the available information in the changing optic array that serves perception. Gibson also introduces the concept of affordances, which refers to properties of stimulation that are useful to the observer. For example, a flat, firm, horizontal surface offers the affordance of sitting. Evidence supporting direct perception is marshalled and the theory of information pickup is outlined. The final part of the book is concerned with "Depiction" and the analyses of static and moving pictures.

Gregory, R. L. (1966). *Eye and brain. The psychology of seeing.* London: Weidenfeld & Nicolson. This is perhaps the most widely read and readable book on vision. Gregory places his selected topics in an historical setting and conveys his enthusiasm for his subject. It commences with the nature of light, the evolution and structure of eyes, and the neurophysiological activity that takes place in visual areas of the brain. The aspects of visual perception that are selected are brightness, movement, colour and illusions. With regard to illusions, Gregory presents his theory that they are due to inappropriate constancy scaling. There are also chapters on perceptual learning and the relation of art to reality.

Hochberg, J. (1986). Representation of motion and space in video and cinematic displays. In K. R. Boff, L. Kaufman, & J. P. Thomas (Eds.), *Handbook of perception and human performance, Volume I.* New York: Wiley. Julian Hochberg provides an extensive examination of both static and dynamic modes of representing space and events that occur within it. Video and film both operate with sequences of discrete displays that create the appearance of motion. Hochberg rejects Gibson's theory of invariants in moving pictures and suggests that perceptual psychology has much to learn from filmmakers and those who generate animated computer graphics.

Pirenne, M. H. (1970). *Optics, painting and photography.* Cambridge: Cambridge University Press. Maurice Pirenne's excellent monograph returns to original sources to integrate ideas of geometrical optics with pictorial representation. Like Gibson, he believes that "all methods of representational painting rest on empirical optical facts". The book describes image formation in cameras and eyes, and presents results from Pirenne's own explorations using pinhole photography. The sections on illusionistic paintings (like Pozzo's painted hemicylindrical ceiling in the church of St. Ignazio in Rome) and on viewing perspective pictures askew are particularly recommended.

Representations of Space

Alberti, L. B. (1956). *On painting.* Translated by J. R. Spencer. New Haven, Conn.: Yale University Press. Alberti's seminal theory of painting, originally written around 1435, is made accessible through this translation from Italian and Latin manuscripts. In it the mathematics, methods and means of linear perspective are enunciated.

Ames, A. (1925). Depth in pictorial art. *Art Bulletin, 8,* 5–24. Ames describes the range of techniques that artists can use to produce impressions of depth, their relative efficacy, and the observational procedures which enhance the represented depth.

Ames, A., Proctor, C. A., & Ames, B. (1923). Vision and the technique of art. *Proceedings of the American Academy of Arts and Science, 58,* 3–47. The optics of cameras are contrasted to those of the eye with regard to aberrations, distortions, retinal sensitivity and binocular vision. The authors conclude that "a pictorial representation of nature to be technically satisfactory from an artistic point of view should be similar in its general characteristics to the pictures we receive on our retinas while holding one center of focus".

Arnheim, R. (1956). *Art and visual perception. A psychology of the creative eye.* London: Faber & Faber. Rudolf Arnheim's first synthesis of Gestalt principles of perceptual organisation and art. The chapters cover topics of balance, shape, form, growth, space, light, colour, movement, tension and expression. Children's drawings are analysed alongside examples of major art works. Arnheim speaks for many students of the psychology of art when he states "art may seem to be in danger of being drowned by talk".

Baltrusaitis, J. (1976). *Anamorphic art.* Translated by W. J. Strachan. London: Chadwyck-Healey. This book rekindled the modern fascination with anamorphoses. It provides a lucid history of accelerated and decelerated perspectives, linear, conical and cylindrical (mirror) anamorphoses, and the principles on which they are based. The interaction between philosophers and artists in the 17th century is illuminating, as is the analysis of Holbein's *The Ambassadors*.

Boring, E. G. (1942). *Sensation and perception in the history of experimental psychology*. New York: Appleton-Century. This is a standard history of perception. The chapters most relevant here are those on visual perception of bidimensional space and on visual perception of depth and distance. The constant concern with the geometry of retinal projections is evident from the former, and the development of concepts in perceptual constancy are presented in the latter.

Deregowski, J. B. (1980). *Illusions, patterns and pictures: A cross-cultured perspective*. London: Academic Press. This book brings a refreshing cross-cultural approach to the experimental study of geometrical illusions, pattern recognition, and representation pictures.

Descartes, R. (1664/1972). *Treatise of man*. French text with translation and commentary by T. S. Hall. Cambridge, Mass.: Harvard University Press. Descartes presents his theory of vision in this treatise. He refines Kepler's analysis of image formation in the eye, speculates upon the mechanism for accommodation, introduces a theory of binocular combination, and suggests how the perception of size is dependent on cues for distance as well as retinal size.

Dubery, F. & Willats, J. (1983). *Perspective and other drawing systems*. Revised edition. London: The Herbert Press. Lucid descriptions of different systems of projection onto a flat surface are given. There are also descriptions of Brunelleschi's experiments, mechanical aids to drawing, shadow projections, and modern mixed systems of projection.

Edgerton, S. Y. (1975). *The Renaissance rediscovery of linear perspective*. New York: Basic Books. Samuel Edgerton examines the influences that led to the emergence of linear perspective in the early 15th century. Principal amongst these was the dissemination of earlier works on cartography and perspectivas (books on optics). Brunelleschi's experiments and their formalisation by Alberti are especially well presented.

Gibson, J. J. (1971). The information available in pictures. *Leonardo, 4,* 27–35. The projective theory of pictures is contrasted with convention theory. The latter holds that pictures are comprised of arbitrary symbols, the rules of which need to be learned.

Goodman, N. (1971). On J. J. Gibson's new per-spective. *Leonardo, 4,* 309–360. A reply to Gibson (1971) by one of the foremost proponents of convention theory. Goodman states: "A symbol may inform in as many different ways as there are contexts and systems of interpretation."

Hagen, M. A. (Ed.) (1980). *The perception of pictures. Volume I. Alberti's window: The projective model of pictorial information*. London: Academic Press. A collection of penetrating essays examining the relationship between optical projection and pictorial representation. The chapters by Sedgewick, on the geometry of spatial layout in pictorial representation, by Edgerton, on the Renaissance artist as quantifier, and by Perkins and Hagen, on convention, context, and caricature, are of especial interest. Gibson's Foreword to the book lists 10 different meanings that have been applied to the term image.

Hagen, M. A. (Ed.) (1980). *The perception of pictures. Volume II. Dürer's devices: Beyond the projective model of pictures*. London: Academic Press. This volume presents alternatives to the projective model. Hagen outlines a perceptual theory of pictorial representation, Hochberg compares pictorial function with perceptual structures, and others examine picture perception from developmental and cross-cultural perspectives.

Homer, W. I. (1964). *Seurat and the science of painting*. Cambridge, Mass.: MIT Press. An assessment of the scientific influences of Helmholtz, Rood, Blanc, and Sutter on the development of Seurat's pointilliste technique.

Ittelson, W. H. (1968). *The Ames demonstrations in perception*. New York: Hafner. Ames graduated from being a neo-Impressionist artist to ophthalmologist. He devised many ingenious perceptual demonstrations, like the distorted room and the rotating trapezoidal window, which formed the basis for his transactional theory of perception. The demonstrations are described in this book in a way that permits their construction.

Kennedy, J. M. (1974). *A psychology of picture perception. Images and information*. London: Jossey-Bass. John Kennedy's treatment of picture perception owes a debt to both Arnheim and Gibson. From a starting point of Gibsonian optics he develops the idea that pictures are bearers of information, and that codes of depiction can be used like language. He presents evidence to support his views from children's drawings and cross-cultural research.

Kroy, W. & Langerholc, J. (1984). Ambiguous figures by Bosch. *Perception & Psychophysics, 35,* 402–404. An analysis of the multiple ambiguities that can be extracted from Hieronymous Bosch's drawing *The Owl's Nest.*

Kubovy, M. (1986). *The psychology of perspective and Renaissance art.* Cambridge: Cambridge University Press. The arrow in the eye (as depicted in a Mantegna painting) is taken as a metaphor for the art of perspective. The author then blends analyses of Renaissance paintings with modern studies of visual perception.

Leonardo da Vinci (1721). *A treatise of painting.* Translated from Italian. London: Senex & Taylor. The original Italian version of the book was compiled from several of Leonardo's manuscripts over a century after his death, and this book is its first translation into English. It examines drawing, composition, light and shadow, and colours and colouring, and contains many insights into the nature of perception as well as painting.

Rock, I. (1984). *Perception.* New York: Freeman. A textbook on perception emphasising the perceptual constancies. Rock treats perception and art at an early stage, and then describes illusions, motion perception, and visual orientation. He concludes with his theory that perception is a process like intelligence, making sense of a seemingly ambiguous input. The book is well illustrated and includes a stereoviewer for observing the stereograms it presents.

Swanston, M. T., Wade, N. J., & Day, R. H. (1987). The representation of uniform motion in vision. *Perception, 16,* 143–159. This article develops a theoretical model of the perception of motion in three-dimensional space. It incorporates information from the main articulating parts of the body, like the eyes in the head, and the head in space.

Varley, H. (Ed.) (1983). *Colour.* London: Marshall. A wide-ranging and well-illustrated survey of colour, from the nature of light to its applications in industry. The sections on art, colour printing and colour television provide a good introduction to these topics.

Varnedoe, K. (1986). The artifice of candor: Impressionism and photography reconsidered. In P. Watch & T. F. Barrow (Eds.), *Perspectives on photography. Essays in honor of Beaumont Newhall.* Albuquerque: University of New Mexico Press. It has often been argued that the Impressionists were influenced by the emergence of snapshot photography. Varnedoe proposes the converse, namely that the use of nonstandard viewpoints in photography derived from the use of unusual stationpoints in some Impressionist paintings.

Wade, N. J. (Ed.) (1983). *Brewster and Wheatstone on vision.* London: Academic Press. The book reprints the original 19th century papers by Wheatstone and Brewster concerned with stereoscopic vision, the optical instruments they invented, and subjective visual phenomena. Their theoretical approaches to space perception are contrasted.

Wade, N. J. (1987). On the late invention of the stereoscope. *Perception, 16,* 785–818. Theory and research on binocular vision before the stereoscope was invented in the early 19th century is presented. Many of the earlier binocular instruments and diagrams of binocular combination are illustrated.

Photography and Vision

Ames, A. & Proctor, C. A. (1923). Aberrations of the eye. *The American Journal of Physiological Optics, 4,* 3–37. The article is mainly concerned with experimental studies of spherical aberration, but some work on chromatic aberration is described.

Frisby, J. P. (1979). *Seeing. Illusion, brain and mind.* Oxford: Oxford University Press. This ambitious book attempts a synthesis between visual neurophysiology, simple visual phenomena and computational vision. The illustrations are good, and stereoscopic depth effects can be observed with the red-green viewer provided.

Hammond, J. H. (1981). *The camera obscura. A chronicle.* Bristol: Adam Hilger. A delightful history of pinhole cameras from the fifth century BC in China to present-day observatories. The use of the camera obscura as an aid to art is discussed.

Helmholtz, H. von (1895). *Popular lectures on scientific subjects.* First series, new edition. (1898) Second series, new edition. Translated by E. Atkinson. London: Longmans, Green & Co. Helmholtz's popular lectures were published in two series, each of which has a chapter of particular pertinence to the topics here under discussion. In the first series is one on "The recent progress on the theory of vision", which is in three parts. The first part is on the eye as an optical instrument, and the others are on the sensation and on the perception of sight. The second series contains an essay "On the relation of optics to painting", in which form, shade, colour and harmony of colour are analysed. Helmholtz states: "I have arrived at my studies by a path that is but little trod, that is, by the physiology of the senses ... The physiological study of the manner in which the perceptions of our senses originate, how impressions from without pass into our nerves, and how the condition of the latter is thereby altered, presents many points of contact with the theory of the fine arts."

Marynowicz, W. (1969). *Photography as an art form.* London: MacLaren. The book is concerned with the artistic application of photography, and deals with portraiture, still-life, pictorialism, colour, and tone separation. Whole page photographs are accompanied by details of the camera, photographic materials and processing employed.

Michaels, D. D. (1985). *Visual optics and refraction. A clinical approach.* Third edition. St. Louis: C. V. Mosby. A textbook for ophthalmologists which provides detailed descriptions of optics and aberrations of the eye.

Newhall, B. (1982). *The history of photography from 1839 to the present.* Completely revised and enlarged edition. London: Secker & Warburg. An authoritative history of (principally) black-and-white photography. Most of the text and illustrations concern the period up to about 1950.

Roth, I. & Frisby, J. P. (1986). *Perception and representation: A cognitive approach.* Milton Keynes: Open University Press. The first part of the book is about conceptual categories and how they are formed. The second and third parts address the problem of representation in vision. Roth describes the cognitive approach to object recognition, and Frisby provides an excellent introduction to computational vision.

Scharf, A. (1968). *Art and photography.* London: The Penguin Press. A history of the complex interplay between photography and painting, confined mainly to British and French works. The chapter on the representation of movement, illustrated with photographic sequences taken by Marey and Muybridge, and the cinematic influences on futurism, are useful.

Trevor-Roper, P. (1988). *The world through blunted sight. An inquiry into the influence of defective vision on art and character.* New and revised edition. London: Allen Lane. An ophthalmologist directs his eye at art and raises many questions that are frequently overlooked. The sections on myopia and Impressionism, on colour defects and art, and on the El Greco fallacy, are particularly recommended.

Vaizey, M. (1982). *The artist as photographer.* London: Sidgwick & Jackson. Photographs have been used by artists ever since they were available. The many uses to which they have been put, from *aide mémoire* to photorealist painting, are charted here. There is appended a useful chronology of art and photography.

Wald, G. (1972). Eye and camera. In R. Held & W. Richards (Eds.), *Perception: Mechanisms and models.* San Francisco: Freeman. A comparison of the eye and the camera at the levels both of optics and of processing light. The optical aberrations of the eye are described together with some of the means of compensating for them.

Weale, R. A. (1982). *Focus on vision.* London: Hodder and Stoughton. The book describes the structure of the eye, circadian effects of light, developmental changes in eyes and vision, and some aspects of perception. It concludes with a brief discussion of illusions in art.

Weaver, M. (1986). *The photographic art. Pictorial traditions in Britain and America.* London: The Scottish Arts Council and The Herbert Press. An exhibition catalogue containing many black-and-white reproductions by well-known photographers from Fox Talbot to Diane Arbus.

Young, T. (1801). On the mechanism of the eye. *Philosophical Transactions of the Royal Society, 91,* 23–88. Young's Bakerian lecture to the Royal Society describes his ingenious experiments to establish that accommodation is achieved by changes in the curvature of the crystalline lens.

Zakia, R. D. (1975). *Perception and photography.* Englewood Cliffs, N.J.: Prentice-Hall. A book addressed to photographers and designers describing the Gestalt principles and their operation in pictures. It is stronger on design than on perception.

Pictorial Allusions

Brewster, D. (1819). *A treatise on the kaleidoscope.* Edinburgh: A. Constable. Brewster invented the kaleidoscope around 1815. The manner of its invention and the optical principles involved in its construction are described in this short book, together with some of its applications.

Carello, C., Rosenblum, L., & Grosofsky, A. (1986). Static depiction of movement. *Perception, 15,* 41–58. The authors examined experimentally different ways of representing human movement in single pictures. Different pictorial devices (like multiple outlines or speed lines) were presented in isolation or in combination with others. Pictorial devices were effective if they corresponded to the event (like running) represented.

Hockney, D. (1986). *Photographs.* Washington, D.C.: International Exhibitions Foundation. A catalogue for an exhibition of David Hockney's composite photographs, some of which are illustrated. The photographs display a subtle use of pictorial space, presenting an assemblage of fragments derived from slightly different activities performed in the same environmental space. There is appended an essay on photography by Hockney. He remarks "I have never used a tripod – this work is not about that, it's about your eye moving, your head moving, and your body moving".

Kepes, G. (Ed.) (1965). *The nature and art of motion.* London: Studio Vista. A collection of essays on the visual representation of motion. Those by Wallach, on the visual perception of motion, by Gibson, on constancy and invariance in perception, and especially by Rickey, on kinetic art, are of interest.

Leeman, F., Elffers, J., & Schuyt, M. (1976). *Hidden images. Games of perception, anamorphic art, illusion from the Renaissance to the present.* Translated by E. C. Allison & M. L. Kaplan. New York: Harry N. Abrams. A brief history of perspective is presented before describing a range of systematic distortions that can be applied, like anamorphoses. It includes a sheet of reflecting plastic so that the reader can fold it to observe the many cylindrical anamorphoses that are printed in an appendix.

Mulvey, F. (1969). *Graphic perception of space.* London: Studio Vista. A graphical exploration of the factors that influence the perception of space in pictures.

Penrose, R. (1975). *Man Ray.* London: Thames and Hudson. The vast range of Man Ray's work is surveyed. Of greatest interest is his creative use of photography in terms of the images captured, the techniques for manipulating them (like solarisation), and the combination of photography with graphics.

Weber, E. A. (1980). *Vision, composition and photography.* Berlin: de Gruyter. A guide to visual communication. The text and illustrations are integrated well, with consideration of colour and black-and-white photography. The principles of composition are based in part on Gestalt psychology and in part on the author's intuition.

Weschler, L. (1984). *David Hockney. Cameraworks.* London: Thames & Hudson. This large format book presents an extensive selection of Hockney's collages using Polaroid and conventional colour prints. He represents both landscapes and inhabited spaces. The latter are more subtle because of the complex interplay of represented postures and expressions over time. Weschler relates the multiple viewpoints and sequenced combinations to their earlier expression in cubism and futurism. Hockney commented: "I'm trying to convey what it's like for both viewer and subject to be moving through space."

3 LITERAL PICTURES

Language is generally accepted as the feature that distinguishes *Homo sapiens* from other species. That is, we can produce sequences of vocalisations that communicate to others ideas we have, and we can comprehend such vocalisations made by others. The origins of language are shrouded in mystery, but it probably served the purposes of coordinating the cooperative activities of groups of people, and of sharing the ideas afforded by an enlarged cerebral cortex. Our interest, however, is in the transmission of information in written form, rather than via speech. Here, one can be a little more precise about the origins of writing systems, because some examples of early scripts have survived. Written scripts have been invented independently in several different cultures, perhaps the oldest derived from Sumeria over 5000 years ago.

Pictorial images have a longer history: carvings on horn extend 30,000 years into the past, and cave paintings were produced 20,000 years ago. With this longer history of pictorial imagery, it is not surprising that the earliest written scripts were pictographic. That is, an object or an idea was represented by a simplified picture. If our ancestors had been as interested in pipes as we were in Chapter One, the pictograph for a pipe might have been like one of the examples in Figure 3.1. It is not clear what these pictorial images have in common, since they do not necessarily conform to the stereotypical view – with the asymmetrical axis of the represented object in the picture plane. Anyone who would recognise one of these as a mark signifying the object "pipe" would need to share some common knowledge regarding the conventions used in the abstraction. Even pictographs represent complex instances of perceptual abstraction, and this is the simplest type of script! There are many shortcomings with pictographic writing systems, the principal one being that they are confined mainly to objects – abstract ideas cannot be communicated unless there is a sophisticated convention that is shared by those using the system. If this is the case, then the main advantage of any writing system, the semi-permanent storage of information, could readily be lost. None the less, early scripts were primarily concerned with property inventories and transactions, and pictographs might have been adequate for this purpose.

Logographs (logograms or ideographs, as they are also called), which are considered to be the next phase of development in writing systems, represent the words of a spoken language by a symbol that is not pictographic. Modern Chinese script is of this form, although it was previously pictographic. The present logographic symbols have become so stylised that it is very difficult to relate them to the earlier pictographs. Having a logograph for each word in the language presents a near insurmountable problem for the writer (and the lexicographer) because the vocabulary is vast. Nor will the written language reflect the subtleties and complexities of the spoken language. An advantage that does accompany logographic writing systems is that the same symbol can be used by speakers of different languages, just as the number system we employ is not restricted to English users. A given Arabic numeral, say 7, can be understood by users of many languages even though the specific words for it will differ.

The next phase of development in writing systems was syllabic, in which each syllable in the language is represented by a symbol or character. As long as the number of syllables in the language is not too great this system can be relatively economical. In Japanese the two Kana systems consist of 46 syllables, which make for usable syllabaries, unlike English which has several thousand syllables. English, in common with many other languages, uses an alphabetic writing system. Since we use it we tend either to take it for granted or to assume that it is universal! Alphabetic systems were used by the Phoenicians about 3000 years ago, and in these the individual characters (letters) represent basic sounds in the spoken words. Two of the alphabetic systems now in use both derive from the Greek alphabet (which developed from the Phoenician), and they are the Roman and the Cyrillic. They both afford a tremendous economy on writing and reading, because the number of characters is so small – just 26 in the English modification of the Roman alphabet. It is relatively easy to learn to discriminate the individual letters from one another (for reading) and to master the manual skills of producing them (for writing). these tasks are performed by young children in our society. Thus, by linking sounds to visual symbols the alphabetic writing systems can encode the complexities of spoken communication economically. Moreover, they can approach the richness of speech, by having written

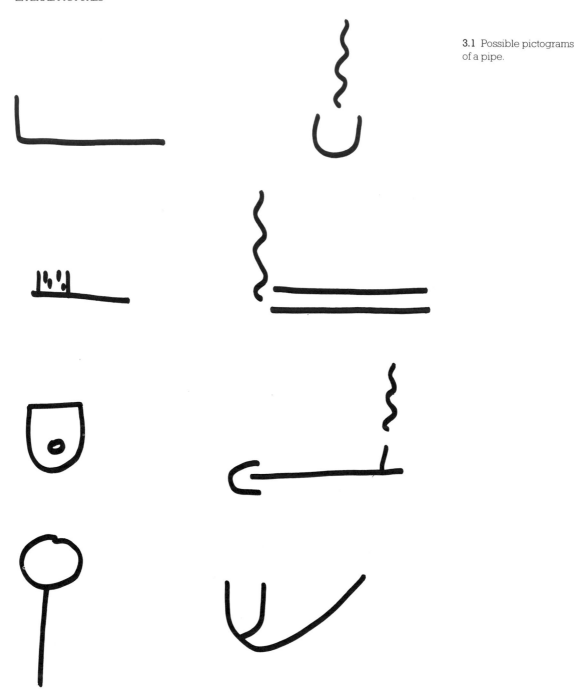

3.1 Possible pictograms of a pipe.

symbols for abstract ideas, and for the relations between ideas and events. The transmission of ideas in this way places fewer visual demands upon the reader, and so the majority of thought processing during reading can be addressed to the message itself, rather than to translating the written symbols.

Because writing systems transmit information in an orderly sequence they require some surface upon which the symbols can be written. While some early scripts involved the incision of symbols in hard or hardening materials (like cuneiform writing on clay tablets), the advantages of a flexible flat surface were discovered thousands of years ago. The use of papyrus by the Egyptians dates back almost 5000 years. The marks could then be made with some suitably opaque fluid, like paint, applied with a brush or reed. Thus, virtually from the origin of writing systems the symbols were essentially made in two-dimensional form. Indeed, the feature that distinguishes *Homo sapiens* from other species, in terms of visual perception, is the analysis of two-dimensional stimuli. Only humans produce pictorial images (of which script is a special case) in two dimensions, and they have evolved the facility for analysing pictorial images at the graphical image level. The allusion in representational pictorial images is to three-dimensional space, whereas that in written words is to ideas – concepts that are associated with the word.

This chapter is concerned with the graphical relationship between words and their referents. The illustrations all use words as elements within them. The first section ("Word and image") pursues the paradoxes presented by Magritte in his painted pipe picture, as discussed in Chapter One. In fact the puzzle is turned on its head by inventing a script that moulds letter shapes back into a pictographic form. The second section ("Word as image") also has pictographic elements, because the graphical features of letters and words echo their meanings. This does not apply to concrete words alone, as it is particularly suited to words that define shapes. The third section ("Words as patterns") uses words as pattern elements; they are arranged sequentially or in arrays and either convey their meaning in the overall shape, or the meaning will be embedded within the design. The final section ("Literal portraits") uses words in the most fluid manner. Rather than presenting a word in a novel form or repetitively, text is employed. The text itself will convey within it a portrait, and the text will allude to the work or life of the individual portrayed.

3.2 *The integrity of words. (Homage to Magritte.)*

Word and Image

In Chapter One the nature of perception was illustrated by reference to pictorial images of pipes. A curved briar was selected because of its similarity to the shape of Magritte's painted pipe in his *The Perfidy of Images*. The painting was considered particularly apposite because of its inscription – "This is not a pipe." Magritte was drawing attention to the way in which objects are represented as words and as pictorial images. It was argued that the pictorial image of a pipe and the written word "pipe" are both processed at the graphical image level; however, the pictorial image alludes to the three-dimensional properties of the object represented, whereas the word alludes to the category of objects represented. In short, the word has more ready access to the mental image level. Magritte's painting is so arresting because of the way it jolts our preconceptions regarding these two forms of representation. It can also be considered as questioning the way in which we treat different shapes as equivalent when they are letter-forms, but not necessarily when they are pictorial images. On the one hand, a given letter or word can be written in a wide variety of ways and still be recognised as the same letter or word. On the other, different pictorial images are likely to be seen as representing different objects, or the same object from different viewpoints.

The game that Magritte played with words can also be played pictorially. Figure 3.2 is called *The integrity of words*, and the words "une pipe" are depicted in two ways, one corresponding to Magritte's handwriting and the other in a form that the reader may never have seen before. The letters of the uppermost one are manipulated to have the outline of Magritte's curved briar pipe. Even though the letters are depicted in this novel way they are still readily recognisable as forming the words "une pipe". To perform this task of visual recognition is remarkable in its own right – it says something about the way in which letters can be considered as visually equivalent, after the manner of the discussion of the pictorial images of objects. Thus, the words combine the two levels of representation – the pictorial and the linguistic. This, too, as in Magritte's painting, is reflected in the inscription: "This is a pipe". However, the inscription is also ambiguous: it could be stating that the words "une pipe" are present, or it could be making an equivalence between the shape of the words and that of a real pipe. Is this pictorial image any more pipe-like than Magritte's?

In fact, the conflicts can be generated in textual terms alone, since text presents similar pattern recognition problems to those for pictorial images of objects. There is, however, one important difference: text is inherently two-dimensional. The problems of viewpoint, mentioned in the context of pipe images, rarely apply to images of text. Despite this, it has proved equally difficult to define the shape of individual letters. That is, the range of shapes that can be recognised as representing a given letter is vast, and has not proved amenable to pictorial definition.

The conflict that Magritte created between word and image can be represented in text alone. Compare the following two statements:

> This n'est pas un mot.
> Ceci n'est pas Français.

We can also ask whether Magritte ever had a pipe. Was he painting an object or a mental image or even a pictorial image? In the case of Figure 1.4 a real briar pipe was photographed (assuming that you are prepared to take my word for it). Unlike Magritte's pipe, mine can be handled (see Figure 3.3). If Magritte was painting a pipe of his dreams then the inscription was perfectly correct!

While the relationship between the form and shape of objects or people is not exact, it does exist, and it can be related to the level of the optical image. The same cannot be said for the relationship between words and objects. What does the word "pipe" have in common with my curved briar? With the exception of such contrived manipulations as Figure 3.2, the word does not share any of the optical image features of the object. The verbal label is arbitrary, and needs to be learned if it is to serve any function. Magritte's choice of the "pipe" on which to play his discordant tune was anything but arbitrary. The word pipe has multiple meanings. One of the most basic of these is a simple tube or cylinder, and the stark geometrical features of these were considered to have an aesthetic appeal earlier in the century, when Magritte was producing his first works on this theme. He was obviously not resonating to the aesthetic conceptions of his day, rather the reverse. This is but one meaning of pipe; others include a musical instrument, a means of conveying

3.3 Photograph of a hand-held pipe.

liquids or gases, in addition to a pipe for burning dried leaves. Moreover, it can be a verb as well as a noun.

When the meaning is restricted to a pipe used for smoking there is no single object to which the word refers. I might be able to say that a picture of a pipe looks like my pipe, because the image represents a specific instance of the category. The word, on the other hand, represents the entire category – all smoking pipes – of which there is an astonishing variety. Even for object words the level of abstraction is much broader than with pictorial images. Thus, not only is the level of abstraction greater for words, but the graphical latitude in depicting them is also vast. The range of printed letter-shapes is enormous, and these are more amenable to classification than are handwritten letters. Novel letter-shapes are constantly being produced, but the more exotic ones – like those in Figure 3.2 – require the context of the word for their recognition. For example, if the "U" in the bowl of the word-picture was presented in isolation it probably would not be recognised as a letter "U"; there is no difficulty in seeing it so in the context of the other letter-shapes.

In the same way, the uncertainty in recognising a word can be resolved by the context in which it is placed – the phrase or the sentence.

In creating novel letter-shapes it is possible to create a conflict between the elements that compose the letter and the letter-shape itself, especially if the former are themselves letters. For example, in Figure 3.4 we have two pipes and two tubes; the

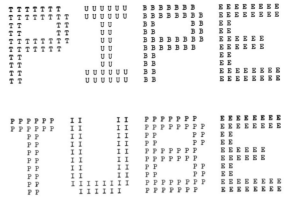

3.4 Letter-shapes from letters.

```
E E E E E E E E E      P P P P P P      I I I I I I I I I      P P P P P P P P P
E E E E E E E E E E    P P P P P P      I I I I I I I I I I    P P P P P P P P P P
E E            E E     P P            I I            I I    P P
E E            E E     P P            I I            I I    P P
E E            E E     P P            I I            I I    P P
E E            E E     P P            I I            I I    P P
E E E E E E E E E E    P P            I I I I I I I I I    P P P P P P P P
E E E E E E E E E      P P            I I I I I I I I I    P P P P P P P
E E                   P P            I I            P P
E E                   P P            I I            P P
E E                   P P            I I            P P
E E                   P P P P P P    I I            P P P P P P P P P
E E                   P P P P P P    I I            P P P P P P P P P P
```

3.5 Backward pipe.

```
P I P E      P        P I P E      P I P E
I     P      I        I     P      I
P   I        P        P   I        P
E P I P      E        E P I P      E P I P
P            P        P            P
I            I        I            I
P            P        P            P I P E
```

3.6 Word pipe.

```
T U B E      T        T U B E      T U B E
U     B      U        U     B      U
B   U        B        B   U        B
E B U T      E        E B U T      E B U T
B            B        B            B
U            U        U            U
T            T        T            T U B E
```

3.7 Pipe-tube.

letters of one make up the letter-shapes of the other. Our initial impression is of the overall letter-shapes – PIPE above and TUBE below, although the smaller letters defining them can disrupt our recognition for a short time. The same theme is played with a backward pipe in Figure 3.5. In these two examples the whole letter-shape has been made from individual letters, whereas the elements are themselves words in Figure 3.6. The word elements reinforce the meaning of the overall or global word-shape, but they interfere with its recognition, because the elements are themselves meaningful (although the word elements need to be read in different directions). The disruption is more severe when the word elements conflict with the global word shape, as in Figure 3.7. The disturbance of recognition caused by the word elements can easily be removed by making them more difficult to discern; squinting to defocus the elements makes the word-shape easily discernible. Finally, the letter elements themselves can be used to provide a pictorial image of my pipe, as is shown in Figure 3.8. Here the differential density of the image, which provides the tonal variation, is created by the use of the individual letters P,I,P, and E in upper and lower case letters and by overtyping them.

To represent my pipe in words alone would need a great deal of verbal elaboration in order to distinguish it from other pipes. The elaboration concerns not only the obvious aspects, like the material from which it is constructed and its curved form, but also its precise spatial dimensions. In representing specific instances of objects, pictorial images are economical whereas words are not; the reverse applies to the representation of general cases. Therefore, pictorial images provide us with spatial representations of the object whereas words result in representations of categories of objects that operate at the mental image level.

This distinction presents problems for both the writer and the artist. The writer can call upon a storehouse of linguistic tools of varying degrees of abstraction, and mould them into the form that is required. Only those features of the object that are relevant to the narrative need be described; indeed, heightened importance can be placed on them by writing about them in isolation. The graphic artist, on the other hand, must ask: how can the pictorial image transcend the specific instance? How can general ideas be represented pictorially?

3.8 *Pipescript.*

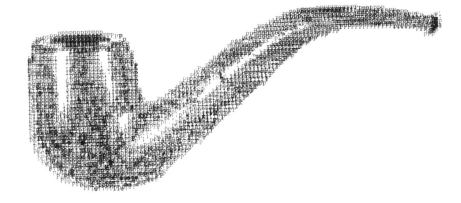

Word as Image

Letters and their groupings into words are pictorial images. They are two-dimensional shapes which we have learned to analyse at the level of graphical images and interpret at the mental image level. Letters and words rarely reflect the intermediate stages of image processing that have been described above. Even pictographs (or pictograms) represent objects as abstracted pictorial images. They do not share the optical image properties of the object represented. It is, however, possible to produce pictorial images of words that do echo properties of their referents. In this case, the meaning of the word should be evident from its overall pictorial shape, before the individual letters have been recognised. In practice, the processes of letter and word recognition occur with such alacrity that the appreciation of the multiple meanings will seem simultaneous. However, in some of the illustrations the process of word recognition is likely to be retarded by the manner in which the letter shapes have been modified.

Words could also be made to reflect the visual image level, although no examples of this are possible in a book: the word can take the three-dimensional form of the object. Of course, the word becomes redundant under those circumstances. If the object itself can be perceived there is little need for an alternative symbolic manner of presenting it.

The pictorial characteristics of words can be modified in such a manner that they represent aspects of the graphical image. Pictorial images are considered to be processed at the graphical image level. Accordingly, many perceptual phenomena that have been demonstrated at this level could be

3.9 *Pomme.*

THIGH CALF FOOT FOOT CALF THIGH

3.10 *Legs.*

3.11 *Mug.*

3.12 *Grey scale.*

represented by their names, rather than as abstract line drawings. In other words, the pictorial images as words represent the phenomena they describe, and a number of such illustrations will be presented in this section.

Concrete nouns provide the most straightforward source for word-image manipulations. This was one reason why Magritte chose a mundane and relatively unambiguous object, like a pipe, to confront the observer with the puzzle of pictorial images. In pictograms, it is likely that the stereotypical viewpoint for the object will be represented in some simplified shape. In other words, the problem of projected shape (the optical image) that is inherent in all pictorial images of solid objects will be minimised by representing the object in the shape most likely to be recognised. The same general constraint will apply to the word-pictures shown here. For example, in Figure 3.9 we see the shape of an apple, which is made up of the letters spelling the English word for this fruit. At a slightly more complex level, the legs shown in Figure 3.10 are made up of the words for their constituent parts. In both cases, the shapes are recognisable if the figures are viewed from beyond reading distance, so that the individual letters are not discriminable. Some other examples of word-pictures can be seen in Figures 3.11–3.14.

It is of interest that Magritte did not use this device to draw attention to the arbitrariness of the linguistic labels that are applied to objects. He almost always used inscriptions in his own handwriting, rather than any stylised lettering.

In addition to concrete nouns there are many words which have clearly defined spatial referents, and these spatial characteristics can be blended with the letter or word forms. For instance, the spatial concept of tangency can be incorporated in the word "tangent" (Figure 3.15), or eccentricity in "eccentric" (Figure 3.16). In the case of "concentric" (Figure 3.17) the word can be read in two directions, one around the circumference and the other radially from the outside towards the centre. Further exam-

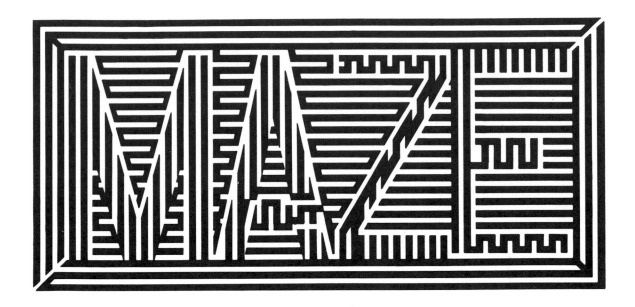

3.13 *Labyrinth.*

ples of words as pictorial images which augment their spatial characteristics are given in Figures 3.18–3.20. In each case the letters themselves are composed of pictorial elements that depict the geometrical meaning of the words. This can also be achieved with words that do not have such a specific spatial reference, as in Figure 3.21.

The individual letters are either readily recognisable or separated from one another in each of the previous figures, but this might not be so for Figure 3.22. Its title gives some clues, as do the arrow-like extremities, but the difficulty arises from segregating the shapes of the individual letters. A further clue is that each letter is tilted a little more than its neighbour on the left. As a final clue, the arrow-like N-dings of the words act rather like logograms symbolising the relationship of one direction to another.

Despite having an alphabetic writing system we still employ a variety of logograms in our script. In addition to our number symbols and the arithmetic operators (+, −, ×, /), the symbols for punctuation are logograms (Figure 3.23) as are those for currency (Figure 3.24). Logograms are also used extensively in areas in which no assumptions regarding a

3.14 *Two footballs.*

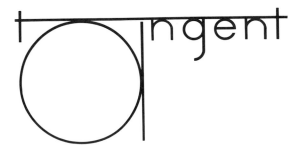

3.15 *Tangents.*

103

eccentric

3.16 *Eccentricity.*　　　**3.17** *Concentricity.*

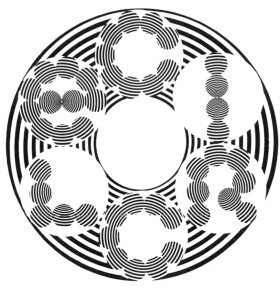

3.18 *Triangles.*

3.19 *Circles.*

3.20 *Ellipses.* **3.21** *Tear.*

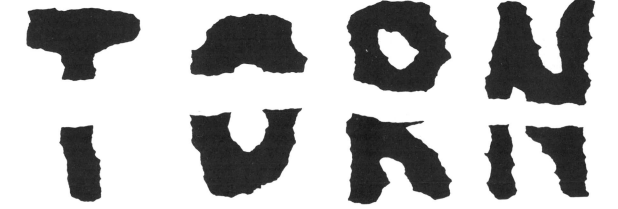

3.22 *Directional difference.*

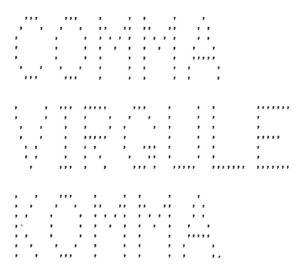

3.23 *Punctuation.*

```
£ £ £ £      £ £ £     £ £        £ £       £ £ £     £ £ £ £
£ £ £ £ £   £ £ £ £ £  £ £        £ £      £ £ £ £   £ £ £ £
£ £ £ £    £ £ £ £    £ £        £ £      £ £ £ £     £ £ £ £
£ £ £ £    £ £ £ £   £ £ £ £ £  £ £ £ £   £ £ £ £     £ £ £ £
£ £ £ £     £ £ £    £ £ £ £ £  £ £ £ £   £ £  £ £   £ £  £ £
```

3.24 *Sterling.*

common language can be made – as in the case for internationally agreed road signs. Another such area is that dealing with dangerous materials, such as radioactive isotopes (Figure 3.25).

Words refer to processes and phenomena as well as to objects and spatial relations. In the context of vision, many of the phenomena investigated are concerned with graphical image processing. The phenomena are elicited on two-dimensional surfaces as pictorial images, and some of them are amenable to representation literally. For example, the processing of pictorial images generally requires that they are optically in focus, although this might not prove too easy for Figure 3.26. The mechanism of focusing in the eye was described in Chapter Two, and it is called accommodation. The states of curvature of the lens when focusing on near and far objects are shown in Figure 3.27, together with their consequences. Accommodation functions to focus light on the retina for further processing, so that the fine spatial detail in it can be resolved. The detection of spatial detail is called visual acuity (Figure 3.28), and it is often measured with charts consisting of letters or patterns varying systematically in size. One such chart was devised by Landoldt, and it was made up from circles with small gaps in them, rather like a letter C. The location of the gap could be to the left, right, top or bottom, and the observer's task was to identify its location. Another way of determining the resolving power of the eye is to present observers with patterns of evenly-spaced, parallel lines (called gratings). When the lines are very thin and densely packed it becomes impossible to discriminate between a grating and an equally illuminated patch of grey. The variation in the density of the lines is referred to as spatial frequency (Figure 3.29), and certain recent theories of vision suggest that complex patterns are analysed in the visual system in terms of their constituent spatial frequencies – rather like the analysis of a complex sound in terms of its constituent pure tones.

Some visual phenomena themselves can be depicted in their own terms, and the following are examples of this dual representation. Figure 3.30 consists of grids made of white on black or vice versa; in the case of the former, dark grey dots will be seen at the white intersections of the Hermann grid, whereas there are light grey dots at the black intersections in the Hering grid. These two visual

3.25 *Hazard warning.*

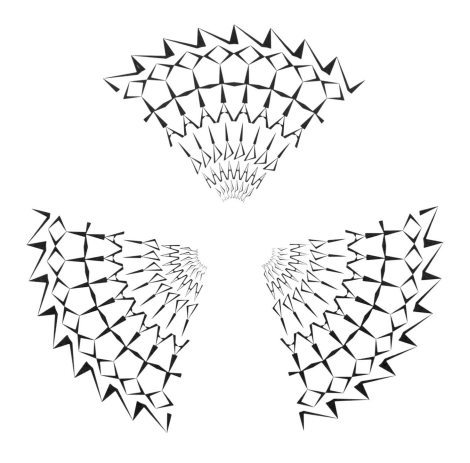

3.26 *Sharply defined.*

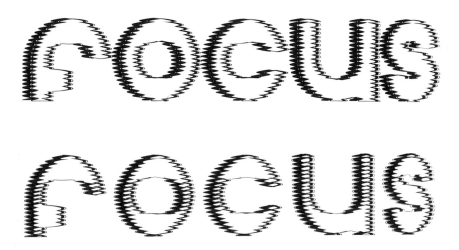

FAR

F A R

3.27 *Lenticular accommodation.*

scientists gave the phenomena their names over a century ago. The illusory contours shown in Figure 3.31 have a shorter history in visual science. Where discontinuities in a pattern exist there is a tendency for them to be smoothed out by the visual system – often creating the illusion of contours where none exist physically. Various of the pattern properties that induce illusory contours are shown here.

A more conventional geometrical illusion is described and depicted in Figure 3.32: the vertical and horizontal extents are physically equal, but the vertical looks longer. Moreover, the magnitude of the illusion is indirectly indicated in the figure, too: the word VERTICAL is written five times, but HORIZONTAL is written only four times. With this particular configuration the vertical extent is overestimated by approximately 20 per cent. The vertical–horizontal illusion is an example of an illusion of extent, somewhat like the Ponzo illusion described in the "Allusions" section in Chapter One. Figure 3.33 provides an example of an illusion of orientation.

Some of the most commonly represented ambiguities in pictorial images are the reversing figures – simple outlines which can be perceived in alternative depth planes. Three examples are given here, each named after those who initially des-

3.28 *Landoldt sees.*

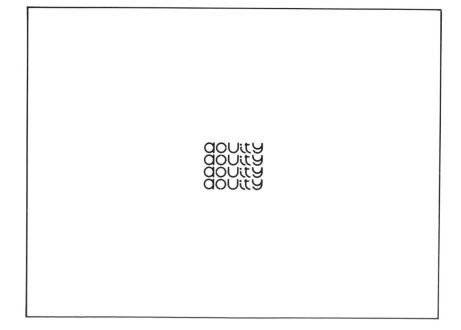

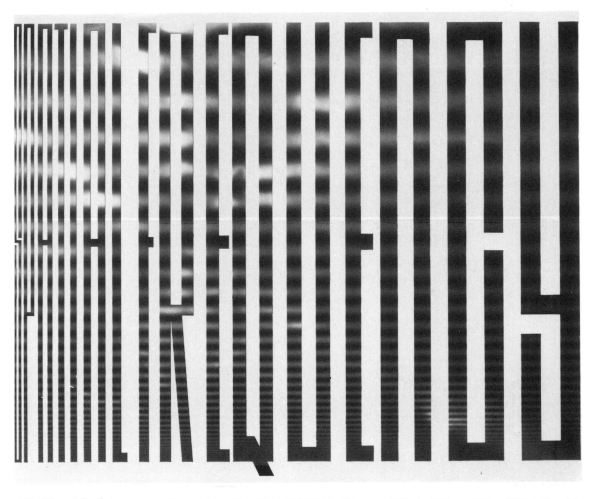

3.29 (Above) *Gratings.*

3.30 (Right) *Illusory dots.*

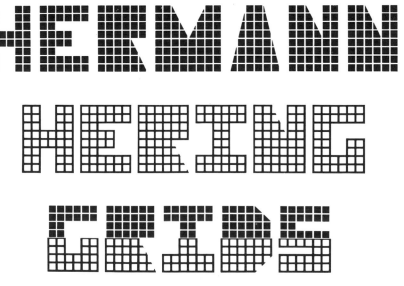

3.31 Subjective or illusory contours can be produced in a number of ways, several of which are illustrated here.

3.32 *Meridional variation.* The vertical and horizontal letters (and words) are the same length, but the verticals look longer. The vertical separations between the letters are less than those for the horizontal letters, so that the word VERTICAL is repeated five times, for only four of the HORIZONTAL. If VERTICAL had been typed only four times (making the line 20 per cent shorter) then the two extents would look about equal.

cribed them – the Necker cube (Figure 3.34), the Mach book (Figure 3.35), and the Schroeder staircase (Figure 3.36).

Thus far, all the word-pictures have been congruent – the overall shapes have echoed the meanings of the words. Such congruence is by no means necessary, as was hinted in the "Word and image" section earlier in this chapter. Indeed, again it is surprising that Magritte did not use the technique of word-picture discordance to emphasise the conventional nature of verbal labels. In *The Key of Dreams* he divided the picture plane into four quadrants and painted a pictorial image in each; three were accompanied by inappropriate written labels, and the fourth was appropriate. We see in Figure 3.37 a pictorial shape of a jug that is made up of the word "bird", which was one of the discordant relationships Magritte painted. The recognition of both the pictorial image and the written word are probably disturbed by this discordance. Within cognitive psychology this would be considered as a general example of the Stroop effect. In the 1930s Stroop found that the time taken to name the colour of a simple pictorial image depends upon its shape. For instance, it would take less time to say that the colour of the upper rectangle in Figure 3.38 is white than it would for the lower word-shape. The colour name "black" inhibits the naming of the colour in which it is written, because the two are discordant. The word is read implicitly even though it is not necessary for the task on hand, and this can retard responding. This is not so for the upper rectangle because its shape is not competing with the colour of the paper.

The Stroop effect is not confined to colours and colour names – it occurs with letters and letter-shapes too (Figure 3.39). Recognising a letter that is made up from its own letter-shape (like the first O in STROOP) is faster than when it is made up from another letter (like the second O). There is an additional dimension in Figure 3.39, because the letter elements themselves spell a word "TROOPS" that conflicts with the proper name "STROOP" and is an anagram of it. However, the effects are often more lasting when the word can have a variety of meanings, so that a number of discordances can be alluded to simultaneously. In Figure 3.40 the contrasting forms of the words are immediately evident, but the additional contrasts, like the directions in which the underlying letter elements are written

3.33 The short line elements are inclined slightly clockwise or counter-clockwise, while their centres are aligned vertically. None the less, the letters appear to be inclined in the direction of the line elements.

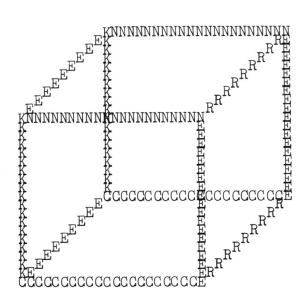

3.34 *Necker cube.* If the outline is seen as a representation of a cube, then it might appear to fluctuate in depth, with the near face directed left and downwards or right and upwards.

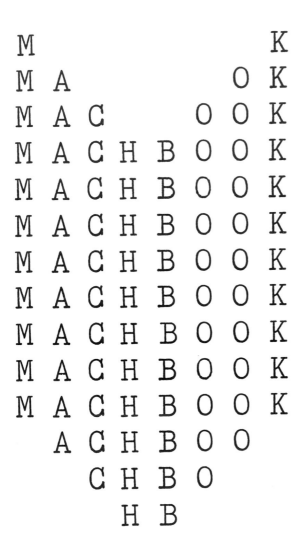

3.35 *Mach book.* If the arrangement of letters is seen as a book, then the spine might appear directed either closer or farther away than the extremities.

and the presence of a single lower-case letter in each word, take a little longer to appreciate.

Words as Patterns

Pictorial images are marks made on some surface, and writing represents conventionally accepted marks that are usually related to spoken language. Written symbols have been made on a wide variety of surfaces, as have other pictorial images. It is not surprising, therefore, to find that the implements used to produce written symbols are also enlisted to create pictorial images. This relationship is to be expected when using a pen or pencil, but less so for instruments designed to produce written script alone. For example, typewriters were designed to produce legible text of a given typeface in a repeat-able form with constant spacing, etc., and little else. None the less, the facility for repeatability and alignment have been used to create patterns in which the letters or words are elements. A word can be typed many times, without spaces separating each repeat, so that a background pattern is created; repeating this process, with the paper displaced slightly (as in Figure 3.41) will produce interference patterns of the type that are called moiré fringes. They are usually produced by displacing one pattern of black and white lines with respect to another, but the effects are rather more subtle with words, because of the way in which the overlapping letters interact. If this effect had been produced by black and white lines as wide as the type then only vertical moiré fringes would have been produced. Here there is a

3.36 *Schroeder staircase.*
A representation of a stair
or steps like this can be
seen in two ways, either
from above or below.

3.37 *The jug.* One quadrant of Magritte's *The Key of Dreams* consists of a painted jug above the words "the bird". The jug represented here is the same shape as Magritte's, but it is defined by its false label.

3.38 The Stroop effect: less time is required to name the upper central area "white" than the lower region of white. The conflicting linguistic information in the word delays the appropriate colour name for the surface.

```
TTTTT  RRRRR  00000  00000      PPPPP  SSSSS
T          R  0          0      P          S
TTTTT      R  00000  0      0   P      P   SSSSS
    T      R  0      0      0   P      P   S
TTTTT      R  0      0   00000  PPPPP      S
```

3.39 *The Troops effect.*

114

3.40 *Opposing qualities.*

3.41 *Interference fringes.* When two regular, repetitive patterns are inclined slightly with respect to one another they produce interference or moiré fringes.

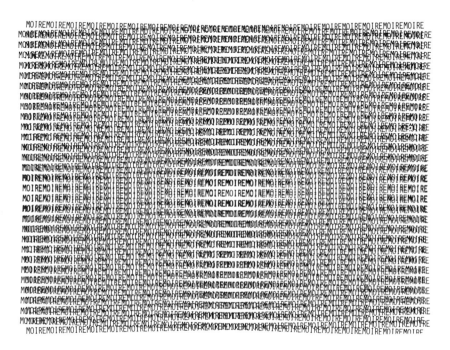

strong impression of concentric circles around the words that are in closest register.

In Figure 3.42 the spaces between the lines are abolished, as well as those between the words. This provides a relatively uniform background against which very small differences in contrast can be detected. The term threshold is used to denote the limits of perception – so a stimulus at or near the threshold of vision will be visible at some times but not at others. Thresholds are fundamental features of any sensory system, and they have been referred to by a variety of names, one of the oldest of which is "limen", from Latin. In this figure the word LIMEN is embedded near its threshold! There are, in fact, two limen – an upper and a lower: the upper limen is slightly brighter than the background and the lower limen is slightly darker.

When the regularity of the spacing in typed words is disturbed in some manner, as in Figure 3.43, a strong impression of a three-dimensional surface can be produced. The size of the elements provides a suggestion of relative distance and this is enhanced by the twisting of the typescript. Manipulations of elements in terms of their size and orientation is a feature of some forms of geometrical abstraction, particularly of the works produced by Bridget Riley (see Figure 3.44): although the letters themselves are all arranged in a rectilinear way, the impression of curvature can still be produced. This is even the case when the letters are typed in

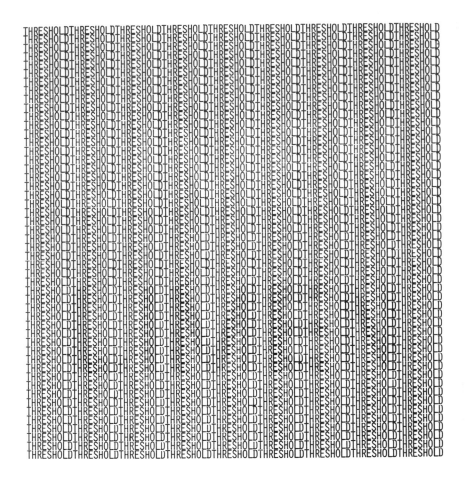

3.42 *Just noticeable differences*. The background pattern is made up of the word THRESHOLD, which refers to the limits of discriminability within a simulus dimension. These limits or LIMEN are just detectable changes, like those that can be seen here: there is an upper (brighter) and lower (darker) LIMEN visible in the pattern.

3.43 *Twisted awry.*

3.44 *New wave.*

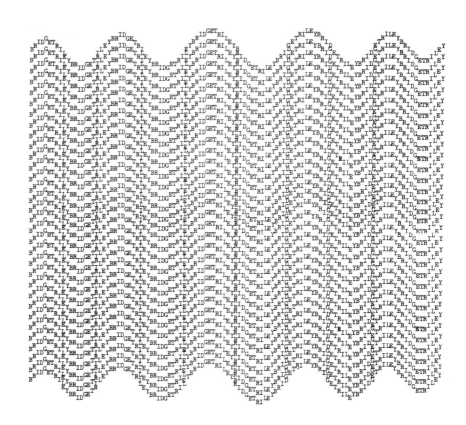

3.45 *Right justified.* The words are arranged in a regular geometrical sequence so that all blocks form rectangles. Despite this, the non-fixated regions of the pattern appear to be curved rather than rectilinear.

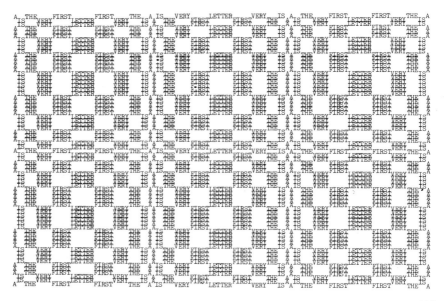

rectangular blocks (Figure 3.45): fixating the centre of the figure results in the extremities appearing . curved. Whenever fixation moves to a region that formerly appeared curved it will revert to recti-linearity.

The typewriter (or the printer on a computer) can be used as a rather crude drawing device. For example, the outline and salient features of an object can be defined by letters, as is shown in Figure 3.46. Only a gross impression is produced by using a single letter, especially when the paper is kept in a fixed relation to the carriage, as was the case here. When the full keyboard is used, together with over-typing, a much more detailed pictorial image can be produced (Figure 3.47). If this figure is viewed slightly out-of-focus, or from several metres dis-tance, a relatively solid impression is created by the varying densities of the typed marks. Indeed, it is remarkable how much information about identity can be introduced into a portrait using typed letters, even accepting the constraints of normal sequential typing and even using a restricted range (and order) of letters. The portrait of Peter Mark Roget pre-sented in Figure 3.48 consists of the letters THE-SAURUS typed in that order from left to right; the only differentiating feature is the separation of suc-cessive letters. While no one is able to say whether

it is a good resemblance of Roget, it is certainly recognisable as similar to other portraits that were made of him.

All the pattern elements in this section, up to now, have been produced on a typewriter. It is also possible to make word-patterns with specially writ-ten letter forms. The concentric design in Figure 3.49 probably appears like an abstract pattern. There are some clearly defined geometrical shapes present in it, but they might not look letter-like. This is the pattern that would be produced if a single word was viewed in the device it describes: the word KALEIDOSCOPE is written from the outside towards the centre. Each word is formed in a 15° sector of the circle, but all neighbouring words are reflected with respect to one another. Thus the pattern corresponds to that produced by placing the word in a kaleidoscope, and the device was given that name by its inventor because it was derived from the Greek for "to see beautiful forms".

The letter shapes in Figure 3.50 are even more esoteric, because they have been moulded to the

3.47 (Facing page) *Charles Babbage.*

3.46 *Model T.*

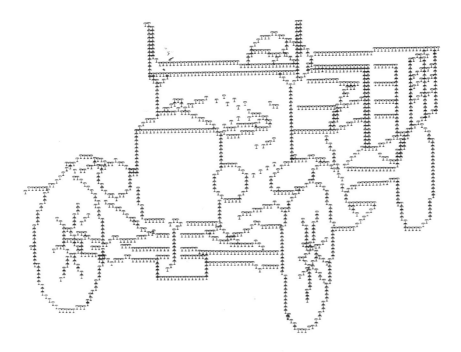

3.48 *Thesaurus of Roget.*

profiles of a face. In following the contours of the face some of the letters are difficult to recognise, particularly the "I" which falls at the lips. However, this unusual letter shape can be accommodated quite readily because the context in which it has been placed (i.e., the other letters) reduces or removes the uncertainty regarding its identity. If it is accepted that the shapes spell a word, and that the

other letters can be recognised, then there is no alternative to it being an "I", since it must be a vowel.

Finally, the letter shape, word arrangement and the total configuration can combine to augment a particular idea or concept. In Figure 3.51 the individual letters are "blocked", as though they were made in angular three-dimensional form. The squared backgrounds are black above and white

3.49 *To see beautiful forms.* This is the English equivalent to the word KALEIDOSCOPE (derived from Greek) which is drawn in multiple reflections and rotations as it might be seen in the instrument itself.

3.50 *Outlines.*

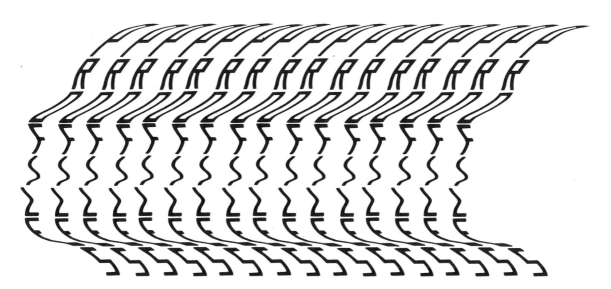

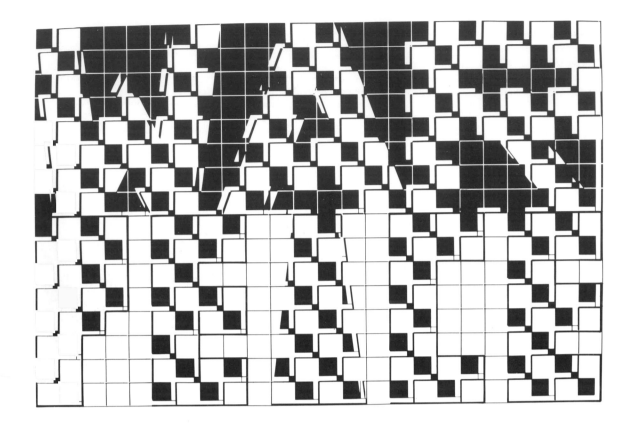

3.51 *Strategic studies.* The motif of a board game is used to convey the war games that often constitute peace studies.

WAR is presented against a black background, whereas PEACE is placed in a white context.

below, with the letters rather like parts of a chess board; this pictorial imagery is intentional as the words describe the conflicts and resolutions that have been characteristics of human societies. In Figure 3.52 the letters are aligned in concentric squares of varying size, and the three faces are the sides of a cube. It is only reasonable, therefore, that the letters spell the name Pablo Picasso. It should also be noticed that the angle of regard for the letters of "Pablo" are different to those for "Picasso", reflecting the multiple viewpoints incorporated in the early cubist paintings.

The use of words as patterns provides a vehicle for considering some aspects of letter and word recognition. However, letters and words are rarely used in isolation, in the manner of these illustrations. Rather, they comprise the parts of a message, to be communicated to others. In the next section we will examine some more complex interactions between words and images, namely, when the words are conveying some message that complements the pictorial image carried by them.

Literal Portraits

It is only appropriate to open this section with a portrait of the most literary of playwrights – William Shakespeare. Several portraits of Shakespeare exist, and there has been much debate concerning the one most likely to have been a good resemblance. The one most often reproduced is the engraving by Martin Droeschout that was printed in the First Folio edition of his plays, published in 1623. It is this portrait that is alluded to visually in Figure 3.53. When it is viewed from a distance the familiar collared portrait of the bard will be seen, but it will be virtually impossible to discern on closer detailed inspection. The pictorial image is carried by text, written by Ben Jonson, that appeared opposite the Droeschout engraving in the First Folio. Jonson was musing on the impossibility of Droeschout's task: he agreed that the facial likeness had been achieved,

but what of the bard's wit and wisdom? These, Jonson said, could only be appreciated from his writing – hence the entreaty to the reader to read Shakespeare's plays rather than look at his portrait; only that way would the nature of the man be understood. In one sense this figure fulfils Jonson's request – if the text can be read the face is illegible and vice versa.

3.52 *Cubism.*

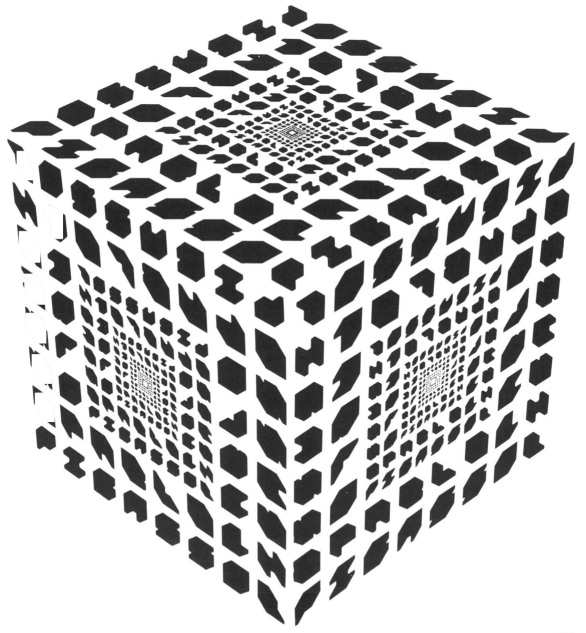

To the Reader.

This Figure, that thou here feeſt put,
It was for gentle Shakeſpeare cut;
Wherein the Grauer had a ſtrife
with Nature, to out-doo the life :
O, could he but haue drawne his wit
As well in braſſe, as he hath hit
His face ; the Print would then ſurpaſſe
All, that vvas euer vvrit in braſſe.
But, ſince he cannot, Reader, looke
Not on his Picture, but his Booke.

B. I.

3.53 Droeschout's Shakespeare.

This illustration conveys the flavour of what I call "literal portraits". They consist of two elements, a portrait and some appropriate text. The text can be simple and contrived, as in Figure 3.54, which just contrasts the words "positive" and "negative"; these terms take on far greater significance in the context of photography, particularly when the portrait they carry is that of the inventor of the negative/positive process – William Henry Fox Talbot. The arrangement of pictorial images facing one another in this way signifies the manner in which positives were originally made by contact printing the negatives – they were placed with the light-sensitive parts in contact, so there was a left-right reversal, reversing that produced in the camera. Talbot called his photographs calotypes (printed by the sun), but

3.54 *Talbotypes (William Henry Fox Talbot).*

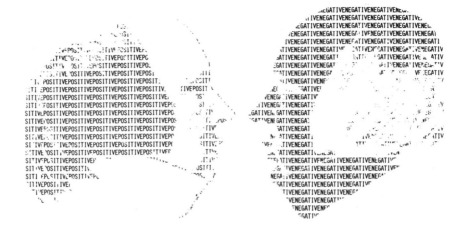

some of his supporters considered that they should be referred to as talbotypes, so that they could be contrasted with daguerreotypes, which were positives imaged on metal plates. Talbot announced his process for making photographic images in 1839, just after Louis Daguerre had published the details of his technique.

Another combination that can be employed to make literal pictures is to use some text written by the person whose portrait is carried in it. For example, the text shown in Figure 3.55 is taken from a late-16th century book on vision by Giovanni Battista della Porta, who is portrayed within it. The text is describing a test for eye dominance that Porta devised, and which is still used. If you look at a point on a wall a few metres away, using both eyes, and then align a finger or a pencil with it, the alignment will remain when one eye is closed but not for the other. The eye that maintains alignment is the dominant one for sighting. Porta believed, falsely, that people who were right-handed were also right-eyed. This is so for some people but by no means for all.

The pictorial images embedded in literal portraits are sometimes easy to decipher, as with Figure 3.54, and at other times difficult, as with Figure 3.53. For the latter, the observer tries to decode the marks in order to segregate them in some coherent way which would result in a recognisable pictorial image. Similar problems of segregation and reconstruction were involved in deciphering the early writing systems. One of the most debated examples of deciphering concerned the Rosetta stone (Figure 3.56), which was dis-

covered by Napoleon's army in Egypt at the end of the 18th century. The inscriptions on the stone consist of the same message in three scripts – hieroglyphics uppermost, then demotic and finally Greek. The first successes at deciphering the hieroglyphics were due to Thomas Young, but it was the Frenchman, Jean François Champollion, who finally cracked its code, and it is Champollion's portrait that is embedded in Figure 3.56.

Thomas Young made many notable contributions to the study of vision as well as language. Perhaps of greatest significance were his experiments on colour mixing, from which he concluded that only three colour receptors would be needed to account for human colour vision. Young was following in the line of Isaac Newton, who had shown, a century before, that the sun's light could be separated into its prismatic spectrum, and then recombined. Newton eschewed speculative theories of natural phenomena, as was evident from his statement "I do not invent hypotheses". This phrase, in his own hand and in Latin, provides the background in which his portrait is embedded (Figure 3.57).

Newton's scepticism was similar to that of René Descartes, some decades earlier. Descartes sought a fundamental starting point that was beyond question from which to construct a view of the world and man's place in it. His origin was the knowledge of his own thought-processes: "Cogito ergo sum". But he would not have been able to think without his senses, without some intercourse with his surroundings – or if he could he would not have been able to communicate his thoughts. Consequently, Descartes'

deque paginas videre valuerit, nisi breui temporis momento
videndi virtutem à dextro oculo subtrahat, mutuetq́; sinistro.
Idem in alijs sensibus euenire videmus, si dextra aure aliquem
loquentem audiuerimus, non poterimus alterum sinistra admit-
tere, & si vtrunque audire velimus, neutrum audiemus, vel si ali
quod dextra audiemus, tantundem sinistra deperdemus. Sic etiā
si vna manu scribere, altera lyram tangere, aut aureos nume-
rare nequimus. Alterum argumentum erit, si quis baculum an-
te se locauerit, & illum perpetuo alicui rimæ è regione existenti
obiecerit, notaueritq́; locum, quando sinistrum oculum clauserit, non videbit baculum ab opposita rima dimotum, ratio est,
quia vnusquisque dextro oculo cernit, vt dextram manum, & pede
vtitur, & qui sinistro oculo manus aut pede pro mortuo habe-
tur. At si dextrum oculum clauserit, illico baculus ad dextram
partem accedit. Tertium erit argumentum quòd natura duos
oculos alterum à dextris, alter à sinistris ho-
minem ab incursantibus defenderet, & in animalibus clarius
apparet, siui per semipedem inter se distant, vt in bubus, equis,
& leonibus videre est, in quibus alter alteri oppositus est, vel à
dextris, vel à sinistris videndum sit. Virtus, quia velocissimè ac-
cedens, animal sua munia obire potest, vnde non simul videre
possunt rem eandem. Et si quis situm oculorum in homine in-
spiciat non in recta linea sunt, vt sine oculorum contorsione rē
eandem inspiciant, etsi in recta linea videntur in radice tamen
cohærent. Sed quæso quæ tam dira hominum insania est ima-
ginari spiritus deferre spectra per foramina neruorum opticorum, & naturales spiritus intellectualia simulacra deferri? quomodo per foramina neruorum opticorum transeunt, si nobis di-
ligentissimè intuentibus vix occurrerunt, & adeò tenuissimi, vt
obtutum effugiant, si verè foramina dici possunt, & sunt Medi-
corum plerique, qui perforatos esse negent? Quomodo se simul

3.55 (Facing page) *Eye dominance (Giovanni Battista della Porta).* The text is taken from Porta's book *De Refractione*, in which he described a test for determining eye dominance that is still used today.

famous dictum has been modified in Figure 3.58, to read "I am seen therefore I am": existence is then defined by the perception of others – as is Descartes' portrait, which is carried by the text.

Moving to more modern times, our view of man-

kind has been deeply influenced by an understanding of our biological heritage. Charles Darwin (Figure 3.59) provided the evidence to support a theory of evolution, but he also wrote extensively about the facial expressions in man and animals. Here he is shown frowning in text that is describing the features of this expression.

Another giant of 19th century science was Hermann von Helmholtz (Figure 3.60). He was at the first rank in both physics and physiology, and the text in the figure is taken from his *Handbuch der Physio-*

3.56 *Hieroglyphics (Jean François Champollion and the Rosetta Stone).*

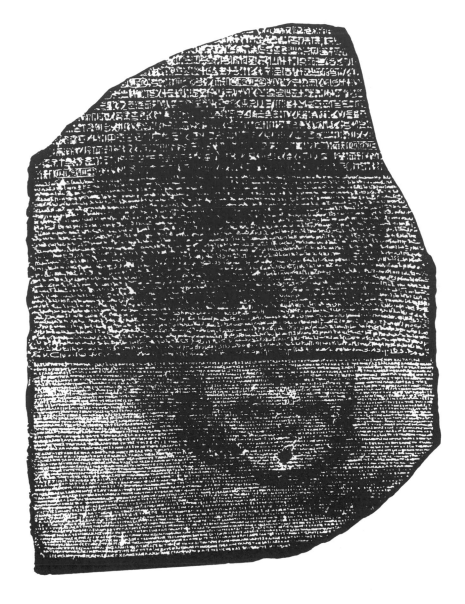

3.57 *Hypothesis non fingo (Isaac Newton).*

logischen Optik. This extract is from the concluding chapter of the third volume, and he is discussing the nature of perception. Helmholtz was a philosophical empiricist, more influenced by the British empiricists than the Continental nativists. Here he is summarising his belief that the senses provide us with tokens of what is in the world, and we need to use our intelligence to relate the tokens to external space. It is as though we carry out some form of rapid unconscious problem solving to piece the tokens together, he considered. A similar form of problem solving is required to combine these fragments of Helmholtz's portrait. However, I have argued earlier in this book that this particular theoretical approach to the perception of space is inappropriate, because of its reliance on the concept of a static retinal image: it represents the analysis of pictorial images rather than of objects in space. Pictorial images and their analysis at the graphical image level do involve interactions with mental images in a way that is not as necessary at the visual image level. The experimental examinations of visual phenomena carried out by Helmholtz were made more rigorous by the psychophysical methods described in the mid-19th century by Gustav Theodor Fechner (Figure 3.61). Fechner was a physicist and a philosopher, and he sought to determine the laws that relate the physical and the mental domains. He formulated a logarithmic relation

3.58 (Facing page) *Dual aspect (René Descartes).*

Conspicior ergo sum. Conspicior ergo sum. Conspicior ergo sum. Conspicior ergo sum.
Conspicior ergo sum. Conspicior ergo sum. Conspicior ergo sum. Conspicior ergo sum.
Conspicior ergo sum. Conspicior ergo sum. Conspicior ergo sum. Conspicior ergo sum.
Conspicior ergo sum. Conspicior ergo sum. Conspicior ergo sum. Conspicior ergo sum.
Conspicior ergo sum. Conspicior ergo sum. Conspicior ergo sum. Conspicior ergo sum.
Conspicior ergo sum. Conspicior ergo sum. Conspicior ergo sum. Conspicior ergo sum.
Conspicior ergo sum. Conspicior ergo sum. Conspicior ergo sum. Conspicior ergo sum.
Conspicior ergo sum. Conspicior ergo sum. Conspicior ergo sum. Conspicior ergo sum.
Conspicior ergo sum. Conspicior ergo sum. Conspicior ergo sum. Conspicior ergo sum.
Conspicior ergo sum. Conspicior ergo sum. Conspicior ergo sum. Conspicior ergo sum.
Conspicior ergo sum. Conspicior ergo sum. Conspicior ergo sum. Conspicior ergo sum.
Conspicior ergo sum. Conspicior ergo sum. Conspicior ergo sum. Conspicior ergo sum.
Conspicior ergo sum. Conspicior ergo sum. Conspicior ergo sum. Conspicior ergo sum.
Conspicior ergo sum. Conspicior ergo sum. Conspicior ergo sum. Conspicior ergo sum.
Conspicior ergo sum. Conspicior ergo sum. Conspicior ergo sum. Conspicior ergo sum.
Conspicior ergo sum. Conspicior ergo sum. Conspicior ergo sum. Conspicior ergo sum.
Conspicior ergo sum. Conspicior ergo sum. Conspicior ergo sum. Conspicior ergo sum.
Conspicior ergo sum. Conspicior ergo sum. Conspicior ergo sum. Conspicior ergo sum.
Conspicior ergo sum. Conspicior ergo sum. Conspicior ergo sum. Conspicior ergo sum.
Conspicior ergo sum. Conspicior ergo sum. Conspicior ergo sum. Conspicior ergo sum.
Conspicior ergo sum. Conspicior ergo sum. Conspicior ergo sum. Conspicior ergo sum.
Conspicior ergo sum. Conspicior ergo sum. Conspicior ergo sum. Conspicior ergo sum.
Conspicior ergo sum. Conspicior ergo sum. Conspicior ergo sum. Conspicior ergo sum.
Conspicior ergo sum. Conspicior ergo sum. Conspicior ergo sum. Conspicior ergo sum.
Conspicior ergo sum. Conspicior ergo sum. Conspicior ergo sum. Conspicior ergo sum.
Conspicior ergo sum. Conspicior ergo sum. Conspicior ergo sum. Conspicior ergo sum.
Conspicior ergo sum. Conspicior ergo sum. Conspicior ergo sum. Conspicior ergo sum.
Conspicior ergo sum. Conspicior ergo sum. Conspicior ergo sum. Conspicior ergo sum.
Conspicior ergo sum. Conspicior ergo sum. Conspicior ergo sum. Conspicior ergo sum.
Conspicior ergo sum. Conspicior ergo sum. Conspicior ergo sum. Conspicior ergo sum.
Conspicior ergo sum. Conspicior ergo sum. Conspicior ergo sum. Conspicior ergo sum.
Conspicior ergo sum. Conspicior ergo sum. Conspicior ergo sum. Conspicior ergo sum.
Conspicior ergo sum. Conspicior ergo sum. Conspicior ergo sum. Conspicior ergo sum.
Conspicior ergo sum. Conspicior ergo sum. Conspicior ergo sum. Conspicior ergo sum.
Conspicior ergo sum. Conspicior ergo sum. Conspicior ergo sum. Conspicior ergo sum.
Conspicior ergo sum. Conspicior ergo sum. Conspicior ergo sum. Conspicior ergo sum.
Conspicior ergo sum. Conspicior ergo sum. Conspicior ergo sum. Conspicior ergo sum.
Conspicior ergo sum. Conspicior ergo sum. Conspicior ergo sum. Conspicior ergo sum.
Conspicior ergo sum. Conspicior ergo sum. Conspicior ergo sum. Conspicior ergo sum.
Conspicior ergo sum. Conspicior ergo sum. Conspicior ergo sum. Conspicior ergo sum.
Conspicior ergo sum. Conspicior ergo sum. Conspicior ergo sum. Conspicior ergo sum.
Conspicior ergo sum. Conspicior ergo sum. Conspicior ergo sum. Conspicior ergo sum.
Conspicior ergo sum. Conspicior ergo sum. Conspicior ergo sum. Conspicior ergo sum.
Conspicior ergo sum. Conspicior ergo sum. Conspicior ergo sum. Conspicior ergo sum.
Conspicior ergo sum. Conspicior ergo sum. Conspicior ergo sum. Conspicior ergo sum.
Conspicior ergo sum. Conspicior ergo sum. Conspicior ergo sum. Conspicior ergo sum.
Conspicior ergo sum. Conspicior ergo sum. Conspicior ergo sum. Conspicior ergo sum.
Conspicior ergo sum. Conspicior ergo sum. Conspicior ergo sum. Conspicior ergo sum.
Conspicior ergo sum. Conspicior ergo sum. Conspicior ergo sum. Conspicior ergo sum.
Conspicior ergo sum. Conspicior ergo sum. Conspicior ergo sum. Conspicior ergo sum.
Conspicior ergo sum. Conspicior ergo sum. Conspicior ergo sum. Conspicior ergo sum.
Conspicior ergo sum. Conspicior ergo sum. Conspicior ergo sum. Conspicior ergo sum.
Conspicior ergo sum. Conspicior ergo sum. Conspicior ergo sum. Conspicior ergo sum.
Conspicior ergo sum. Conspicior ergo sum. Conspicior ergo sum. Conspicior ergo sum.
Conspicior ergo sum. Conspicior ergo sum. Conspicior ergo sum. Conspicior ergo sum.
Conspicior ergo sum. Conspicior ergo sum. Conspicior ergo sum. Conspicior ergo sum.
Conspicior ergo sum. Conspicior ergo sum. Conspicior ergo sum.
Conspicior ergo sum. Conspicior ergo sum. Conspicior ergo sum. Conspicior ergo sum.
Conspicior ergo sum. Conspicior ergo sum. Conspicior ergo sum. Conspicior ergo sum.
Conspicior ergo sum. Conspicior ergo sum. Conspicior ergo sum. Conspicior ergo sum.
Conspicior ergo sum. Conspicior ergo sum. Conspicior ergo sum. Conspicior ergo sum.
Conspicior ergo sum. Conspicior ergo sum. Conspicior ergo sum. Conspicior ergo sum.
Conspicior ergo sum. Conspicior ergo sum. Conspicior ergo sum. Conspicior ergo sum.
Conspicior ergo sum. Conspicior ergo sum. Conspicior ergo sum. Conspicior ergo sum.

...opment of an o..
...as structure, so with the ..
...it is advisable to follow as nearly
...same plan. The earliest and almost sole ..
...on during the first days of infancy, and the
...exhibited, is that displayed during the act of scre
...and screaming is excited, both at first and for so..
...terwards, by every distressing or displeasing sens..
...and emotion,—by hunger, pain, anger, jealousy, fea..
At such times the muscles round the eyes are str..
...contracted; and this ... T ... explains to a ..
...extent the ... d ... an ... g ...e remai.. d.
...ur lives. I ... ly o...erved my own
...n under the age of one week to that of
...e months, and ...and that when a scre..
...e on gradually ...o first s..n was the co
...le corrugators, ...ch produced a sligl
...ly followed by the contraction of t..
...les round the ...es. When an infant is
...e or unwell, little frowns—as I recor..
...may be seen incessantly passing lik..
...face; these being generally, but ..
...sooner or later by a crying-fit. F..
...for some time a baby, between sev..
...sucking some milk which was co..
...asing to him; and a steady litt..
...all the time. This was never..
...rying-fit, though occasionally
...ch could be observed.
...it of contracting the
...fants during inn..

3.59 *The expression of the emotions in man and animals (Charles Darwin).*

...ungen, die wesen..
...e Ideenassociatio.. ..
...g zu setzen. Daß ..
...geschichtlichen Übersichten schon
...chten einzelner Physiker und P..
...., wie WHEATSTONE, VOLKMANN, H. MEY..
...mehr Opposition als Anerkennung fanden, so gu..
...n von der Abneigung unseres Zeitalters gegen philoso..
...sche Untersuchungen, davon herrührt, daß es an..
...enden Darstellung aller Erscheinungen dieses Gebietes f..
...n Seiten der unerledigten Erscheinungsgebiete immer w..
...zen gegen diejenigen, welche von den genannten Forsch..
...n. Ich habe deshalb die vorliegende Gelegenheit benut..
...Gebiet nach dieser Richtung hin durchzuarbeiten und eine
...on zu geben.
...mir einen kurzen Überblick der zur Erklärung von mir
...ipien zu geben. Der Hauptsatz der empiristischen Ansicht..
...empfindungen sind für unser Bewußtsein Zeichen
...ng verstehen zu lernen unserem Verstande über..
...as die für den Gesichtssinn erhaltenen Zeichen betrifft, su
...chsten nach Intensität und Qualität, das heißt nach Helligkeit
...und außerdem muß noch eine Verschiedenheit derselben
...e abhängig ist von der Stelle der gereizten Netzhaut, ein
...calzeichen. Die Localzeichen der Empfindungen de..
...und durchgängig von denen des linken verschieden.
...außerdem den Grad der Innervation, die wir..
...lichen lassen. Die Anschauung der Raumverhäl..
...sind nicht notwendig aus den Gesichtswah..
...nicht aus diesen allein herzuleiten, da..
...genau und vollständig auch unter Vermit..
...können also für unseren
...nen wir offenbar ler..
...er anderen Sin..
...n

3.60 *Tokens of sensation (Hermann von Helmholtz).*

between stimulus and sensory intensities, and the text in the figure is a later discussion by Fechner of objections to his law.

Helmholtz's inferential approach to vision has been adapted by modern cognitive theorists, such as Frederick Bartlett (Figure 3.62), Donald Broadbent (Figure 3.63) and George Miller (Figure 3.64). Another offshoot from this is the computational approach, which is concerned with modelling the process of perception in machines. Kenneth Craik (Figure 3.65) was one of the forerunners of this enterprise, and its recent standard-bearer was David Marr (Figure 3.66). Both of these scientists died tragically young.

The visual phenomena studied by these psychologists have generally been those occurring on two-dimensional surfaces – that is, pictorial images. Another visual scientist, Richard Gregory, has written about the odd features of pictures, as is evident from the text in Figure 3.67. He is describing the paradoxes of pictures, and the depth of the problems involved in analysing them. Accordingly, it seems appropriate that the background text in which he is represented is itself in apparent relief! Perhaps it is not strictly accurate to state, as he does, that "No eyes before man's were confronted by pictures", as there are many examples of markings

3.61 *(Facing page) Psychophysics (Gustav Theodor Fechner).*

Schon oben (S. 151) habe ich vorgreiflich dieser Formeln in diesem Sinne gedacht; es wird jetzt etwas näher darauf einzugehen sein.

Wie nun wäre es, wenn jemand dem Gesetze der Schwere keine fundamentale Gültigkeit für die Fallbewegung beilegte, und die bekannten darauf bezüglichen einfachen Formeln als unrichtig corrigirte, weil sie die Abweichungen vom Gesetze nicht in sich aufnehmen, weil das Gesetz, selbst beim ganz exceptionellen Falle in absoluter Luftleere niemals genau zutrifft, der Luftballon, der Dampf sich gar in die Luft erheben, die untern Theile der Zimmerdecke nicht herabfallen u. s. w. Auf ganz denselben Standpunkt aber versucht uns Müller bezüglich des Weber'schen Gesetzes mit seinen Formeln zu stellen, d. h. anstatt die Complication mit Nebenbedingungen, denen es unterliegt, zu analysiren, soweit es möglich ist, erklärt er die ganze Complication für das, woran man sich in der Empirie zu halten und wovon man in der Theorie auszugehen habe, und stellt unbestimmte Formeln auf, welche dem Bedürfniß in dieser Hinsicht entsprechen sollen. Man frage sich aber, was aus empirischer und theoretischer Betrachtung der Fallbewegungen herauskommen würde, wenn man die entsprechende Behandlung darauf anwenden wollte.

In der That stellt Müller, um mit dem Weber'schen Gesetze auch dessen Abweichungen durch eine allgemeinere Formel als meine auf das Gesetz gegründete Maßformel zu repräsentiren, statt dieser folgende Formel als sog. „corrigirte Maßformel" auf, (p. 229):

$$s = \varkappa \log \varphi \, (r).$$

A THEORY OF REMEMBERING

'schema'. It is at once too definite and too sketchy. The word is already widely used in controversial psychological writing to refer generally to any rather vaguely outlined theory. It suggests some persistent, but fragmentary, 'form of arrangement', and it does not indicate what is very essential to the whole notion, that the organised mass results of past changes of position and posture are actively *doing* something all the time; are, so to speak, carried along with us, complete, though developing, from moment to moment. Yet it is certainly very difficult to think of any better single descriptive word to cover the facts involved. It would probably be best to speak of 'active, developing patterns'; but the word 'pattern', too, being now very widely and variously employed, has its own difficulties; and it, like 'schema', suggests a greater articulation of detail than is normally found. I think probably the term 'organised setting' approximates most closely and clearly to the notion required. I shall, however, continue to use the term 'schema' when it seems best to do so, but I will attempt to define its application more narrowly.

'Schema' refers to an active organisation of past reactions, or of past experiences, which must always be supposed to be operating in any well-adapted organic response. That is, whenever there is any order or regularity of behaviour, a particular response is possible only because it is related to other similar responses which have been serially organised, yet which operate, not simply as individual members coming one after another, but as a unitary mass. Determination by schemata is the most fundamental of all the ways in which we can be influenced by reactions and experiences which occurred some time in the past. All incoming impulses of a certain kind, or mode, go together to build up an active, organised setting: visual, auditory, various types of cutaneous impulses and the like, at a relatively low level; all the experiences connected by a common interest: in sport, in literature, history, art, science, philosophy and so on, on a higher level. There is not the slightest reason, however, to suppose that each set of incoming impulses, each new group of experiences persists as an isolated member of some passive patchwork. They have to be regarded as constituents of living, momentary settings belonging to the organism, or to whatever parts of the organism are concerned in making a response of a given kind, and not as a number of individual events somehow strung together and stored within the organism.

Suppose I am making a stroke in a quick game, such as tennis or cricket. How I make the stroke depends on the relating of certain

3.62 *Schema of Sir Frederick Bartlett.* The concept of schema was advocated by Bartlett, as is described in this text from his book *Remembering: A Study in Experimental and Social Psychology.*

3.63 *Channel capacity (Donald Broadbent).* The text is taken from Broadbent's book *Perception and Communication.* Here the viewer must carry out a task like that advocated for the listener in the text in order to perceive the portrait.

24   PERCEPTION AND COMMUNICATION

Monitoring of several channels with response to one at a time.— The situation which we will now consider is much closer to real life than those which have gone before. In the present case the listener hears speech from a number of different sources, but ignores any messages which are not for him. He is therefore carrying out a combination of the two simpler tasks: he may listen to two call-signs simultaneously, but then can ignore one message and deal only with the other. As before, we are interested largely in central processes which may apply to psychology in general rather than to hearing alone. It is more difficult to be sure of the relative roles of sensory and central processes in this case than it was in the simpler ones, but some such distinction can be made by considering the types of score and the effect of instructions. There are comparatively few results from this type of situation on the effect of varying the amount of information presented to the subject. Many data are to be found, however, on the familiar question of the physical methods used to present the messages: and in addition there are results on the effectiveness of certain types of message in securing response.

The spatial arrangement of the sound sources is again important. It will be remembered that spatial separation is highly beneficial when only one message is to be answered, but not when both are to receive a response. In the monitoring situation, which combines both the other tasks, separation is on the whole desirable but not altogether so. Webster and Thompson found that six channels were handled better when fed through six loud-speakers rather than one, and also that provision of ' pull-down ' facilities was helpful. Spieth, Curtis and Webster found that three loudspeakers were better than one. This was not because of differences in the quality of the sound produced by different echoes in different places, because separation was still useful when the channels were made artificially different in quality by putting different band-pass filters in the circuits. Increasing the angle of separation from 10° to 90° between neighbouring speakers was also helpful. Poulton found that when two loudspeakers were operating fairly continuously, separation was helpful if only one speaker was to be monitored but if both were to be monitored the effects were more equivocal. Fewer messages were misheard with separated speakers, but no fewer were completely missed.

3.64 *The magical number seven, plus or minus two (George Miller).* Miller wrote a very influential article with this title, and so his portrait is defined by SEVEN in a background that is slightly larger and smaller, numerically.

that have evolved on the flat surfaces of animals (like the shapes on the wings of butterflies). It would be more accurate to say that no hands before man's have intentionally produced pictorial images that represent other things.

Theories of perception have also been influenced by the psychology of language, most notably by the theories of Noam Chomsky. Chomsky has introduced a wide range of novel terms into the analysis of language, some of which are included in Figure 3.68. The surface structure of this list is not

punctuated, but the terms will be suitably segmented in alphabetic sequence with respect to its deep structure. The portrait is part of the deep structure, too, in so far as it appears to be behind the text. The only words presented that are not related to this theoretical edifice are "Noam Chomsky" and "verbarian", the latter meaning a coiner of phrases.

Before leaving scientists for artists we will see one more portrait – that of Sigmund Freud (Figure 3.69). Freud's models of motivation and personality affected both art and literature in the first half of this

3.65 *The recognition of identity (Kenneth Craik).* The text is taken from Craik's book *The Nature of Explanation.* Recognition presents a major problem for any theory of vision, but particularly for the design of artificial devices to process optical input. Here the recognition can take place at the level of the category grouping – of a face. Identity would only be possible in those who had either seen Craik or seen portraits of him.

ABSTRACTION AND BRAIN MECHANISMS

As remarked above one of the characteristics of memory and perception is the recognition of identity or of similarity. To recognise a thing is surely to react to it, internally or overtly, as the 'same thing' to which we reacted on a previous occasion.

In the above sense mechanical devices can show some degree of recognition. A photocell can respond in the same way to apples having the same colour, a penny-in-the-slot machine to similar coins, and so forth. Men and animals are capable of this, but of much more. The progressive stages of recognition may be classified as:

(1) Those in which all the conditions of stimulation are identical, within the limits of discrimination of the organism;

(2) Those in which there are differences in the peripheral stimulation, but in which these may be 'corrected' by other sensory impulses so as to lead to the production of an identical pattern of central stimulation;

(3) Those in which such correction is inadequate or lacking, so that there are points of difference between the stimulation on two occasions, these points of difference being perceptible by the organism, yet the thing recognised as the same in certain important aspects; and

(4) Those in which the differences extend to all direct sensory qualities and physical constituents, so that the likeness of the two objects is confined to some abstract characteristic such as triangularity, number, and other spatial or temporal relations or vague qualities such as intellectual difficulty.

How should we set about designing a mechanism to respond to these different kinds of identity, and identity in diversity?

century. Indeed, his influence now is far more widespread outwith psychology than within it. Freud's model of motivation was essentially mechanistic, and it is often represented graphically in terms of concentric or overlapping circles. Thus, it is within such a graphical scheme that his portrait is presented. The overbearing and enclosing effects of socialisation define the superego. The ego, that part of the self presented to the external world, is orderly and well-formed – unlike the id, which is primitive and generally unseen. These oversimplified characteristics of his system are also echoed in the scripts used – the dominant and aggressive forms of "super-ego", the neat, presentable "ego", and the unschooled "id", which was written with the left hand!

The final literal portraits are of artists. The cubist word-picture in the previous section (Figure 3.52) was made up of the words PABLO PICASSO. Figure 3.70 is a modification of this design so that portraits of Picasso are incorporated in each face of the cube. The portraits have been taken from three stages of his life: the young man in the lower right, in middle

4.2 IMAGE SEGMENTATION

Perhaps the best way to introduce the whole question of the 2½-D sketch is to describe in some detail the impasse that it was intended to resolve. The neurophysiologists' and psychologists' belief that figure and ground constituted one of the fundamental problems in vision was reflected in the attempts of workers in computer vision to implement a process called *segmentation*. The purpose of this process was very much like the idea of separating figure from ground, the idea being to divide the image into regions that were meaningful either for the purpose at hand (which for computer vision might be assembling a visual comp) or in their correspondence to physical objects or their parts.

Despite considerable efforts over a long period, the theory and practice of segmentation remained primitive for two reasons. First, it was well-nigh impossible to formulate precisely in terms of the image or even of the physical world what the exact goals of segmentation were. What, for example, is an object, and what makes it so special that it should be recoverable as a region in an image? Is a nose an object? Is a head one? Is it still one if it is attached to a body? What about a man on horseback?

These questions show that the difficulties in trying to formulate what should be recovered as a region from an image are so great as to amount almost to philosophical problems. There really is no answer to them—all these things can be an object if you want to think of them that way, or they can be a part of a larger object (a fact that is captured quite precisely in Chapter 5). Furthermore, however these questions were answered in a given situation did not help much with other situations. People soon found the structure of images to be so complicated that it was usually quite impossible to recover the desired region by using only grouping criteria based on local similarity or other purely visual cues that act on the image intensities or on something like the raw primal sketch. Regions that have "semantic" importance do not always have any particular visual distinction. Most images are too complex, and even the very simplest, smallest images like one depicting just two leaves (Marr, 1976, fig. 13) often do not contain enough information in the pure intensity arrays to segment them into different objects.

3.66 *Marr's vision.* The text is taken from David Marr's book *Vision*, and it is addressing the problem of how a shape can be segregated from its background, as is required in order to see the portrait embedded in the text.

age above, and as an old man in the lower left face of the cube. He was most widely known to the general public in the middle phase of his life, and so this portrait is more prominent than the others. Indeed, the portrait itself has been "blocked", that is, reduced to small squares of black on white, although this is difficult to see in the relatively small print presented here.

Picasso's art was distinctly personal, even though it was produced in vast quantities. Victor Vasarely, on the other hand, wanted to remove the imprint of personality from his works of art. They should be in a form that can be manufactured, and available to the public at large. His works are hard-edged, geo-metrical and visually arresting. His concern was with very simple geometrical shapes, like squares, circles, triangles and ellipses, and he varied the sizes, colours and relations between these in a variety of ingenious ways. Vasarely produced a large number of works in stark black and white, and these were often visually vibrant – they would appear to move or the shapes would seem to reorganise themselves in novel configurations. These marked the art form called Op (for Optical) about which more will be said in the next chapter. Figure 3.71 is a homage to Vasarely: it uses his favoured shape elements – circles and squares – and it is in highly-contrasting black and white. In fact, it reverses the contrast into

3.67 *The intelligent brain.* The text is taken from Richard Gregory's book *The Intelligent Eye.*

Pictures have a double reality. Drawings, paintings and photographs are objects in their own right – patterns on a flat sheet – and at the same time entirely different objects to the eye. We see both a pattern of marks on paper, with shading, brush-strokes or photographic 'grain', and at the same time we see **that these compose a face**, a house or a ship on a **stormy sea. Pictures are unique** among objects; for they are **seen both as themselves and as** some other thing, **entirely different from the paper or** canvas of the picture. **Pictures are paradoxes.**

No *object* **can be in two places at the same** time; no object **can lie in both two- and three-dimensional** space. **Yet pictures are both visibly** flat **and three**-dimensional. **They are a certain** size, yet also **the size of a face** or a house **or a ship.** Pictures are **impossible.**

No eyes before man's were confronted by pictures. Previously, all objects *in themselves were im***portant or could** be safe**ly** ignored. But pictures, thou**gh trivial in them**selves, mere **patterns** of marks, are **important in showing** *absent* things. **Biologically this is most odd. For millions** of years animals had been **able to respond only to present** situations and the immediate **future.** Pictures, **and other sym**bols, allow responses to **be** directed to **situations** quite different from the present; **and may give perceptions** perhaps not even possible for **the world** of objects. Apart from pictures and other symbols, the **senses direct** and control behaviour according to the **physical** *properties* of surrounding objects – not to **some other**, real or imaginary, state of affairs. Perhaps man's abili**ty to** respond to absent imaginary situations in pictures **repr**esents an essential step towards the development **of** abstract thought. Pictures are perhaps the first step away from immediate reality; and without this, reality cannot be deeply understood.

two parts, so that the lower half is the opposite of the upper. The squares are outnumbered by the circles, but they are arranged in an orderly sequence so that they spell the artist's name. However, hovering even more subtly in the pattern is a portrait of Vasarely, with his broadly framed spectacles spanning the boundary between the two halves. It might be

necessary to view this figure from several metres in order to see the hidden portrait.

The final portrait in this section is a further homage to Magritte, which is only appropriate since the book commenced with a discussion of his pipe-puzzle. A pictorial portrait presents the painter or photographer with the problem of transcending the

3.68 *Deep structure (Noam Chomsky).*

3.69 *Ideologist (Sigmund Freud).*

3.70 *Cubist (Pablo Picasso).*

particular in order to capture some enduring characteristic of the sitter. The painter has more freedom in this regard than the photographer, and so the latter often uses props or poses to emphasise a desired aspect of the sitter. Magritte was not a flamboyant person, indeed the reverse. His personal image as a bowler-hatted man and his many pictorial images of bowler-hatted men, impersonally submerged in a mechanical world, display his concern with individual identity. Moreover, a portrait is always a pale reflection of the portrayed – it is flat and inert. Despite this, it can be recognised as being a picture of a specific individual. But what about the pictures that do not enable recognition even at this level? It is this aspect that is presented in Figure 3.72, derived from Magritte's painting entitled *The Great War.* In the painting a bowler-hatted man has

his face obscured by an apple, complete with stalk and leaves. Clearly it is impossible to determine the identity of the subject from the picture. But there is no doubting the signature that falls throughout the pictorial image – it is that of Magritte, as he produced it on numerous paintings. The signatures are in outline in some parts, white in others, but black only on the lower right, where convention usually requires it (though Magritte rarely complied with this convention). The picture is entitled "This is not Magritte". To what does this apply? The portrayed bowler-hatted man? The artist who produced the image of the apple and man? The signature? The whole work? It is left for the spectator to decide.

3.71 (Overleaf) *Towards plastic unity.*

3.72 (Overleaf) *Ceci n'est pas Magritte.*

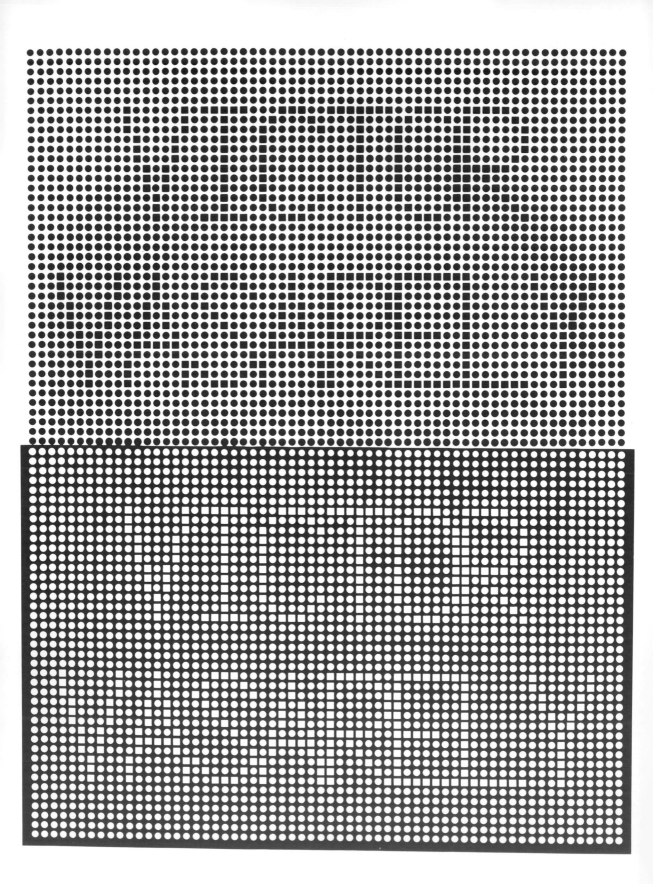

Bibliography
General

Carr, T. H. (1986). Perceiving visual language. In K. R. Boff, L. Kaufman, & J. P. Thomas (Eds.), *Handbook of perception and human performance. Volume II.* New York: Wiley. Thomas Carr has reviewed the extensive experimental literature on reading written language. He initially contrasts auditory and visual language and then describes writing systems generally, with emphasis on the special properties of English. The interpretation of pictographic (or semasiographic) and logographic symbols precedes a consideration of words as pictures. In this context he remarks "research on reading is very active, knowledge is so far quite tentative, and almost every topic is under dispute some way or another". Alphabetic letter strings have provided the focus for much psychological research on reading, and the experimental procedures applied to word recognition and the Stroop effect are critically examined. The final sections are concerned with eye movements, context effects and comprehension.

Gaur, A. (1984). *A history of writing.* London: The British Library. Albertine Gaur treats writing systems as one amongst several modes of information storage and transmission. She places the origin and development of writing systems in the context of "idea transmission". A classification of scripts is presented, together with others that have foiled attempts to decipher them. The social, political and aesthetic aspects of writing and literacy are also traced.

Harris, M. & Coltheart, M. (1986). *Language processing in children and adults. An introduction.* London: Routledge & Kegan Paul. The first part of this book provides a good introduction to pictographic, logographic, syllabic and alphabetic writing systems. Language learning in its spoken and written forms is discussed in the second part. The authors propose that there are four phases in learning to read English: developing a sight vocabulary, discriminating from within it, recoding words phonologically, and finally recoding words on the basis of letter shapes. Disorders of reading are also discussed.

Kennedy, A. (1984). *The psychology of reading.* London: Methuen. Alan Kennedy has produced a very readable book on reading. Reading is examined with regard to the perceptual, cognitive, and skill factors involved in it. The origins of writing systems are related to other graphical means of representing ideas. Both perception and reading are viewed from a cognitive perspective.

Kostelanetz, R. (Ed.) (1970). *Imaged words and worded images.* New York: Outerbridge and Dienstfrey. This is a delightful collection of word pictures, generally produced by mechanical means (e.g., by typewriter). Kostelanetz refers to these works as "word-imagery".

Mayer, P. (1984). Some remarks concerning the classification of the visual in literature. *Visual Poetics, 12,* 5–13. Peter Mayer has displayed an abiding interest in the visual aspects of literature. In this article he presents a classification of letter and word shapes which includes ornamental and artificial letters, penetrated words, telling typefaces, letter shifts and reversals, visible puns, logograms, ideograms, pictograms, framed and filled forms.

Wade, N. J. (1985). Literal pictures. *Word & Image, 1,* 242–272. An article presenting a variety of word pictures, some of which are reproduced in the present book. It was "writing" this article that stimulated my interest in letter shapes.

Word and Image

Hammacher, A. M. (1974). *Magritte.* London: Thames & Hudson. Part of this book is addressed to Magritte's use of words, as is Gablik's book cited earlier. Both authors suggest that Magritte's word pictures were influenced by the writings of Foucault and Wittgenstein on the relativity of language.

Mayer, P. (1968). Framed and shaped writing. *Studio International,* 110–114. An early form of the circular classification scheme for letter shapes, together with examples of them drawn from historical and modern sources.

Word as Image

Briggs, J. R. (1977). *Letter-forms and lettering.* Poole, Dorset: Blandford Press. A brief history of writing is presented. Attention is then directed mainly to manipulations of the Roman alphabet, with a final section on some non-latin scripts.

Hess, S. (1972). *The modification of letterforms.* New York: Art Direction Book Company. Manipulations of the shape of Roman letters in terms of proportions, pattern, slope, surface and prospect are described and illustrated.

Witten, I. H. (1985). Elements of computer typography. *International Journal of Man-Machine Studies, 23,* 623–687. A tutorial article that marries moveable type with computer software. The terminology of typography is explained with reference to computer processes, and some examples of exotic text are illustrated.

Words as Patterns

Hefting, P. (1985). Jurriaan Schrofer. *Graphis*, *25*, 74–85. Jurriaan Schrofer is a Dutch artist who produces both two- and three-dimensional word structures. Some examples of his work are shown in this article.

Igarashi, T. (1987). *Igarashi alphabets*. Zurich: ABC Editions. Numerous photographs of Igarashi's ingenious two- and three-dimensional letter forms are presented. The sculptured letters utilising reflections are especially attractive.

Kim, S. (1981). *Inversions. A catalog of calligraphic cartwheels*. Peterborough, New Hampshire: Byte Books. Scott Kim designs words in ways that can be read from opposite directions. Sometimes they can be read from the left or right but mostly from above or below. Many examples are presented here, and some links with music and art are made.

Riddell, A. (Ed.) (1975). *Typewriter art*. London: London Magazine Editions. The astonishing variety of marks that can be produced by typewriters is here displayed along with a very brief commentary.

Wozencroft, J. (1988). *The graphic language of Neville Brody*. London: Thames & Hudson. Neville Brody's lettering and graphics have had a great impact on magazine and advertising presentation. This book shows many examples of the letter shapes he has employed.

Literal Portraits

Arnold, H. J. P. (1977). *William Henry Fox Talbot. Pioneer of photography and man of science*. London: Hutchinson Benham. A biography of Talbot describing his interests in mathematics, chemistry and optics prior to his photographic discoveries.

Bartlett, F. (1932). *Remembering: A study in experimental and social psychology*. Cambridge: Cambridge University Press. The concept of schema, developed by Bartlett in this book, has been influential in analyses of both perception and art. Page 201 of the book provides a background for Figure 3.62.

Broadbent, D. E. (1958). *Perception and communication*. Oxford: Pergamon Press. Donald Broadbent developed an information processing model of perception based upon studies of auditory communication. Page 24 of the book provides the background for Figure 3.63.

Craik, K. J. W. (1943). *The nature of explanation*. Cambridge: Cambridge University Press. Kenneth Craik combined his fascination with instruments and his studies of vision to propose that perception involves forming internal models of the world. These ideas of internal representation have proved central to cybernetics and artificial intelligence. Page 69 of the book provides the background for Figure 3.65.

Darwin, C. (1872). *The expression of the emotions in man and animals*. London: John Murray. Charles Darwin's fruitful foray into comparative psychology provides (on page 225) the background for Figure 3.59.

Fechner, G. T. (1882). *Revision der hauptpuncte der psychophysik*. Leipzig: Breithopf & Hartel. Fechner published his *Elements of Psychophysics* in 1860, in which he proposed a logarithmic law relating the magnitudes of sensation and stimulation. The *Revision* incorporated reactions to criticisms of his law, and page 202 provides the background for Figure 3.61.

Helmholtz, H. von (1866). *Handbuch der physiologischen optik*. Dritte Band. Leipzig: Voss. Helmholtz's *Handbuch* remains an essential text for students of vision despite its age. Page 974 provides the background for Figure 3.60.

Miller, G. A. (1957). The magical number seven, plus or minus two: Some limits on our capacity for processing information. *Psychological Review*, *63*, 81–97. This article describes many experiments on perception and memory indicating that humans can process around seven items or chunks of information at one time.

Porta, G. B. (1593). *De refractione. Optices parte*. Naples: Carlinum and Pacem. Porta had earlier written a book on natural magic, but this book on optics represents his more orthodox scientific work. Page 143 of this study provides the background for Figure 3.55.

4 VISUAL ALLUSIONS

Whenever we look at pictorial images we are alluding to features they do not contain. In Chapter Two the principal allusion discussed was that to three-dimensional space: a variety of procedures can be adopted that result in the pictorial image providing a closer approximation to the perception of objects in space. The concern in Chapter Three was with more arbitrary, but no less important, allusions – those to the meanings conveyed by written words. The illustrations presented in this chapter are more closely akin to the literary allusions mentioned in the Introduction. That is, they are visual allusions that can be interpreted in several ways, some of which will be more immediately evident than others.

The first section is concerned with allusions to visual processes themselves. It was suggested in the "Pictorial representations of space" section in Chapter Two that some modern movements in art have tried to represent aspects of our own graphical image processes: rather than producing pictorial images that act as a substitute for some other objects, they have attempted to draw upon, and manipulate, processes occurring when we actually look at pictures. The pictorial image then becomes a reflection of the processes occurring in the perceiver when observing pictures. It will be shown how a variety of such processes can be alluded to by particular pictorial patterns.

The second section uses some of these patterns in combination with photographic images, in order to introduce pictorially recognisable content into the illustrations. There are many techniques that can be enlisted to combine graphic and photographic images, and some of these are described in Appendix Two, together with some suggestions for producing graphic designs.

The combination of photographic images with graphic designs can be applied to accentuate the photographic image and it can also be utilised to render the photographic image more difficult to discern. It is in this direction that my interests lie, and here the visual allusions are most effective. Examples of photographic images that are almost hidden will be shown in the third section. There is a variety of ways of making them emerge from the graphic design conveying them, as will be described. It may well be the case that these allusory pictorial images are more memorable than

clearly defined ones because of their transient and shadowy existence.

The final section extends this approach of combining pictorial images by utilising graphical designs that have been drawn specifically for the photographic images with which they are married.

Allusions to Visual Processes

It was suggested in the "Pictorial representations of space" section in Chapter Two that the pictorial art of the 20th century can be thought of as reflecting a concern with graphical image processing. That is, the picture plane has been treated as an object in its own right and the interplay of marks on the flat surface has become a major preoccupation – as in the emergence of abstract art. The artificiality of the medium has been both appreciated and extended. This is, of course, a gross over-simplification. There are so many styles that have danced with vigour, if often only briefly, on the stage of 20th century art that it is unsuitable to characterise them this generally. None the less, there is an attraction in pursuing the argument. For example, cubism can be seen as denying the single station point so that multiple viewpoints can be incorporated within a single pictorial image. The surrealist painters wallowed in the ambiguity afforded by the two-dimensional picture plane. Abstract art, particularly abstract expressionism, has capitalised upon the multiple interpretations that can be made of shapes and lines. However, it is geometrical abstraction that offers the clearest example to support my thesis. Many works of geometrical abstraction are concerned with the interplay of sharply defined shapes themselves – with the Gestalt grouping principles that will be described later in this section, but attention will be addressed principally to one branch of this general style.

If it is argued that the artist can represent aspects of the graphical image – of the processes involved in perceiving pictures themselves – then the next question is: what aspects? There are many phenomena that can be elicited in the perception of pictorial images – textbooks on perception are replete with examples of them. Which ones are to be selected for depiction? There is no single answer, because many different phenomena have been manipulated in this regard. Perhaps the artistic

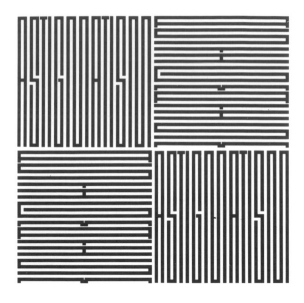

4.1 *Eye chart.* Differences in the clarity of the vertical and horizontal lines will reflect the existence of regular astigmatism. If the horizontals are sharply focused and the verticals somewhat blurred this is called "with-the-rule", its converse being "against-the-rule".

4.2 Astigmatic effects are more easily discernible with patterns consisting of densely packed fine lines, like these concentric squares. The pastel colours sometimes reported in between the blurred contours are seen more easily than in coarser patterns, like those in Figure 2.32.

movement that has had the greatest success, some would say notoriety, at such depiction is "op art". Op art is an offshoot of geometrical abstraction that reached its peak in terms of popularity in the 1960s. Op is an abbreviation for Optical, because it was thought that the works produced dazzling effects optically. This was a mistaken assumption, since many of the effects are a consequence of processes occurring in the visual system, after the optical energy has been transformed into neural signals. None the less, the label has stuck, and it has a certain appeal: op art works do dazzle, they do play upon processes of pictorial perception because of the way the high contrast (mostly black and white) lines and shapes are arranged. The pictures engage the observer by making them a part of the work. To make these points more apparent (literally), various of the phenomena manipulated in op art will be described and illustrated.

If the term optical is to be applied strictly in op art then the works would capitalise on the optical aberrations of the eye, as described in the "Photography and vision" section in Chapter Two. That is, the spherical and chromatic aberrations and astigmatism found in all eyes to various extents would be rendered more visible by the arrangements of the lines – their widths, orientations and separations. Of these aberrations the one that has been manipulated most frequently is astigmatism. Thus, for example, in Figure 4.1 the vertical and horizontal lines might not appear equally distinct: for some people the verticals will look sharper and blacker whereas others will see the horizontals having more clearly defined edges. In each case, if the page is rotated by 90° the lines that were formerly blurred will now appear well-defined, and vice versa. This shows that the differences in appearance are not due to the manner in which the figure was printed, but reside in some property of the eye – namely the one that is written four times in the figure itself. Astigmatism is classified clinically as being with or against the rule, and this distinguishes between the appropriate focusing of horizontal and vertical lines, respectively. Consequently, the two orientations of words in Figure 4.1 represent the two principal categories of astigmatism. It is of interest to note that the individual letters themselves can generally be read more easily when they are elongated vertically rather than horizontally, and this is independent of any astigmatism present, assuming that it is not so severe that the lines cannot be resolved at all.

Astigmatism is corrected optically by means of cylindrical lenses, which compensate for the differences in focusing for contours at right angles to one another. It is likely that any appreciable astigmatism that you have has been corrected optically, as will be evident if you look at Figure 4.1 without spectacles. Moreover, the effect of the spectacles can easily be seen by holding one of the lenses in front of the figure and then rotating the lens: the lines in the pattern will vary in clarity in a systematic manner. For some positions of the lens both sets of orientations in the pattern will be somewhat indistinct, whereas at others one set will be sharply defined and in higher contrast than those at right angles.

This effect will perhaps be more evident in Figure 4.2, because the lines in the concentric squares are more regular. There may be another effect that can be seen with this figure, too: when one set of lines is blurred the white spaces between them may appear in pastel shades of pinkish or greenish. Again this can be shown to be due to processes in the observer rather than the pattern, because rotating the pattern will shift the contours that appear with faint colours in the spaces between them. The colours that are seen are probably a consequence of the chromatic aberration of the eye. Under normal circumstances we are not aware of the effects of our chromatic aberration. However they can be exposed when looking at patterns like this, provided there is some degree of astigmatism in the eye. In fact, they can also be exposed in people who have no visually measurable astigmatism by inducing one artificially: if they look at the pattern with a cylindrical lens in front of the eye, the lines that are clearly defined appear black and white whereas the blurred ones often appear to have pastel shades, mostly of reddish or greenish, between them. It is likely that the chromatic aberration is expressed more clearly because of the harsh optical demands made by such patterns on the astigmatic eye. When the contours in one orientation are focused appropriately, the out-of-focus orthogonals will also be affected by chromatic aberration. The colour effects can be reduced or removed by viewing the pattern through a pinhole, so that both sets of contours remain in focus or, of course, by wearing any optical prescription to correct for astigmatism.

The scientist Thomas Young first described the condition of astigmatism, at the beginning of the 19th century. He measured it in his own eyes, although little attention was paid to the phenomenon until a few decades later, when an appropriate correction for it was appreciated. Thomas Young is represented in Figure 4.3, enclosed by horizontal and vertical lines, arranged in the shape of concentric diamonds.

The type of astigmatism discussed so far is generally a consequence of the non-spherical shape of the eyeball. For a given individual the axis of astigmatism is tied to the orientation of the eye so that particular contour orientations in objects or pictorial images will be degraded optically, unless a correction is worn. There are, however, other forms of astigmatism that occur in all our eyes, and these are not fixed in relation to the eye in the same way as regular astigmatism. Moreover, these additional forms, which will be called transient astigmatism, are much smaller than regular astigmatism. When you look closely at Figure 4.4 the circles will probably vary in clarity around their circumferences: sometimes it will look as though there are one or more lightish propellers or spokes radiating from the centre, and these will probably rotate as well. The rotations are usually quite rapid, and they occur about once or twice a second. The lighter spokes correspond to those parts of the pattern that are sharply focused, while the other parts are slightly blurred. This difference occurs independently of regular astigmatism, although anyone with any marked and uncorrected regular astigmatism will see one predominant spoke, rather than several rotating ones.

Transient astigmatism occurs because of minor instabilities in the ciliary muscles which control the curvature of the crystalline lens. Whenever there is any accommodation, to focus on near objects, the ciliary muscles contract in order to increase the curvature of the lens, which increases the optical power of the eye. Any asymmetry in the action of the ciliary muscles leads to minor variations in the curvature of the lens in one or more orientations. These variations lead to the transient astigmatism. Under normal circumstances we are totally oblivious of such small changes in the optical characteristics of our eyes, because the objects we look at rarely have the pattern characteristics that elicit their expression, and the patterns are usually viewed at an appreciable distance. The transient astigmatic effects do not occur when the lens is in a relaxed state, viewing objects at optical infinity (beyond six metres), and it becomes increasingly evident with viewing near objects or pictorial images. Op artists

4.3 *The astigmatic Thomas Young.*

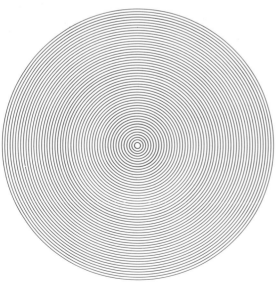

4.4 Transient astigmatism can be made apparent when looking at the centre of a pattern of fine concentric circles: wispy spokes might appear to extend from the centre, and these will seem to rotate. Transient astigmatism occurs because the tension applied to the lens during accommodation is not even around its circumference, and so the optical power is not the same in all orientations. Accordingly, some orientations are clearly resolved and others are slightly blurred, and their axes change over time. It is these differences, which are very small, that become discernible in patterns like concentric circles.

have been particularly successful in rendering this minor modulation of the eye's optics dazzlingly apparent. This has applied with respect to regular geometrical patterns having very fine lines that vary in orientation.

The widest range of orientations can be found in circular and radiating patterns (see Figures 4.5 and 4.6). In both cases the distinctness of sets of lines will vary over time, so that there is the appearance of motion within the pattern: for the circles it is like a propeller rotating, whereas for the radiating lines it is more like arcs of circles changing their locations. These are relatively simple patterns, but the effects are seen most readily where there are few departures from regularity. Nonetheless, it is possible to introduce figurative aspects into the pictorial images, as in Figures 4.7 and 4.8.

The effects of any transient astigmatism can be exposed most easily with very fine lines, and with these it is most effective when there is some variation in line width. Therefore, curved lines will be at their narrowest at their inflection points – where the direction changes most rapidly. For example, in Figure 4.9 the apparent motion seems to be confined to the centre and the circular regions where the radiating curves change direction. Note also that there is a very strong allusion to solidity in this design – the curves appear to lie on a surface that varies in depth. However, the·surface is a very unusual one because the contours that define a hump on one side allude to a hollow on the other! This is an example of an impossible object of the type described in the "Allusions" section in Chapter One, and it was photo–graphically modified to produce Figure 1.1.

When the radiating lines vary abruptly in orientation, as in Figure 4.10, the allusion to solidity is reduced, whereas the pattern appears to undergo some perplexing movements: circular areas seem to be rotating in opposite directions to their neighbouring regions. It looks as though there is a sequence of ratchet-like movements, in addition to any fluctuations in the clarity of the lines. When the radiations themselves define an identifiable shape, as with the facial profiles in Figure 4.11, there is less likelihood of seeing the inflections in depth. Another feature that is displayed in this figure is the effectiveness of approximately equal black and white areas in exposing the transient astigmatism. Both the upper and lower components consist of the same contour boundaries, but these are enclosing black and white areas above and only the outlines below.

4.5 Transient astigmatic effects are seen most readily in the regions of the pattern having the narrowest black lines.

Here they make the shape of a spiral and so the blurring tends to follow this pattern.

4.6 Radiating lines also render visible small changes in the optical characteristics of the eyes. In this case, the

blurred regions are like petals extending from the central parts of the pattern.

4.7 *Sunset strips.* The variations in the overlap of the two patterns make the horizontal spokes darker than the other orientations, and so the changes due to transient astigmatism tend to be confined around that axis.

The upper pattern is more dynamic, in that the fluctuations in clarity and the apparent movements are seen more easily in it than in the lower one.

Transient astigmatic effects can also be rendered visible with other patterns besides circular or radiating ones, although they do need to cover a range of orientations. Figure 4.3, of Thomas Young, consists of only two principal orientations – vertical and horizontal – and yet they can fluctuate in clarity, so that the diamond shapes of a given orientation can appear to pulsate, becoming clearly defined and then blurred. The effects are more gradual when the orientation changes in the pattern are less abrupt, as in Figures 4.12 and 4.13.

If artists are representing the graphical image then restricting consideration to the optical transformations of incoming light is clearly too restricted. In the case of astigmatic effects it is assumed that the retinal image has been modified, and that the changes so produced are retained through the

4.8 *Torsion.* When the centre of the pattern is fixated the blurring at right angles to the contours can be seen, but there are some additional effects. The radiating elements of the pattern might appear to rotate, in a ratchet-like manner, which is probably due to involuntary torsional movements of the eyes. Moreover, if you look at the centre and move your head away from the page then parts of the pattern appear to rotate counter-clockwise; head movements towards the page have the opposite effect.

4.9 Smooth changes in direction of radiating lines results in some parts being narrower than those around them. These narrow regions correspond to the inflection points of the curves, and most of the visual motion is confined around them.

4.10 Abrupt changes in the direction of radiating lines enhance the likelihood of seeing ratchet-like rotations of concentric regions.

4.11 *Facet.*

152

4.12 The apparent motion appears to ripple along the inflection points of the wave pattern.

4.13 The central region, in which the lines are thickening, appears to pulsate with prolonged viewing. The points at which the lines start to reduce in thickness are not symmetrical, and define a left-hand facing head.

153

4.14 *Good figure?*

4.15 *Segregation.*

4.16 *Fluctuating crosses.*

visual and graphical image levels. There are many processes that are particularly associated with the graphical image: most of the phenomena investigated by visual scientists are produced on a picture plane (now usually a display screen), and so they are concerned with picture perception. That is, they are analysing characteristics of graphical image processing, rather than visual image processing.

One of the groups of researchers who added most to our understanding of the graphical image, earlier this century, was concerned with how we organise the elements in a pictorial image. For example, Figure 4.14 consists of a series of black shapes; they look rather odd, some being a little letter-like, although the resemblance to our own script appears to be minimal. One thing that does seem evident is that the black shapes are clearly differentiated from their background. In fact, this particular group of researchers gave great prominence to this feature of analysing pictorial images, namely the segregation of a figure from the ground upon which it is placed. A pattern, like the word FIGURE in Figure 4.15, is generally smaller than the background and it has closed contours – that is, all its sides have boundaries. There is typically a complementarity between figure and ground, as is the case here where the letters of the one define the other. This is a description of figure/ground properties in purely pictorial terms. This group of visual scientists stressed that perception involved principles of organisation, too. Thus, the strange shapes in Figure 4.14 do indeed carry a message in script, but the shapes have to be organised in a particular way in order to decode it: the spaces between the black shapes spell the name that has been applied to this group – Gestalt. The German word is used because they were originally from Germany, but also because there is no adequate term in English to convey the nuances of the word: roughly translated it is a configuration. The Gestalt in Figure 4.14 is not simply given by the shapes but it has to be organised by the observer.

The Gestalt psychologists were interested in those pictorial images that have multiple organisations, especially when the alternatives were equally likely to be seen. So, Figure 4.16 is generally described as a cross, defined by radiating lines alternating in visibility with a cross defined by circles. One interesting aspect of such perceptual fluctuation is that only one organisation is visible at one time. This type of figure/ground reversal is demonstrated most frequently with pictorial images

like Figure 1.22, which is seen either as a central vase or facing profiles: the contours defining one also define the other. Even when there are no clear contours separating the parts of the pictorial image, as in Figure 4.17, there is still alternation between the two organisations.

The Gestalt psychologists produced a wide range of pictorial images to demonstrate the manner in which such organisations can take place. Most of the illustrations employed to this effect consisted of small elements, like black dots, squares or lines, that could be easily segregated from the white paper. The arrangement of the elements on the paper can lead to quite different perceptual organisations. For example, when the elements are all the same, as in Figure 4.18, then those that are closer together tend to be organised or grouped together perceptually. This is referred to as the principle of proximity. If the elements themselves differ in some way, as in Figure 4.19, then those that are similar to one another tend to be grouped together perceptually, even though they are nearer to others that are dissimilar along some dimension. This is called grouping by similarity. Symmetry is another dimension that can influence perceptual organisation (see Figure 4.20). In many pictorial images the elements themselves can vary by small amounts that are

4.17 *Facing vases.*

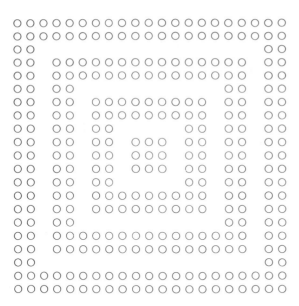

4.18 Proximity: the pattern elements that are near to one another tend to be united in perceptual organisation.

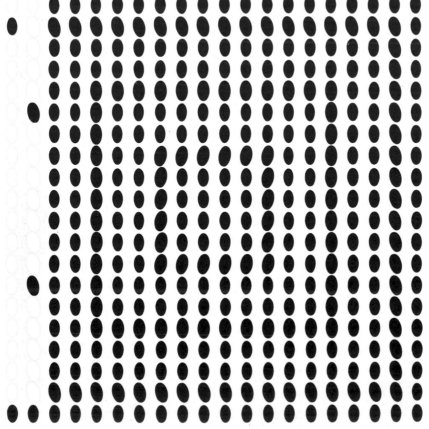

4.19 Similarity: the ellipses of a particular size and orientation tend to be grouped together perceptually. The three groups of larger ones form concentric squares.

4.20 Symmetry: the upper and lower halves are symmetrical but in reversed contrast. However, in each half there are paired symmetries between adjacent shapes of the same colour.

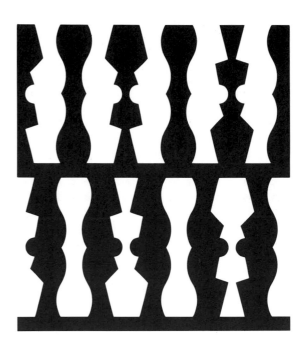

4.21 Good continuation: although the hypotenuses of all the triangular elements are straight there appear to be curves connecting them.

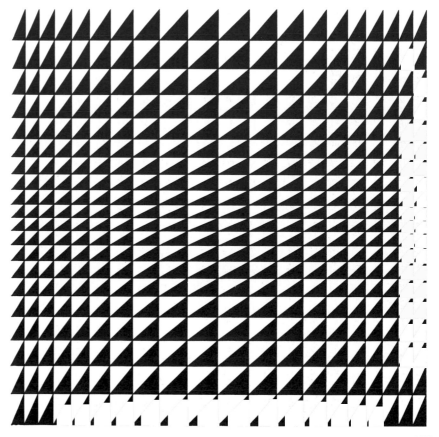

relatively difficult to discriminate. When the elements are arranged in a geometrically regular way, the small differences tend to be smoothed over. For example, the individual triangles in Figure 4.21 differ slightly in height and breadth, but the overall organisation of the pattern is one of curved lines where no curvature is present. This is called the principle of good continuation, and its operation has been evident in many of the pictorial images presented earlier in this book.

These grouping rules, which are only the most prominent of those described by the Gestalt psychologists, seldom operate in isolation. More commonly, they either augment one another (as in Figure 4.22) or compete with one another (as in Figure 4.23). It is in this latter condition that many visual allusions can be generated. That is, by pitting one (or more) of the grouping principles against others then aspects of a pictorial image can be rendered more difficult to see. In Figure 4.24 the black areas tend to be seen as related to one another, but their shapes differ quite considerably. However, the shapes are both similar, symmetrical and in close proximity in concentrically circular regions: around the circumference the shapes are reasonably clearly defined feet, that are pointing in opposite directions to their neighbours. Towards the centre the groupings tend to be more complex, and a variety of possibilities is present. What tends to be lost in this sequence of perceptual organisations is the connection of the circumferential feet to legs that project from the centre! The legs are not all of the

4.22 The hexagons vary systematically in size, and the change in their orientation tends not to be noticed.

4.23 *Christmas boxes.* Each face of the cube carries the same message, though in most cases the similarity of the cube-like elements makes this difficult to see.

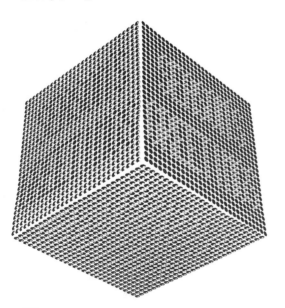

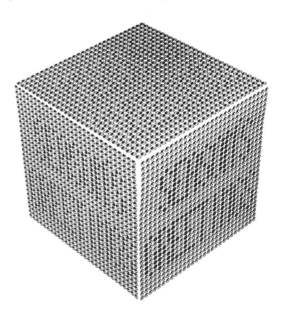

4.24 *Forfeit.* The seemingly abstract design is defined by projecting and overlapping legs, and the central pattern consists of four interlocking feet.

same contrast (i.e. black or white alone), and so the opposite contrasts need to be grouped together in order to see them. If a contour is traced from a foot at the circumference towards the centre then the upper or lower shape of an extended leg will be defined. The neighbouring legs alternate in direction, so determining the particular patterns that have

been blocked in as black. Once they have been traced in this way then they will probably be seen in the design, whereas they were hidden initially. Another type of embedding is present in the centre of the figure. Here there are four feet, of the same dimensions to those around the circumference, but not of the same contrast. The feet are overlapping, each one at right angles to the two it is overlapping, and the extended big toe is white in each case. The difficulty experienced in segregating these four feet attests to the power of grouping by contrast similarity and symmetry.

159

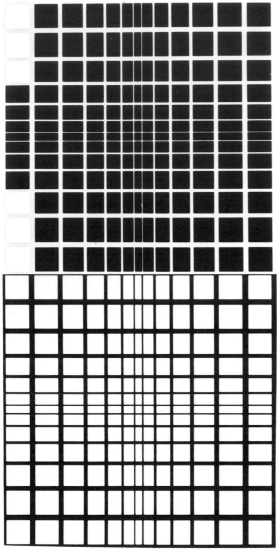

4.25 *Hermann–Hering grids.*

The Gestalt grouping principles often operate in concert with other graphical image phenomena. For example, Figure 4.25 consists of two parts, the elements in one are black blocks, whereas they are white in the other. The black blocks are separated by white lines of varying width, and the white ones by black lines. Illusory effects are produced throughout this pictorial image: light grey dots are seen at the intersections of the black lines and dark grey dots appear at the white line intersections. These dots, which are called Hermann and Hering grids respectively (see Figure 3.30), are a consequence of processes occurring at the graphical image level of visual processing. They are not physically present in the print – a photometer would not record their presence. In this figure the dots are arranged symmetrically. However, when ·the elements are manipulated in size in a more subtle way, as in Figure 4.26, the location of the illusory dots is not so linear. None the less, they are grouped into a set of smooth curves, following the principle of good continuation. Thus, the grouping principles can operate upon phenomena that are themselves a consequence of visual processing. The artist Victor Vasarely has used the Hermann–Hering grids to particularly good effect in his pictorial images, as was alluded to in Figure 3.71.

Essentially any discontinuities can be organised perceptually in this way. The discontinuities can be physical, in the sense that they are a property of the pictorial image. For instance, the dots in Figure 4.27 might appear, on first inspection, to be the same size throughout. However, when the pictorial image is viewed from afar or blurred in some way, then it is evident that some dots are bigger than others. This is because there are larger aggregations of dots that are themselves circular, and form the letters DOT MATRIX. Here there is a physical difference in the size of the dots, but this might not be discriminable for the individual dots. When their effects are averaged, so to speak, by defocusing the pictorial image then the differences are discernible.

Subjective contours occur most commonly in pictorial images when there is some perceived boundary for which there is no physical correlate. In Figure 4.28 two white triangles will probably be seen: their edges are continuities of the sectors of the circles, and the centres of the triangles appear brighter than the backgrounds. This occurs even though there is no difference, physically, between the various regions of white. The phenomenon has

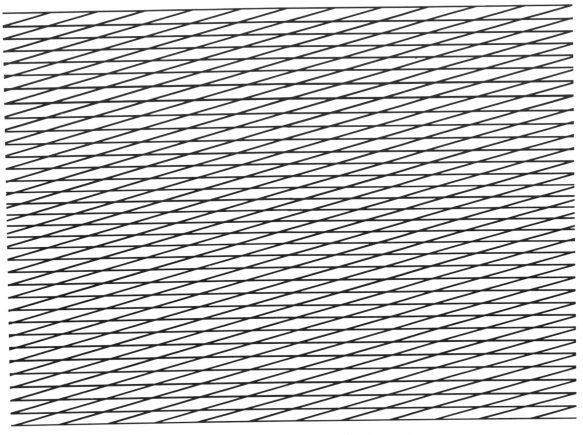

4.26 *Good curve.*   **4.27** *Dot matrices.*

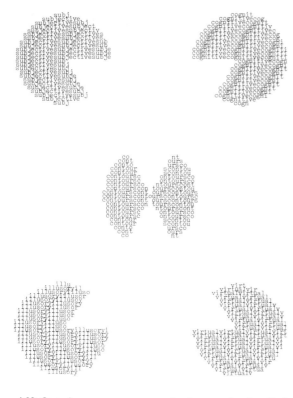

4.28 *One phenomenon or many?* The phenomenon of seeing triangular shapes between the arrangements of words

has been variously called subjective, cognitive, illusory and virtual contours.

4.29 An illusory impossible triangle.

been given a number of names, as is indicated in the figure. It is most often represented as a triangle, the angles of which are formed from incomplete circles, and an unusual variation of this is shown in Figure 4.29. Rather than presenting a pictorial image of a flat triangle, one suggesting the combination of three rectangular sides is shown. However, the three sides could not be assembled appropriately to make an actual three-dimensional triangle – it is an example of an illusory, impossible object (see the "Allusions" section in Chapter One for some more conventional illustrations of impossible objects).

Another way in which boundaries or borders can be produced perceptually using minimal pictorial differences is to produce changes very gradually. So, for instance, the slight thickenings of the vertical lines of Figure 4.30, which would be difficult to see in an individual line, are organised perceptually to produce a defined brightness difference. These effects are called Mach bands, and so the figure both describes and demonstrates the effect. In general, small differences in the pictorial images tend to be enhanced at the graphical image level. This characteristic of graphical image processing will be utilised in many of the pictorial images in the following sections.

The discussion in this section has been confined to one small offshoot of geometrical abstraction called op art. None the less, a similar argument could be applied more generally to geometrical abstraction: the artists in this tradition have been concerned with the pictorial manipulations of shape itself. They have directed our perception to the analysis of these geometrical shapes at the graphical image level, rather than suggesting that the shapes should refer to another alluded space. Because much of the art of this century has been faithful to the picture plane – has been concerned with pictorial images in their own right – then it is reasonable to argue that these artists are tapping processes occurring at the graphical image level in the scheme presented here.

Photo–graphic Combinations

The basic techniques involved in producing graphic designs and in manipulating photographic images are described in Appendices One and Two. This section illustrates some of the ways in which photographic images can be blended with graphic designs.

There are several ways in which the photo image can be combined with a graphic design. The sim-

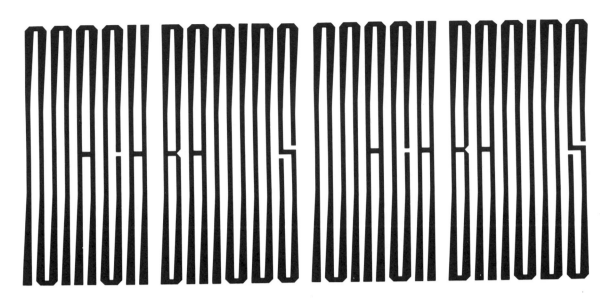

4.30 *Brightness contrast.*

4.31 Combinations of inclined lines with positive and negative photographic images of Lord Rayleigh.

plest is to superimpose a photo (on lith film) on a single design. Figure 4.31 shows the effects of superimposing an inclined grating over a negative and a positive photo. Obviously, the former, which gives a positive print, is more readily recognisable as a face, because the black areas of the positive image are replaced by the pattern.

Under normal circumstances a single superimposition like this would be a preliminary step to further image manipulation. However, it can provide an end in itself if the two components are in har-

a

b

4.32 *Irradiation.* The gaps in the radiating pattern correspond to the dark (negative) regions of a photograph of a face.

4.33 *Faces.* The radiating design corresponds to profiles of a face, while the gaps in them define a frontal view of a face.

mony. The dominance of the facial image can be reduced by printing it in negative, as in Figure 4.32. The white breaks in the radiating zigzags appear amorphous initially, but then the face emerges with the unseen centre of the design localised in an eye. Similarly, with Figure 4.33 the radiating contours are facial profiles and enclosed within them is a full face photo image. Here, the unseen centre of the design is located between the eyes. The photo images in these two examples were reduced to their essential features in the conversion to lith film, so that they could be blended with the drawn designs. Photo subjects do not always have the contrasts to enable such reduction to essentials, and one such example is shown in Figure 4.34. This is a picture of Sir David Brewster superimposed in text from one of his own books. The photographic image was taken from an engraving which contained a great deal of facial detail. It was converted to lith film and much of the detail was retained because it had been in high contrast in the engraving. The negative was combined with a page of text from his book, *The Stereoscope*, written in 1856. (In fact, the text describes his presentation of a stereoscope to Queen Victoria at the Great Exhibition in 1851.) The detail in the image is evident in the fragmentation of some of the text, particularly around his hair; but his eyes, which disclose the "beautiful stereoscope", are more sharply defined. If it proves difficult to see the face with any degree of clarity then place the book upright on a chair, or by a wall, and view the design from afar. The face will then shine out through the text – or, more correctly, the detail of the text will no longer be visible. This same strategy will be recommended frequently for viewing the images in the next section.

Faces are by no means the only images that are suitable for photo–graphic manipulation, but they do have the advantage that we can recognise them as such with the most fragmentary of cues. Indeed, within visual science much experimental attention has been directed towards understanding what it is about faces that makes them such powerful visual stimuli. The face has simple, symmetrical and stereotyped features which are common to all. This geometrical structure might enable us to recognise a pattern as a face very easily. The paradox is that the structural similarity that leads to seeing a visual stimulus as a face embeds within it the structural differences allowing identification of a particular face. That is, different rules might operate for recog-

4.34 *Sir David Brewster. Portrait in text from his book The Stereoscope.*

... stereoscope ...
... not a single instrument ...
... was not till a year after ... ...
... it was exhibited in England. In the ...
... Philosophical ir ... ... hich M. Du...
... ... to ... reat F ... ... , and for ... ...
... ... he ... ... with a ... ... he placed a lens ...
... roscope, with a ... ... lar Daguerreotype
... instrument attracted the ... icular attention of ...
... and before the closing of the Crystal Palace ...
... executed ... beautiful st. ...oscope, which I pre ...
... Majesty in ... ... In onsequence of this ...
... tion of the ... ...t, M. Du... received ...
... from England, and a large number of ...
... introduced into ... ountry. The dem ...
... so great, that opticians of all kin ...
... to the manufacture of the instrument ...
... ...ers, both in Daguerreo... ... and Talbot...
... most lucrative branch of their profession, to
portraits of views to be thrown into reli...
scope. Its application to sculpture, which ...
out, was first made in France, and an artist in ...
copied a statue from the *relievo* produced by the stere...

Three years after I had published a description of
lenticular stereoscope, and after it had been in general u.
in France and England, and the reflecting stereoscope for-
gotten,[1] Mr. Wheatstone printed, in the *Philosophical
Transactions* for 1852, a paper on Vision, in which he says

nising a pattern as a face and for determining the identity of that face.

In the examples presented above a simple derived photo image was matched with a pattern. It can be desirable to manipulate the photo image in the ways described in Appendix One before the stage of pattern combination. This has been done

with Figures 4.35 and 4.36. In the former, the reflected form of the Sydney Opera House was matched in positive and negative. The concentric circular pattern was placed in the enlarger and projected onto the lith image, to convey the idea of the sun setting over the water in the harbour. In order to emphasise the impression of the building

4.35 *Op-era House.*

reflected in the water, a plate of patterned glass was placed over the bottom half of the film, so that it would be exposed unevenly. Figure 4.36 utilised a kaleidoscopic image of the Tay Road Bridge (see Figure 2.71) and superimposed on it a screen varying gradually from light to dark dots. The screen was arranged so that the level at which the dots in the background had equal ratios of black and white was horizontal and corresponded to the water level for the bridges extending to the left and right. This gives an added suggestion of a mirroring reflection in the photo–graphic combinations.

Figure 4.31 showed the effects of superimposing a simple linear pattern over a negative and positive lith image. Rather than presenting these separately, they can be combined to form a single print, as is shown in Figure 4.37. Light and shade in the original photo image have been replaced by lines in different orientations. This general principle of combining negative and positive with their respective patterns can have wide utility. In Figure 4.37 the density of the lines differs from the highlights and the shadows of the face; the shadows and background have thicker black lines. Even when there is no indication which parts would normally be light and which shade, once the composite design has been recognised as a face we have no problem in assigning these values. These same points apply to Figure

4.38, too, although it might be more difficult to recognise the facial image. The possibility of identifying the face is, of course, only open to those who are familiar with it either in real life or from pictures. Here it is a portrait of my colleague Hiroshi Ono. He is a visual scientist who studies the intricacies of binocular vision. Accordingly, the superimposed designs are two sets of concentric circles each of which is centred on an eye.

Clearly the attraction in producing such photo–graphic portraits is that the design can augment the interests of the individual imaged, and this theme is continued in the next illustrations, too. Light and shade can be specified in the final design by the appropriate combination of positive and negative lith images with dense or fine contours in the graphics. In Figure 4.39 the portrait of another visual scientist, Lothar Spillmann, is combined with grid patterns of the type he has studied extensively. The bearded face is easily distinguished from the background and the contrast relations are normal. The same grid pattern was used throughout but in its positive and negative forms. In order to retain the appropriate contrast the positive of the face was matched with the negative of the design, and vice

4.36 (Facing page) *Tay Road Bridge.*

4.37 A combination of the two components shown in Figure 4.31.

versa, keeping their relative locations the same. The resulting two images were registered to form the final image. Essentially the same procedure was followed for Figure 4.40, which is a portrait of the sculptor Marcel Floris. His works consist of ambiguous three-dimensional structures which contain "false angles" – flat portions that have the perspective of solidity and depth. It was thus apposite to combine his facial image with a set of impossible triangles which do not convey consistent impressions of depth. Again, the positive of the face was matched with the negative of the graphic design, and vice versa.

The light and shade in a photo–graphic combination can be manipulated by means of variations in the design itself. In Figure 4.41 the same pattern is used in the positive and negative regions of the photo image, which is of two sisters. The pattern consists of lines varying gradually in thickness from left to right, and its direction was changed in the positive and negative combinations. This has the

4.38 *Binoculus.*

4.39 *Spillmann grid.* Small illusory dots might be seen at the intersections separating the outline rectangles. These are related to the Hermann–Hering grids shown earlier (Figures 3.30 and 4.25), but the variant occurring with outlines in this figure was described more recently by Lothar Spillmann, who is portrayed.

4.40 *The false angles.* The nested impossible triangles contain within them a portrait of Marcel Floris, who has produced many three-dimensional structures which play upon projective ambiguities.

4.41 *Sibling rivalry.* Figures and ground are defined by the same pattern of thickening lines, but they thicken in opposite directions. The resulting impression is of a negative and positive image of the two girls.

4.42 *Homage to Rubin.*

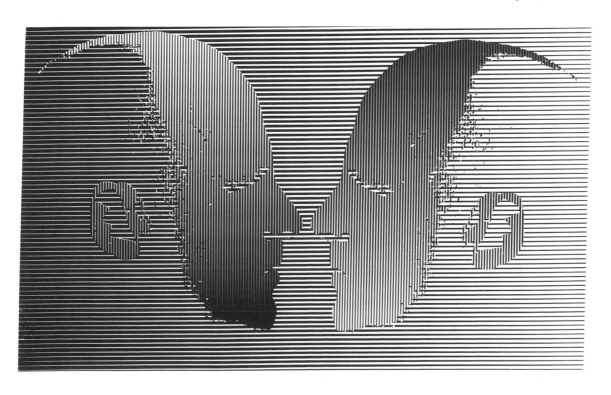

4.43 *Eye contact.*

effect of making the two heads appear in opposite contrasts: although the difference in the width of the lines defining the heads is not too great, it is accentuated by the opposite gradation in the background lines. The same graphic design was incorporated three times in Figure 4.42. The two profiles have the lines running vertically, but thickening in different directions, whereas the lines run horizontally in the background. The positioning of the profiles gives an ambiguous figure, which could be seen as either the two faces or a vase, as discussed in the "Allusions" section in Chapter One.

Figure 4.43 is based on a simple photo in which most of the graphical manipulations have focused on the eyes. Under normal circumstances the eye sockets are in shadow, and this simple fact has proved to be one of the aspects that makes faces so readily recognisable as such. It also accounts for the difficulty we have in identifying pictures of well-known faces when they are presented in the negative form. The photo–graphic image on the right of Figure 4.43 seems starkly attractive in part because the orbits or eye sockets are lighter than the surrounding pattern. This sets up some visual tension which makes it more stimulating than the one on the left. The interplay between the relative light and shade of the eye sockets and surrounds is repeated more focally in the central patterns.

Having derived a photo–graphic image by utilising the transparent areas in the positive and negative, it is possible to take the manipulation one stage further by superimposing another pattern over the combination. If the third pattern is spatially similar to those used in the earlier combinations, then moiré fringes will be produced. This can be seen clearly in Figure 4.44, which has taken the earlier combined images of Lord Rayleigh and superimposed another grating over them. It was the accidental displacement of two photographic negatives of gratings that initiated Lord Rayleigh's interest in interference fringes. He realised that any unevenness in the component gratings would be more easily detected in the moiré fringes than in the originals.

It is often the case that a more pleasing pictorial image can be produced by the superimposition of a pattern over a single image-design combination, so that the moiré fringes occur in part but not over all of the final picture. For instance, Figure 4.45 is a self-portrait in which the moiré fringes are confined to an almost circular background and they are formed from the interaction of spiral and grating patterns. The same process is applied for a far more attractive subject in Figure 4.46. Here the fringes are formed from the interaction of a grating with a curvilinear pattern, so that they vary in direction around the face, often echoing its contours.

The interference of waveforms is something we associate with telecommunications, so it seems

a

b

c

d

4.44 Moiré images of Lord Rayleigh, who described the mathematical relationship between separations of the moiré fringes and the widths and inclinations of the component gratings.

(a) A vertical grating was superimposed on the pattern corresponding to Figure 4.31b, so that moiré fringes occur in the highlighted regions of the represented face. (b) The vertical grating was superimposed on Figure 4.31a, so that the background and shadows of the portrayed face is made up of moiré fringes. (c) The vertical grating was superimposed on Figure 4.37, producing two sets of moiré fringes at different orientations. (d) Another superimposition like (c), but printed in negative to restore relative darkness to the shadow areas of the portrait.

4.45 *Moirébund.*

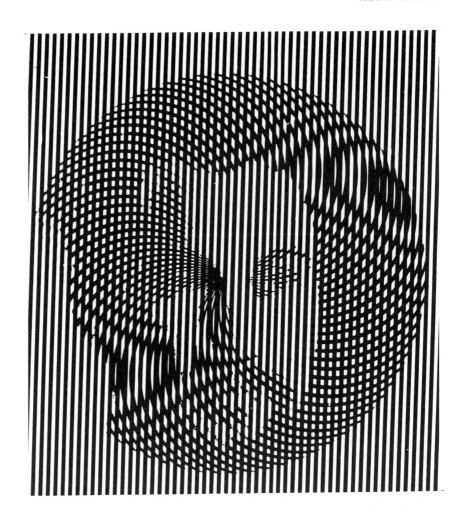

appropriate to include a moiré pattern formed from waves and radiating circles that is blended with an image of a radiotelescope (Figure 4.47).

The photo images with which the graphic designs are blended can themselves incorporate patterns, and these can be used to produce novel photo–graphic images. Figure 4.48 represents a simple pattern superimposed on a photo of striped-stockinged legs. The attraction of this picture is that the moiré fringes follow the contours of the legs, which are immediately recognisable even though their outlines are not visible.

The final figure in this section embodies dot rather than line patterns. In Figure 4.49 the graphic element is a dot pattern that has been superimposed on itself several times to give more complex configurations. The two figures and the background were combined with the same pattern, but in positive and

negative. The dots were enlarged slightly and superimposed over the combined image, producing the variation in texture that distinguishes the figures from the background. There are many variations that can be played on the theme of the photo–graphic combinations described here. Much of the pleasure in photo–graphic imagery derives from discovering personally novel methods and subjects for such combinations.

Hidden Images

Hidden pictorial images are those alluded to almost covertly. They are not always hidden, but they are often not instantly visible. They can be produced by a variety of methods. Embedded images are pro-

4.46 (Overleaf) *Hair style.*

173

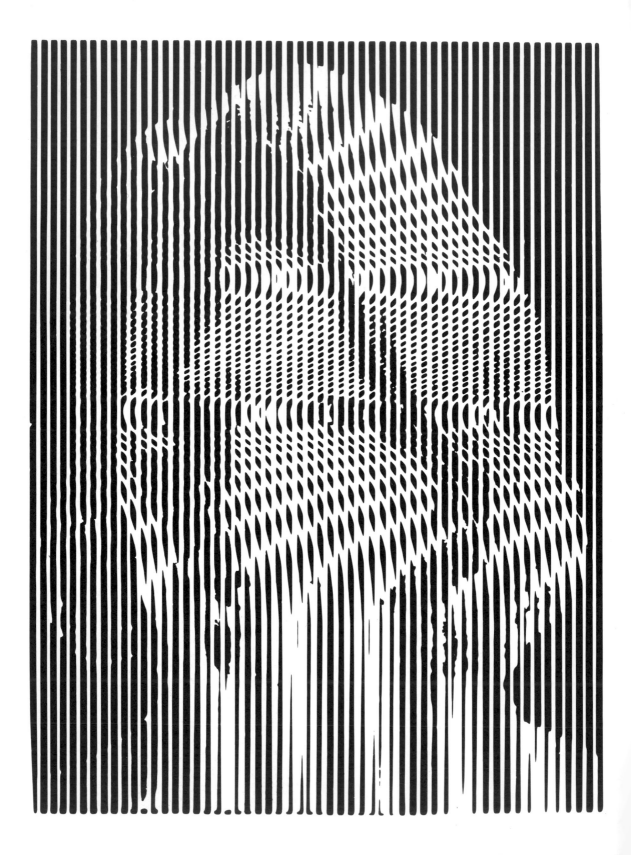

4.47 *Parkes telescope, N.S.W.*

4.48 *Crossed contours.*

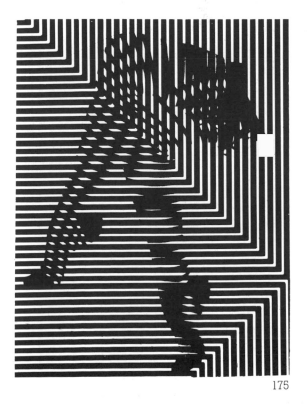

duced in a similar manner to the photo–graphic combinations described in the previous section, but the same graphic design is used both for the combination and the embedding. For example, Figure 4.50 is a portrait of the artist Marcel Duchamp presented in the form of an embedded image. The negative of the face was initially placed over the drawn design and printed on film, forming a positive image. This was then superimposed, slightly out of register, upon the negative of the graphic design to produce the final embedded image. The design itself is suggestive of Duchamp's famous painting *Nude Descending a Staircase*, with the diamonds defining a sequence of positions assumed by the contours of a human figure. This technique was also employed in making Figure 4.51, in which the internal square within the graphic design acts as a frame for the face. The positive of the photo image was first combined with the positive of the checkerboard design, resulting in a negative of the pattern in the

4.49 (Overleaf) *Familiarity.*

4.50 (Overleaf) *Nude descending Marcel Duchamp.*

4.51 *Square-faced.*

4.52 (Below) *Space perception.*

background and transparent areas for the hair and shadows of the face. The positive checkerboard was superimposed once more, so that it was visible fully in the hair and shadowed regions, but it was partly obscured in the other areas, forming the stepping pattern of the background.

If an even simpler graphic design is used in combination with a photo image, then some further aspects of embedding can be explored. A grating was used in both stages of superimposition for Figures 4.52 and 4.53. In the first, a grating was superimposed on the negative of the face – here of the visual scientist Ian Howard. The resulting image consisted of lines, inclined slightly to the horizontal, in the shaded areas of the face. The lined image was superimposed at a slight angle to the original grating so that a single broad, vertical moiré band was

formed that masked part of the face. The area that is masked is dependent upon the positioning of the moiré fringe, and therefore the positioning of the two components with respect to one another. This can be seen in the left and right pictorial images, both of which were derived from the same components but with slightly different superimpositions. It is possible to see much more of the individual facial images by viewing the picture from a distance: parts that appear indistinct on close inspection will reveal detail when seen from afar. The facial image could have been made more uniformly visible by inclining the two lined patterns by a greater degree with respect to one another, so producing multiple moiré fringes. However, it is not always my aim to make images clear and easily discernible. The designs are often successful from my point of view if they make the observer ponder on the nature of the embedded image, and on the sophistication of our vision in recognising it.

4.53 *Sandy.*

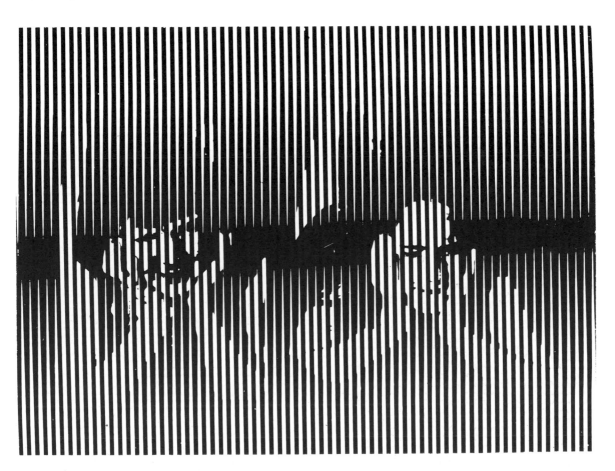

It will be clear from the previous illustration that embedding images in simple patterns offers the opportunity of emphasising some parts of a photo image at the expense of other parts. This has been done with Figure 4.53. The photo image is of two girls lying on a beach. Its negative was superimposed on a grating, and the same design was used for combination at the second stage. The slight rotation of one to the other was arranged to produce

a single broad moiré band near the centre, which gave prominence to the two faces. However, as the two gratings came into register at the upper and lower parts of the picture, then the legs and elbows become indistinct.

Triangular designs were used in the next two examples of photo–graphics – both of which incorporate facial images. In Figure 4.54 the distinction between the positive and negative images of a face can be seen. Although the background patterns are structurally similar, the negative is much more difficult to code than is the positive. The other two

4.54 *Full face.*

4.55 *Windblown.*

quadrants contain the same facial image but it is masked by either embedding or combination. The windblown profile in Figure 4.55 is easily visible in the lower right quadrant, but it becomes increasingly indistinct in the quadrants clockwise of this. In the two on the left the image is embedded in triangles. Indeed, this graphic design was selected because it conveys the impression of windflow around the head. Additionally, the four heads are graphically connected by the whiter lines bisecting each quadrant. The image in the upper right quadrant is the most difficult to see, although it has been formed by combination of the type described in the previous section. If the two graphic designs used in the combination are similar then they act to hide the photo image, or to mask its visibility. It is to this issue that the illustrations in the next section are addressed.

Variations in any of the techniques mentioned in this chapter can yield pictorial images that are initially difficult to see, but which can be seen with perceptual persistence. These composite images can operate at several levels at the same time: they can be seen either as graphic designs, independently of the photo image they carry with them, or as subtly blended pictorial images that are attractive because they are elusive.

The photo images can be hidden because the designs used in their combination are similar, so that the transitions from light to shade, or from figure to ground, are not readily evident. This could be seen in parts of the last two illustrations. Thus, the photographic combinations described in the previous section can yield hidden images if the two designs combined with the positive and negative of the photo image can blend together. One obvious source of graphical blending is to use the positive and negative of the design – provided that they do not differ too much in their pattern density. This has been done for Figure 4.56, which utilises the positive and negative of an eccentric circular design. There is sufficient difference between the two components

for their boundaries to be visible, but the photo image they convey might prove difficult to perceive. The initial impression is of a map or a globe, with continents, islands and peninsulas. This interpretation, strongly suggested by the descending curved strip, is false as the hidden image is a face: the islands are the eye, nose and mouth and the descending curved strip is the line of the jaw.

The same drawn designs have been used in the two stages of combination for Figures 4.57 and 4.58, but their orientations have been changed. Both photo–graphic images are very active visually because patterns with many fine lines varying in orientation generate the astigmatic distortions mentioned in Chapter Two and in the first section of this chapter. These distortions, like the apparent shimmering of spots over the surface, can also act to hide the photo image. That is, the design with which the photo image is blended can produce visual effects that make the visibility of that image more difficult. One of the fascinations in viewing these pictures is

4.56 *Continents of the mind.*

4.57 *Bust of Lenin.*

that the perceptual distortions they generate fluctuate over time, as do the phases of visibility of the hidden image.

Derived designs can be used to create hidden images, and the next two illustrations provide examples of their use. In each case, all the components were captured in the camera at the same locations. For instance, Figure 4.59 contains a photo image of a facial profile in which the hair is covered by a scarf. The derived high-contrast image was separated into three parts by opaquing unwanted areas on three sheets of lith film, and different textures were combined with each one. The textures were derived from seawater, seaweed, and the watery wake of a small boat – all the elements were photographed in the vicinity of a small Scottish island. These textures were combined with the background, face and headscarf, respectively. Although the densities of

the textures are quite different their irregularity assists in making the facial image hidden because alternative interpretations of the seemingly amorphous blobs will often be entertained. The textural structure within Figure 4.60 is simpler than in the previous one, but the photographic subject is considerably more difficult to discriminate. The textures are derived from photographs of limpets on a rock and stones on a beach. The subject of the original photograph is intentionally obtuse: it is of a full face view, but a headscarf is pulled over the eyes so that only the shadow of the nose and lips are present. The background is given by the limpet pattern and the foreground by the stones. The latter define not only the headscarf but also the hands holding it. There are so many images that could potentially be seen in the stony shadows that it is difficult to disregard them, and to interpret the areas they cover

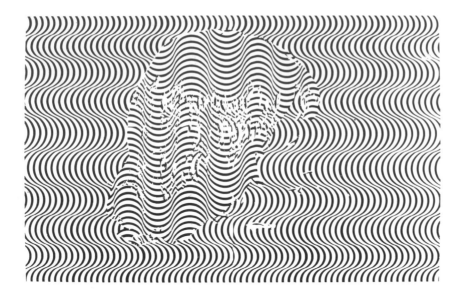

4.58 *Helena.*

4.59 *See Wade.*

4.60 *Masked.*

as uniform. Once the clue to the face – the nose and lips – have been perceived then the other parts, like the two hands, will also emerge from the formerly chaotic distribution of black and white blobs.

The procedures associated with embedded images can be employed to hide photo images in graphic designs. The general principle of embedded images is that the same graphic design is used in successive stages of image processing. This was done with Figure 4.61, using a drawn grid design. These patterns are interesting perceptually because they generate illusory light grey dots at the intersections of the black lines, as described in the "Allusions to visual processes" section earlier in this chapter. However, it is clear that the grid is not uniform throughout, and so the illusory dots only appear within part of it. The photo image embedded

here is of a facial profile in which the eye, nose and lips are signified by the merest discontinuities in the display. The peaked jockey hat, the flowing hair and the chin are defined much more sharply. If the facial image still eludes you then adopt the distant viewing procedure mentioned earlier. Alternatively, if you defocus the image by squinting or by moving the picture around, the face will spring into visibility – only to disappear again with normal observation. The photo image and graphics for Figure 4.62 are stylised stockinged legs and oval shapes. However, here the former has been masked by the latter, with different forms of embedding in the four quadrants.

The essence of the embedding in the previous two photo–graphic images has been the slight displacement of one pattern with respect to another of the same form, but containing the pictorial subject. The closer the registration of the patterns the less discernible is the subject, until it becomes completely masked by the design. This procedure

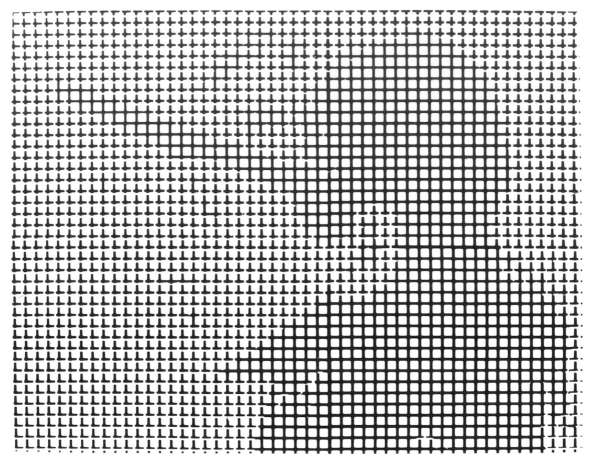

4.61 *Jockey.*

can be taken near to this final state, and yet retain sufficient spatial information for the photo image to be a shadowy presence. Thus, Figure 4.63 appears on first inspection to be a simple pattern of vertical lines, with few if any discontinuities in it. However, there is a facial image present, and it is defined by the small variations in the thickness of the lines. The face can be seen more clearly by moving the book from side to side, by squinting to defocus the picture, or by viewing it from a distance. That is, any procedure that reduces the definition of the lines will enhance the visibility of the hidden image. In order to produce this photo–graphic image the positive of the portrait was first combined with the vertical pattern. The resulting lined image was superimposed over the original grating once more, almost in exact registration. With the aid of a light box it is easy to vary the displacement of the films to

find the degree of masking that is desired in the final image. The films are then fixed in that position with tape, and the composite is contact printed onto film once more.

If the graphic design has a range of orientations in it, then it might prove necessary to increase the displacement in the second combination for the photo–graphic image to be visible. Another aspect of patterns containing lines in different orientations is that any displacement of one to the other will have differential effects throughout. That is, with a con-centric circular pattern, like that in Figure 4.64, a slight displacement will have the greatest effect for lines at right angles to the direction of displacement, and virtually no effect for the lines parallel to it. Here the displacement was in an oblique direction. The centre of the circular pattern lies just to one side of the midpoint between the eyes, and the whole face can be seen by adopting the procedures mentioned previously.

There is an alternative method for producing

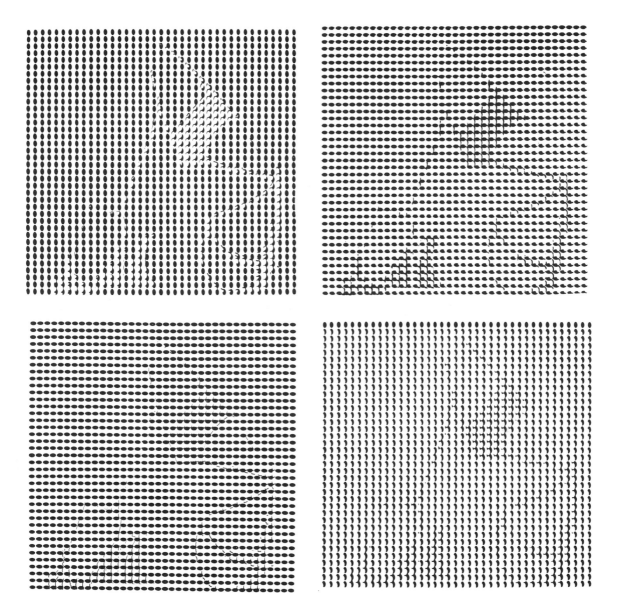

4.62 *Suspendered animation.*

hidden images and it does not correspond to any of the techniques described earlier. It yields effects similar to those for slight displacement, but it does not share the restrictions of the latter, i.e., it can be used with any designs. Basically, the method consists of differentially exposing the pattern in the areas corresponding to the figure and background. It can best be described with the aid of an example.

Figure 4.65 shows a vertical grating in which the black lines thicken slightly in some parts. The line thickening corresponds to the areas formed by two faces. Two components were required to produce this photo–graphic image – negatives of the faces and a grating. The grating was placed in contact with a sheet of lith film and fixed to the baseboard of the enlarger with tape. The negative of the face was placed over these and kept firmly in contact with the underlying film. Thus, light from the enlarger would reach the unexposed film only in those lined areas corresponding to the shadows of the positive photo

image. The film was then exposed for the duration normally suitable for producing a high contrast image. The photographic negative was then removed, leaving the grating in exactly the same position with respect to the underlying, partially exposed film. The film was exposed once more with only the pattern in contact with it, but for a much

shorter time and then it was placed in the developer. The lines corresponding to the facial shadows obviously develop first and fastest. It would be possible to stop the development at this stage, but the outcome would be a simple image–design combination, like the positive lined image in Figure 4.31. However, the development is continued until the lines from the brief second exposure appear and blacken. During this period the lines of the relatively overexposed parts overdevelop and extend into the neighbouring unexposed areas. The development should be stopped before the adjacent lines join one another. In fact, the stopping point will be deter-

4.63 (Facing page)
Subjective vertical.

4.64 *Cyclopean eye.*

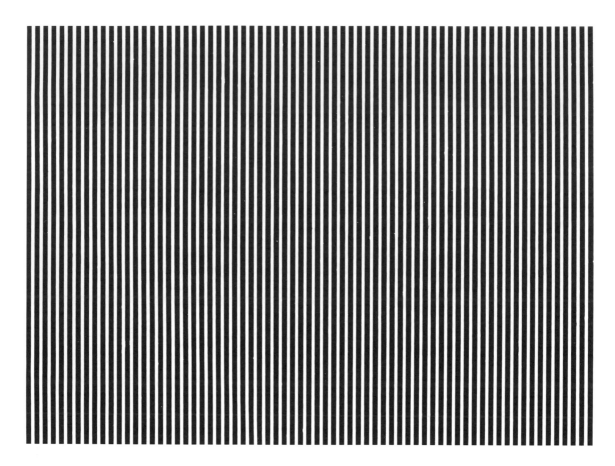

4.65 *Happy faces.*

mined in part by the relative durations of the first and second exposures and also by the degree of thickening desired. The resulting image will be a positive, like Figure 4.65, but on film. In order to print the image on paper an additional print on film is required to make a negative.

This overexposure or "bleeding" method has greater potential than the displacement method for two reasons. Firstly, the variations in the thickness of the lines is gradual rather than abrupt. Secondly, the same method can be applied to a wider variety of drawn designs, including those with differently orientated contours throughout.

A surprising amount of detail can be hidden in a design using this method, even with simple patterns. Figures 4.66 and 4.67 both employ patterns with evenly spaced lines. The first is a pattern of concentric circles with omissions defining the Rubin vase/ faces motif. The circles vary slightly in thickness,

and a map of part of the world can be seen. Within the map a remarkable range of geographical features are provided by very slight line variations. It is possible to allude to pictorial images by having thicker or thinner lines: thus, in Figure 4.67 the letters within the goblet are lighter than the horizontal lines whereas those embedded in the vertical lines are darker. It might be noted that the graphic design here is also a vase/face motif, but one that is inverted. If the figure is inverted then two swan-necked profiles will be seen.

The pattern in which a photographic image is hidden need not itself be regular. In Figure 4.68 the pattern is made up of seemingly random dots. However, embedded in them is a portrait of the neo-Impressionist painter, Georges Seurat. He developed the pointilliste technique, in which small coloured spots of paint defined the surfaces in the scene represented. Here we have a variation on that technique, in which the subject is determined by slight differences in the sizes of the dots – so his face and straggly beard are disclosed when the pictorial image is defocused. In addition to his portrait, which is darker than the background, his signature is present, too. It can be seen in the lower left, and it is lighter than the background.

The size of regular dots is varied in Figure 4.69, although in this case the photographic portrait is produced by making the white dots smaller in the facial region. The series of pictorial images is derived from the same photo–graphic design, but the magnification is varied systematically. When the dots become large enough for their sizes to be discriminated, then the photographic image they carry ceases to be visible. Variation in dot size is the technique employed in photo-mechanical printing,

4.67 (Overleaf) Logo for a conference on visual perception.

4.68 (Overleaf) *Pointillism.*

4.66 *Nation shall speak unto nation.*

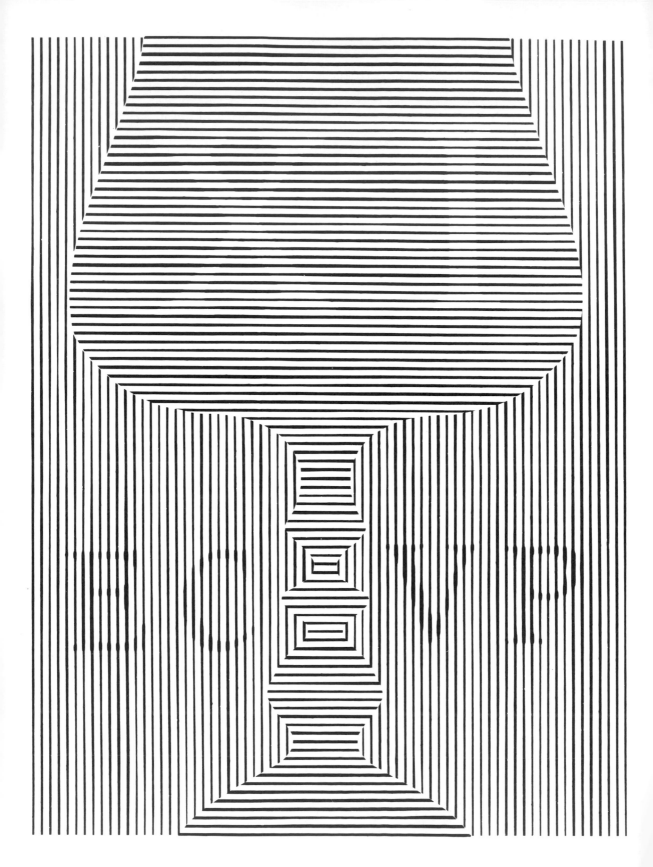

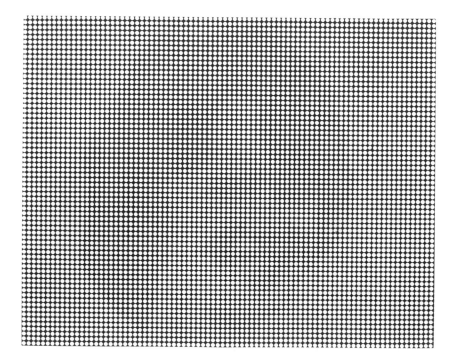

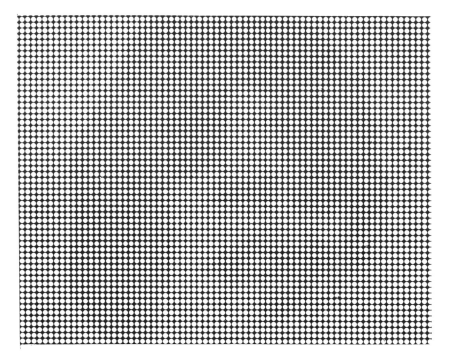

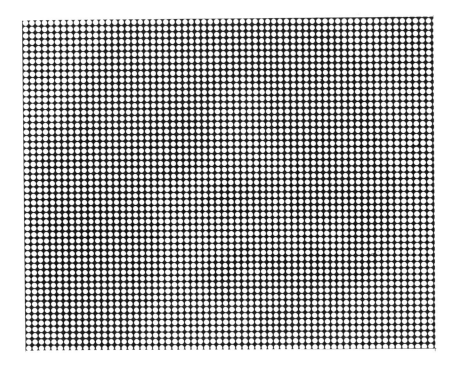

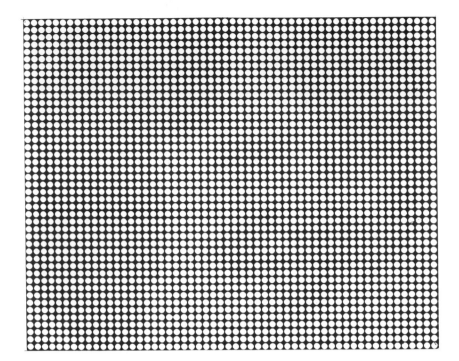

and it forms the basis for most of the pictorial images we see in newspapers and magazines. With this technique the individual dots can vary enormously in size in order to create half-tone effects. The procedure employed to produce Figure 4.69 is the inverse of photo-mechanical reproduction, because the darker regions are defined by smaller white dots rather than larger black ones; it is as though the portrait is carried by the spaces between the dots. Some of these combinations might be below the minimum visible; that is, below the threshold for detecting the small differences in the dot size or their averaged consequences. Figure 4.70 presents a portrait of Bishop Berkeley, who introduced the term "minimum visible" into visual science.

Not all the components of the subject need be hidden in a design. Indeed, if some part of it is readily recognised and the rest is hidden, then the visual tension in the picture will be increased. This was the case for Figure 1.1, which is one of my favourite pictures. At its centre is a well defined left eye, but the rest of the face is not so easily seen. It is all there, though. The right eye is off-centre at the same level as the left one, and the downward radiating lines complement the contours of the nose and lips. This photo–graphic image might require the greatest amount of defocusing to make it visible, but

the solution of the visual conundrum makes it worthwhile.

The visual tension within the photo–graphic image can also be influenced by including graphical features that are visually beguiling. For instance, in Figure 4.71 the graphical design consists of oblique lines varying in direction to produce a pattern of concentric squares. Superimposed on the oblique lines are actual outline squares. However, these latter do not appear to have parallel sides, because the adjacent squares are drawn on lines of different inclination. That is, the design produces the visual illusion that physically parallel lines look inclined to one another. What is not so immediately evident as a consequence of this visual paradox is that a facial image is hidden in the design. It is defined by the slight thickening of the lines, and the right eye is located at the centre of the pattern.

The incorporation of a photo image within a graphic design using any of the techniques described earlier might still result in it being too easily recognisable. If such is the case then further manipulation can reduce it to the limits of visibility.

4.70 (Facing page)
Minimum visible.

4.71 *Visual illusions.*

Alternatively, the previous procedures might be considered as a prelude to a final superimposition in which (almost) all will be hidden! This technique has been employed for Figure 4.72. It incorporates the face of Ian Howard, and a variant of this figure was used as the jacket illustration for his book *Human Visual Orientation*. Since the book is concerned with the ability of human observers to judge and discriminate patterns in different orientations, it

seemed appropriate to embed the author's portrait in a pattern that used lines of different spatial frequencies (thicknesses) and that also induced distortions of visual orientation: the thin lines are vertical, although they might not look so because of their interaction with the inclined lines. Moreover, the thin line segments are aligned vertically, even though they appear to be displaced laterally with respect to their neighbours.

4.72 (Facing page)
Human facial orientation I.

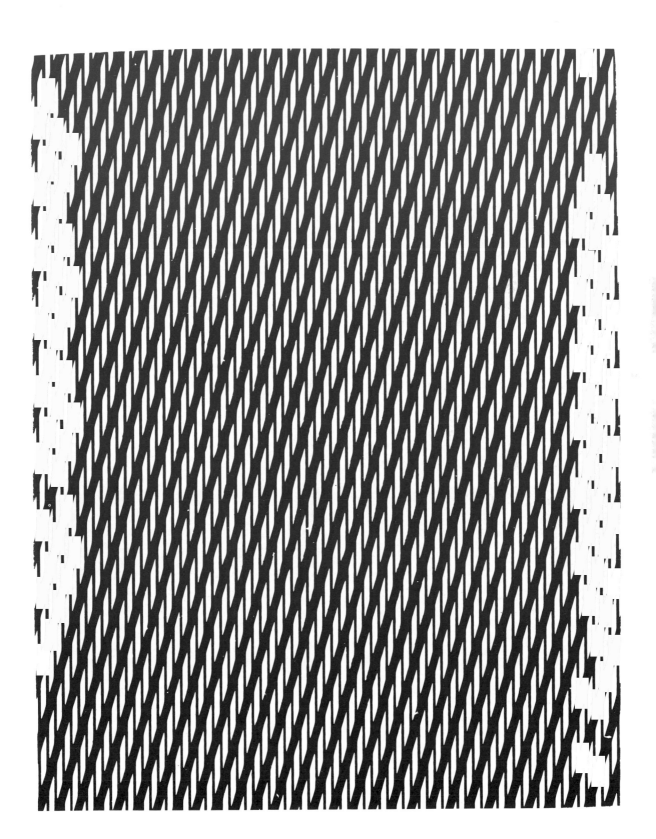

The second superimposed pattern need not be at a slight inclination to the original, as is shown in Figure 4.73. The initial steps involved embedding a positive (on the right) and a negative (on the left) of the portrait within the lines of a vertical grating. Once this had been achieved, the whole design was superimposed upon a pattern of radiating lines, so that moiré fringes were formed near the vertical lines. The resulting pictorial image carries the posi- tive and negative features of the face much more subtly, and the positive is much more readily visible than the negative. The portrait is of the artist Ludwig Wilding, who has produced many beautiful works using moiré fringes, often generating stereoscopic effects, too.

As with the embedded images described earlier, graphic designs need not form the carriers of the hidden images. In Figure 4.74 the texture used for embedding is a diagram of the brain that was taken from Descartes' *Treatise of Man* published over 300 years ago; the pattern contains within it a portrait of

4.73 *Moirémage.*

4.74 *Descartes' brain.*

Descartes. A more modern representation of the brain, or more correctly the visual areas of the brain, is shown in Figure 4.75. The striped patterns correspond to the areas of the visual cortex that are influenced by the left and right eyes. The portraits they carry are of David Hubel and Torsten Wiesel, who first discovered these configurations in the visual areas of the brain.

It might seem unduly perverse to make images difficult to see, when they could be made obvious to the viewer with far less darkroom processing. However, as one who is interested in the process of vision I believe we can learn much from complicating the puzzles posed to our perceptual processes. Being interested in the visual arts I also believe that it is through such perceptual paradoxes that we can appreciate the subtlety of our vision, and revel in the uncertainty of our perception in a way that is seldom available in our everyday world. And finally, as one interested in graphics, I hope that the photo–graphic images can be appreciated as

graphic designs independently of the additional images they secretly carry.

The Sabattier effect, or what for convenience we have called solarisation, can be applied to any of the phases through which a photo image or design passes. Once solarised it can be presented on its own or it can be combined further with other graphic, photo–graphic or solarised images. The technique of solarisation and its applications to photographic images and graphic designs are described and illustrated in Appendices One and Two.

A photo–graphic image derived from any of the methods of combination described earlier can be further modified by solarisation. The process usually results in the photo image becoming more indistinct, but there are exceptions to this. One such exception arises when the combination has been relatively simple – like those described earlier in this chapter, in the initial parts of the section on "Photo–graphic combinations". For instance, if text is used as the graphical element, then the letters can be rendered less stereotyped by solarisation, while retaining the clarity of the subject matter. Figure 4.76 is a portrait

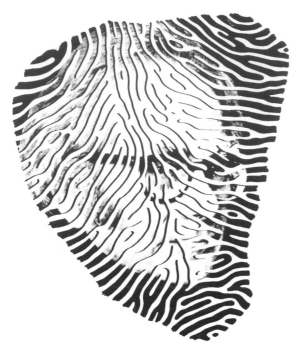

4.75 *Feature detectives.*

4.76 *See more.*

of my colleague Philip Seymour, who is an authority on the subject of reading and visual thinking. The text in which his face has been embedded is taken from the Preface to his book *Human Visual Cognition*. The Sabattier effect has made the text more difficult to read; indeed it looks more like the orthography of a new language than English. Since the book is concerned with the comprehension of written symbols, this degradation of the text seemed most apposite, particularly because it can be read with some persistence.

The previous illustration was a print from solarised film: the Mackie lines were transparent in the film and they appear as black lines on a print. The solarised film can be contact printed onto film once more, so that the paper print from the latter will appear like the initially solarised film. Figure 4.77 is derived from a hidden image: the overexposure technique was applied to a portrayal of a face so that it would be defined by the slight differences in the thicknesses of the inclined lines. The solarisation has transformed the line width variations into very subtle modulations of the Mackie lines. There is a bespectacled face hidden in the lines: by this stage, it is hoped that you are well versed in the art of uncovering it!

A more rigid structure is shown in Figure 4.78 – the Tay Rail Bridge. Four different patterns were combined with the photo–graphic image prior to solarisation. The grids were used to give the suggestion of the lattice-like girders, with the different sizes reflecting the different distances; and gratings in different orientations were used for the wall and road in front of the bridge. Each area was masked in turn, and then the exposed image was solarised.

It is not necessary to solarise the whole design, as often more striking visual images can be created by incorporating a solarised component within a high contrast design. Figure 4.79 contains a portrait that has been combined with a graphic design and solarised, and then combined once more with the same design. In this example, the area corresponding to the head (derived from the photo positive) has been solarised, whereas the background is a continuation of the same design in high contrast black and white rather than in outline. Figure 4.80 shows a portrait of another artist hidden in a pattern of the type he painted. It is Jackson Pollock who emerges from the swirls and splashes, with his laconic gaze, and ever-present cigarette. The painting was, of course, in colour, but only a small detail of it was photographed in black and white. The positive portrait of Pollock was positioned so that a dominant splash in the lower left corresponded to the line of the cigarette, drooping from his mouth, and a print on film was derived. This was then solarised, and

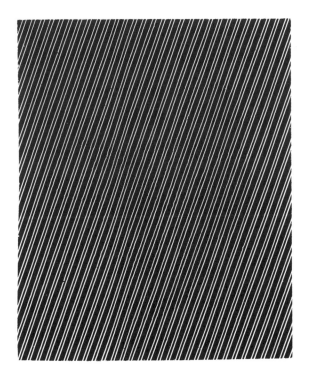

4.77 *Human facial orientation II.*

4.78 *Tay Rail Bridge.*

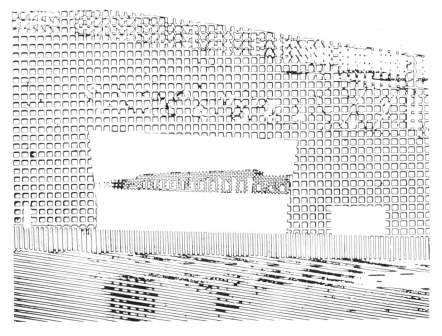

4.79 *Artistic vision.*

repositioned on the original to produce the final pictorial image.

The difficulty with which a solarised photo–graphic image can be recognised relative to a high contrast one can be appreciated in the next two illustrations. Figure 4.81 presents an embedded facial image in combination with its solarised counterpart. The clearly defined hair, and the rather more indistinct profile features of the high contrast image are all but lost in the solarised version. The

same effect occurs with the two components of Figure 4.82. The graphical elements utilised here are more complex than in the previous example, since they carry with them human figures arranged in opposition and in reflection. Indeed, the opposing outstretched feet in the upper pair of figures have been placed so that they occupy the position of the eyes in the photo image. The design and photo–graph were combined using the displacement tech-

4.80 (Facing page)
Abstract expression.

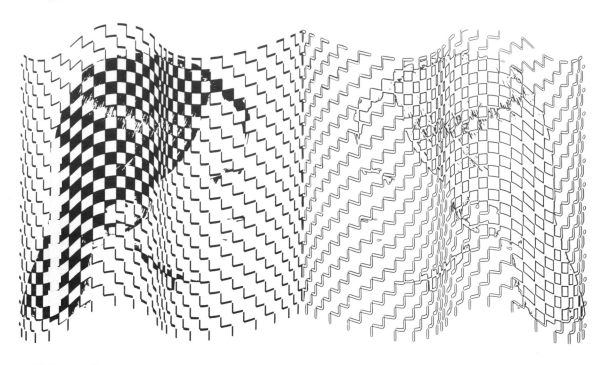

4.81 *Permanent waves.*

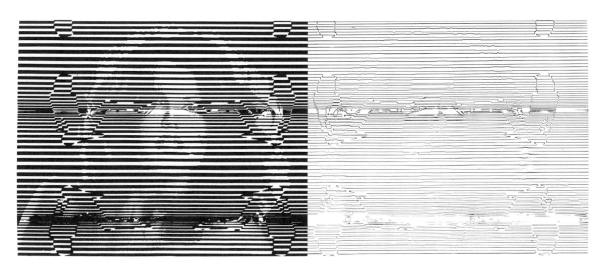

4.82 *Foot lights.*

nique. Because the graphical design has a figural structure associated with it, rather than being uniform, the amount of displacement required to render the face visible was quite large. None the less, when the photo–graphic image was solarised, as in the right half of the illustration, the face is once more virtually hidden. The graphical features on the other hand have greater prominence in the solarised image.

The next two figures were produced in a more complicated way, as they involve combinations of solarised components. Figure 4.83 uses random dot patterns throughout, although some regions are solarised and others are not. Both halves of the photo–graphic image contain a profile face; however, on

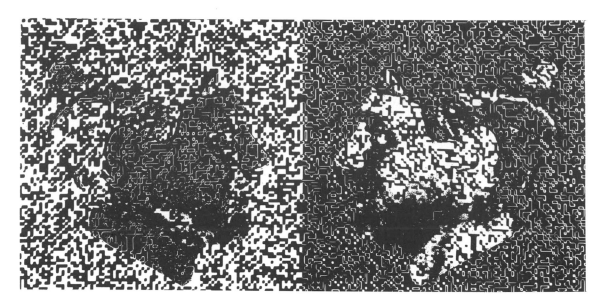

4.83 *Binocular rivalry.*

4.84 *Cyclopean views.*

the left the facial area is solarised and the background is in high contrast, whereas the reverse applies to the right side. These patterns are presented as a pair because random dot arrays have been used extensively in research on stereoscopic depth perception. Typically they are presented in pairs that appear indistinguishable from one another, but when the random dot patterns are presented to different eyes, areas within them appear to stand out in depth, due to the small displacements of these areas in the left and right patterns. Here, however, the two patterns would engage in binocular rivalry because the random dot pattern on the left is reversed on the right, in addition to the reversed contrasts in the two halves.

In Figure 4.84 full-face views are combined with graphics that themselves suggest the structure of eyes. Moreover, the spectacles on the face are framed by the partially overlapping circles in the centre of each one. The graphic design is in high contrast in one half and solarised in the other. Within

4.85 *Observer.*

4.86 (Below) *Bilateral symmetry.*

each of these halves the same solarised image of a face is combined with the underlying design.

The paired, eye-like configuration is used once more in Figure 4.85. Close inspection reveals a figure with outstretched arms as the dominant feature, whereas distant viewing (or using the other means of defocusing the pictorial image) gives an alternative interpretation – of the shaded eyes and nose of a face. The two components utilise concentric circles, one with the figure embedded in it graphically and the other a photo–graphic combination. The same superimposition of the face and concentric circles was used in both halves of the picture, but one was combined with a high contrast design and the other with a solarised one.

Figure 4.86 presents various manipulations of both photo images and solarisations. The faces that are presented in reflection in the upper two designs are combined in the lower one. That is, both faces are presented together, and it might be possible to see each in turn – somewhat like the alternations that occur with the vase/faces figure. The image on the upper right is a combination of two solarised images and that on the left was formed from a solarised and a hidden image. The lower one was derived from two hidden images, and its graphical components, the thick and thin inclined lines, connect with elements in each of the other patterns.

The final two photo–graphic images in this sec-

tion forge a link with the next section. They present graphic designs that are seemingly abstract, but which were initially drawn with the silhouettes of the photo images in mind. For example, in Figure 4.87 the left half represents the original drawn design. It is combined on the right with both a solarised design (the outline pattern) and a photo image. A part of Figure 4.88 was also a drawn design, although which part is not immediately evident. The original graphic design consisted of gently waving lines that were drawn to cover the picture surface, apart from the silhouette of the ballerina. The negative of this drawing was combined with a horizontal grating, which produced the moiré fringes. The photo image was projected onto the area of the silhouette to produce the left image, and this was completely solarised to give the right one. The rhythm of the moiré fringes seems to balance the poise and grace of the ballerina.

Harmony of Figure and Form

The graphic designs used in the previous section were generally abstract. Where they were related to the photographic image that they carried, the relation was conceptual rather than graphical. In this section the graphic designs echo the contours of the photographic images they embody. Accordingly, there is a union between the photo and graphic images. The recurrent theme in this marriage of figure and form is the human body. The photo images have, however, been simplified and stylised

4.87 *Splash.*

4.88 *Pas de deux.*

to conform to the constraints imposed by the graphics. That is, the major concerns are the demands of the graphic design, to which the photo images are required to bend.

None of the techniques used in producing these images differ substantially from those described in the Appendices. Thus, there is little need for commentary. The onus is on you, the observer, to seek the components combined, embedded, hidden or solarised within these pictorial images.

4.89 (Facing page)
Profiles.

4.90 *Rotating faces.*

4.91 *Bali dancing.*

4.92 *Catherine wheel.*

4.93 *Legacies.*

4.95 *Overlays.*

4.94 *Mannequins.*

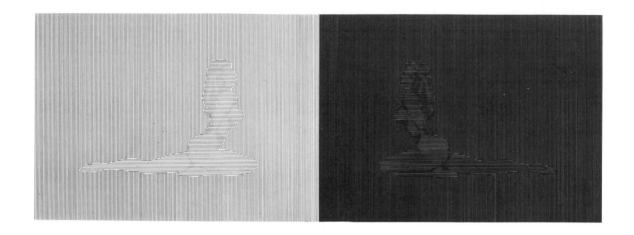

4.96 *Astigmats.*   **4.97** *Prolific profiles.*

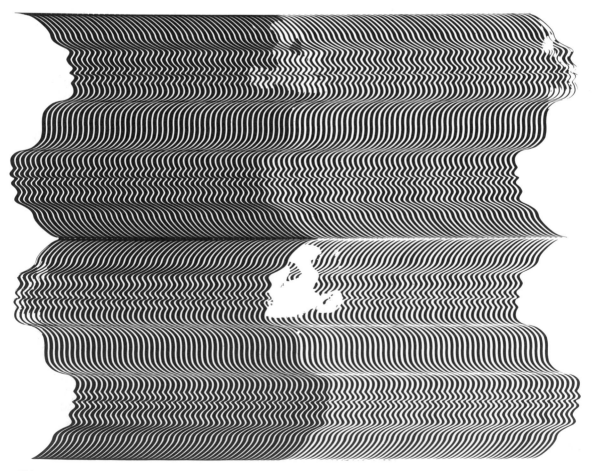

4.98 *A symmetry.*

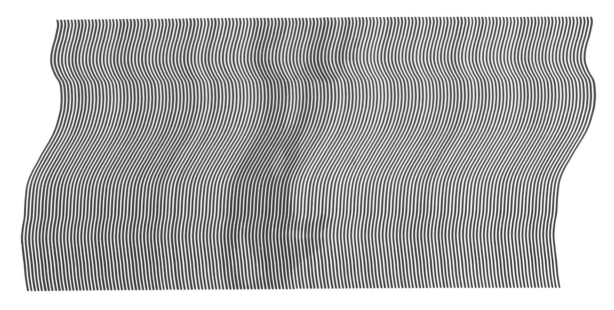

4.99 *Torso.*

4.100 *Trio.*

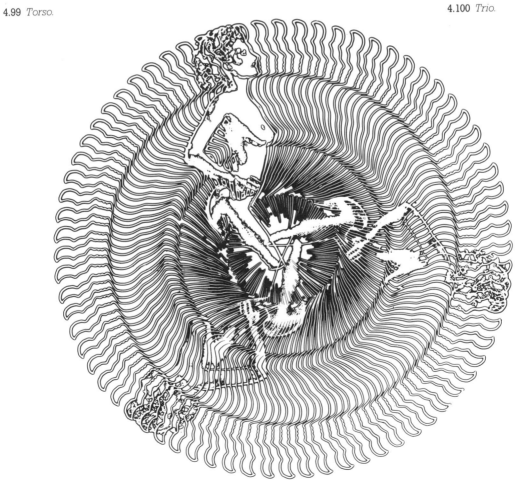

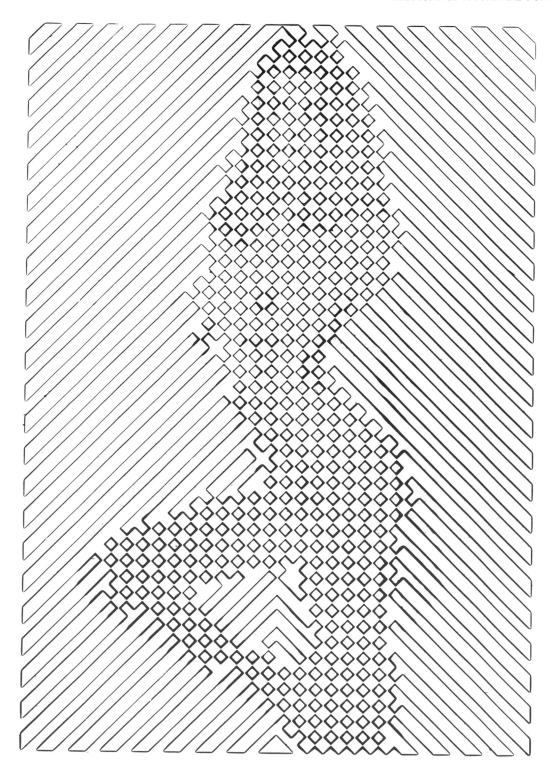

4.101 *Checked mate.*

4.102 *Digital picture.*   **4.103** *Rear view mirror.*

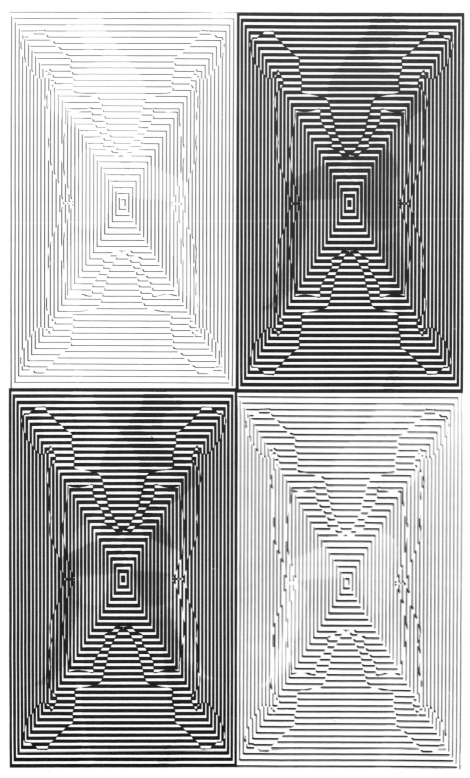

4.104 *Op-positions.*

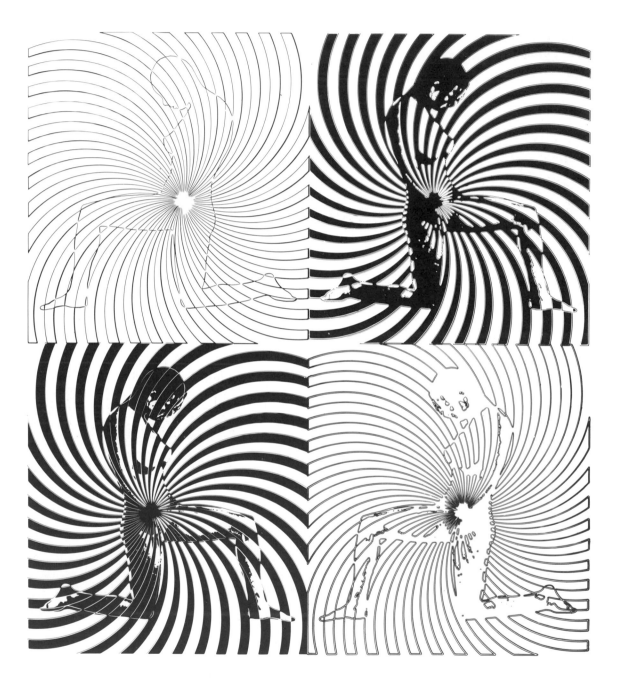

4.105 *Reflections.*

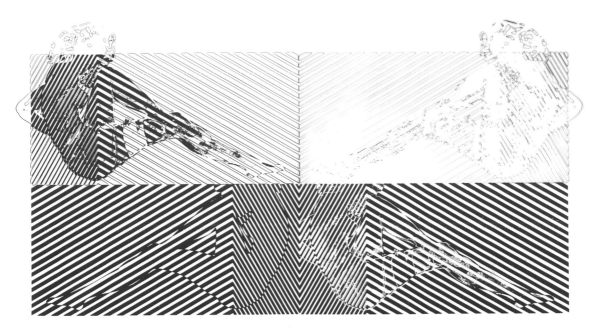

4.106 (Above) *Head lines.*

4.107 (Right) *Ghostly images.*

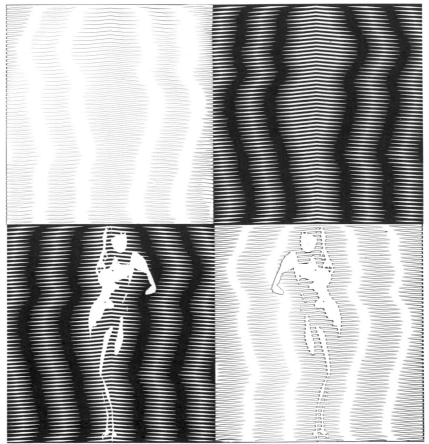

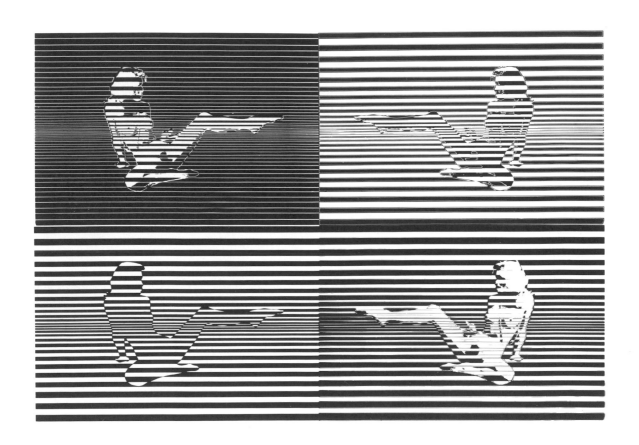

4.108 *Frequently spatial.*

Bibliography

General

Arnheim, R. (1970). *Visual thinking.* London: Faber & Faber. Arnheim argues that visual perception is not the passive recording of stimulus material but an active problem-solving process. One of the principal aspects of the intelligence of perception is taken to be the Gestalt principles of organisation. Many examples of their operation are presented in this book. Arnheim distinguishes between three functions of images: signs, symbols and pictures. He also examines the nature of perceptual abstraction and the use of visual aids in education.

Kanizsa, G. (1979). *Organization in vision.* New York: Praeger. Gaetano Kanizsa is an accomplished artist as well as a perceptual psychologist. His artistic interests have resulted in this book being visually as well as conceptually challenging. He presents a modern version of Gestalt psychology addressed to many problems encountered when viewing pictorial stimuli. He discusses perceptual organisation, apparent motion, colour appearance, transparency, and anomalous contours. Kanizsa is best known in visual science for his work on illusory contours. These are illustrated in numerous figures, and interpreted in terms of amodal completion.

Vitz, P. C. & Glimcher, A. B. (1984). *Modern art and modern science. A parallel analysis of vision.* New York: Praeger. The authors advance the thesis that movements in art since the middle of the 19th century have been fuelled by ideas arising in visual science. They draw support for their thesis from interactions between art and science in the areas of colour mixing, stereoscopic depth perception, Gestalt grouping principles, and illusions of motion. The influences of still and sequenced photography on art are also examined, and many illustrations from both art and visual science are included. The authors state: "Unfortunately modern art history has suffered from its failure to investigate science and technology, which have been the two most dynamic factors of recent history."

Waddington, C. H. (1969). *Behind appearance. A study of the relations between painting and the natural sciences in this century.* Edinburgh: Edinburgh University Press. A geneticist directs a keen eye to the painting of this century, from the emergence of cubism to the flowering of op art. Two major streams are divined – the geometricisers (cubists, de Stijl, futurists and constructivists) and the magicians (Dada and surrealists). Waddington argues that the former were preoccupied with time, trying either to contain it in or to expel it from their canvases. The latter represented a rejection of science and a refuge in popularised Freudian concepts. The geometricisers are said to have been influenced by ideas of relativity in science, particularly in quantum physics. The illustrations presented are of high quality, as are the insightful links made between the two principal means we use to explore our world – observation and experiment.

Wade, N. J. (1982). *The art and science of visual illusions.* London: Routledge & Kegan Paul. This book tries to forge links between art and science in the context of op art. Many original geometrical designs are presented and the effects they produce are described in the language of visual science. Works in the op genre are classified according to the visual effects they elicit, like Gestalt grouping, optical distortions, interference patterns, after-images, subjective contours and binocular rivalry. Geometrical optical illusions are also presented, and a final section combines op patterns with illusion configurations to yield op-tical illusions. The book contains an envelope of transparencies that can be placed over printed designs either to generate moiré patterns or to induce illusions of extent and orientation.

Allusions to Visual Processes

Arnason, H. H. (1977). *A history of modern art. Painting, sculpture, architecture.* Revised and enlarged edition. London: Thames & Hudson. A standard, well-illustrated guide to art from impressionism to photo-realism. It is particularly good on the emergence of cubism.

Barrett, C. (1970). *Op art.* London: Studio Vista. Op art is placed in the broader context of artistic style, deriving influences from Turner and the neo-Impressionists. There are many illustrations of the genre from its heyday during the mid-1960s.

Diehl, G. (1973). *Vasarely.* Translated by E. B. Hennessy. Naefels, Switzerland: Bonfini Press. A collection of, and commentary on, Victor Vasarely's work from 1935 to 1970. The emphasis is on his earlier pictures, although there are some good reproductions of his coloured designs from the 1960s.

Fineman, M. (1981). *The inquisitive eye.* New York: Oxford University Press. Fineman encourages the reader to construct simple pieces of apparatus in order to experience both static and dynamic visual phenomena. There are instructions to see several illusions of movement, to produce Leonardo's window and anamorphoses, as well as illusory contours, impossible figures, figure-ground reversals and grouping effects.

Gombrich, E. H. (1979). *The sense of order. A study in the psychology of decorative art.* Oxford: Phaidon. The book is a series of essays (the Wrightsman Lectures) addressed to the perception of pattern. They are grouped under the headings of decoration, the perception of order, and psychology and history. The sections relating to visual ambiguities and regular geometrical designs are to be found in the second part.

Parola, R. (1969). *Optical art.* London: Reinhold. René Parola states that "today, the science of art cannot be separated from the art of science". He presents mostly his own and his students' designs to show how simple pattern elements can produce increasingly complex visual effects. The book contains colour as well as black-and-white illustrations.

Riley, B. (1971). *Bridget Riley. Paintings and drawings 1951–71.* London: The Arts Council. A well-illustrated exhibition catalogue, charting Bridget Riley's development from drawing to high-contrast black-and-white paintings in the early-1960s. There are also examples of her colour paintings from the late-1960s.

Riley, B. (1978). *Bridget Riley. Works 1959–78.* London: The British Council. A catalogue for an international touring exhibition. In addition to reproducing many of Riley's well-known black-and-white works, there are examples of her paintings of the 1970s in which she tended to use the same repetitive contours (produced using a template) but manipulating the colour relations between adjacent areas. The commentary describes the preliminary studies for some of her paintings.

Thurston, J. B. & Carraher, R. G. (1966). *Optical illusions and the visual arts.* New York: van Nostrand-Reinhold. Optical illusions are broadly defined to include afterimages, contrast effects, shadowing, periodic patterns, moiré, Gestalt grouping, geometrical illusions and reversing figures. Many examples of their expression in the fine arts and photography are shown. A glossary of optical illusions is provided.

Vasarely, V. (1965). *Vasarely.* Neuchatel: Griffon. This book contains many reproductions of Vasarely's pictures together with many of his words. The former are generally more comprehensible. There is a set of transparencies with designs printed on them so that they can be placed on and moved over similar or negative designs printed in the book.

Wade, N. J. (1978). Op art and visual perception. *Perception, 7,* 21–46. The article reprints some well-known black-and-white op art works and relates them to the underlying phenomena they tap. A little history of studies of the phenomena is also given.

Wade, N. J. (1987). Allusory contours. In S. Petry & G. E. Meyer (Eds.), *The perception of illusory contours.* New York: Springer. This is a chapter from a book devoted to illusory (or subjective) contours. It contains many examples of the phenomena, describing the stimulus combinations that can yield them.

Wilding, L. (1987). *Ludwig Wilding retrospektive 1949–1987.* Kaiserlautern: Pfalzgalerie des bezirksverbands Pfalz. Ludwig Wilding is an artist with a keen interest in visual science, which is clearly evident from this comprehensive exhibition catalogue. The works are grouped under four headings: two-dimensional superimpositions (moiré patterns); objects with apparent motion and three-dimensional moiré patterns; pictures and objects for two eyes; and paradoxical objects.

Photo–graphic Images

Brewster, D. (1856). *The stereoscope. Its history, theory, and construction.* London: John Murray. Brewster invented a popular lens model of the stereoscope in 1849, and Wheatstone had earlier (in 1832) invented a mirror stereoscope. Brewster's description of the instrument's applications is useful, although his history is biased against Wheatstone.

Grafton, C. B. (1976). *Optical designs in motion with moiré overlays.* New York: Dover. A collection of 27 printed geometrical designs, together with a single transparency that can be placed over them in turn and moved to produce dynamic moiré patterns.

Larcher, J. (1974). *Geometrical designs and optical art.* New York: Dover. Jean Larcher is a French artist and 70 of his black-and-white op art works are reprinted here, without any commentary.

Oster, G. (1965). Optical art. *Applied Optics, 4,* 1359–1369. Gerald Oster is a chemist and an artist. He has produced many three-dimensional periodic structures that generate dynamic moiré effects when the observer moves. Here he traces the history of the artistic style (backwards in time) and the phenomena manipulated by op artists are briefly described. He also discusses some subjective visual phenomena.

Oster, G. (1968). *The science of moiré patterns.* Second edition. Barrington, N.J.: Edmund Scientific. The mathematics of moiré patterns are described in this booklet before relating them to science, engineering and psychology. A kit of transparencies is included so that readers can generate their own moiré patterns.

Oster, G. & Nishijima, Y. (1963). Moiré patterns. *Scientific American, 208 (5)*, 54–63. The theory and applications of moiré are described. The two-colour illustrations make the principles underlying their expression readily visible.

Hidden Images

Descartes, R. (1664/1909). Traité de l'homme. In C. Adam & P. Tannery (Eds.), *Oeuvres de Descartes. Volume XI.* Paris: Cerf. Descartes' original text and figures are reprinted together with an extensive commentary. Figure 48, depicting the then known anatomy of the brain, provides the background for Figure 4.74.

Howard, I. P. (1982). *Human visual orientation.* Chichester: Wiley. A comprehensive review of research on visual direction and orientation. The geometry of binocular vision is clearly described as are binocular eye movements. The final chapter, on orientation and shape perception, examines the difficulty that we have in recognising polarised (normally vertical) objects when they are inverted.

Hubel, D. H. & Wiesel, T. N. (1979). Brain mechanisms of vision. *Scientific American, 241 (3)*, 130–144. A description of the functional architecture of the visual system, drawing mainly on their own extensive researches for which they were awarded the Nobel prize. Their reconstruction of the ocular dominance pattern over each visual cortical area provides the background for Figure 4.75 (although I have applied artistic licence in rotating the patterns through 90°).

Seymour, P. H. K. (1979). *Human visual cognition.* London: Collier-Macmillan. This book is concerned with the cognitive processes that are initiated by visual stimuli, such as reading. Figure 4.76 uses text from the Preface to the book.

5 PICTURES AND PERCEPTION

In the preceding chapters I have described and displayed a variety of visual allusions that are present in pictures. Allusions to three-dimensional space were examined in Chapter Two, to the meanings of words via letter shapes in Chapter Three, and to the almost hidden images carried in other designs in Chapter Four. In this final chapter I will return to the general issues raised in Chapter One, namely the relationship between pictures and perception. I do not think that the relationship will be adequately understood by restricting consider-

ation to picture perception; we also need to address the problems presented when producing pictures. Thus, my theoretical concern is with the production as well as the perception of pictorial images.

The general model proposed in Chapter One is re-presented here (Figure 5.1), as it will provide the focus for the concluding discussion. The model developed from an analysis of the term *image*, and the model is based on its multiple but qualified use. That is, the term is not used in vague isolation but with more qualified precision. One consequence of

5.1 A re-presentation of the model for perception and picture production introduced in Chapter One.

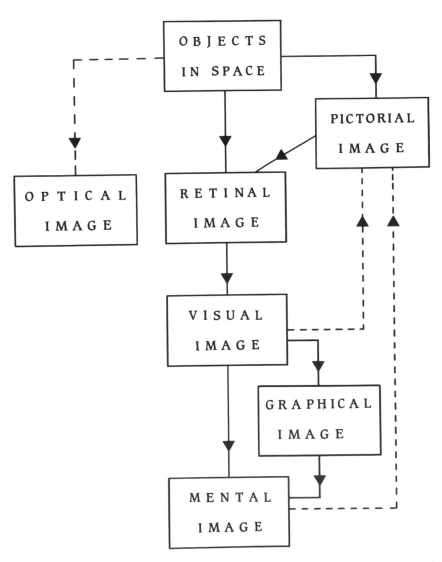

this has been the description of a sequence of image levels that can be applied both to the analysis of vision and to account for different artistic styles. Therefore, although the model is simple the claims made for it are bold. There are virtues in this simplicity in so far as it has laid bare some fundamental misunderstandings about vision and it has also suggested a general development of the manner in which space has been represented in the history of pictorial art. The measure of the model's success will be the extent to which the ideas reflected in it stimulate experiment, debate and criticism.

In recapitulating the essential features of the model I will start with perception because perception precedes pictorial representation. In evolutionary terms perception is prior, and artistically the picture-maker must see the scene and the surface before making marks on the latter. The starting point for perception is the layout and arrangements of objects in space. It is essential that we perceive objects accurately in space so that our actions are appropriate. This three-dimensional starting point is summarised by the phrase *objects in space* in the model. Light reflected from objects can enter the eye to generate a *retinal image*. There has been considerable confusion in the psychological literature concerning the nature of the retinal image, and this confusion has resulted in some muddled thinking about the process of perception. The retinal image refers to the pattern of electro-chemical activity occurring in the light-sensitive receptors in the retina. The concept might be extended to include the neural activity in the retina that follows stimulation of the receptors. It is, perhaps, a mistake to describe it in the singular, as *a* retinal image, because the patterns of electro-chemical and neural activity are continuous. There is no obvious starting point because the retinal receptors are active in the absence of light. However, the retinal image is here defined as the electro-chemical activity that follows stimulation by light. Once stimulated the receptors themselves take an appreciable time to respond and to recover from the incidence of light upon them. Therefore, the dimension of time is integrally involved in the activity I refer to as the retinal image.

The theoretical confusion concerning the retinal image relates to an alternative definition of it – as a time-frozen *optical image*. This conceptual convenience derives from Kepler's description of image formation in the eye, and ever since the 17th century the retinal image has been thought of in similar pictorial terms. In other words, the retina is likened to a curved screen onto which a picture of objects is projected. It is certainly the case that the optical properties of the eye are similar in many ways to those of a camera, but it is a profound error to assume that there is anything akin to a picture in the eye. The retina does not operate on a time-frozen view of the world or even on a sequence of them. The retina works in some ways that are very unlike a camera – not only is it functioning continually over time but it is also moving continually, either because of involuntary eye movements or due to the voluntary pursuit of moving targets. Despite these facts, known to every visual scientist, the optical abstraction of the static image on the retina is still embraced. Indeed, it has become difficult to examine vision theoretically without introducing a pictorial metaphor at the first processing level. It is for this reason that the box containing the optical image in Figure 5.1 leads nowhere. The optical image might have been a convenient abstraction in the past, but it is now a theoretical albatross that distracts visual scientists from the task of understanding vision. The task has not been made any easier by the current preoccupation with computational models of vision, which are essentially involved in the processing of camera-derived time-frozen images.

The retinal image – the electro-chemical and neural activity initiated in the retina – is transmitted to the brain where signals from the two eyes, from their movements and also movements of the head, are integrated in some way to yield a *visual image*. The visual image refers to the perception of surface orientations, textures, locations and motions. Objects will be defined in terms of groupings of coherent surfaces, but the objects are not labelled verbally at this stage. This is the level at which all biological vision operates – the resolution of surfaces in three-dimensional space so that actions appropriate to them can be performed. The visual image, then, provides a three-dimensional representation of the objects in space that have formed retinal images: it is a representation of the immediate surroundings of the observer. The task of visual science should concern the manner in which such representations are achieved.

Any particular significance of the surfaces or objects would not be registered at the visual image level. In order for this to occur the next level, the *mental image*, would need to be accessed. For all species the learned associations between previous visual images and rewards would be formed at the mental image level. For humans, of course, much more can be accomplished at the mental image stage – most specifically the categorisation of surfaces and objects in terms of linguistic categories. These mental images will encompass more general characteristics of the surfaces than is available in the visual image. Thus, there could be more abstract representations of objects than those available from the constrained viewpoint yielding the visual image; this has been called an object-centred description. Within the mental image the representations can be manipulated in the absence of direct input from the visual image: we can imagine novel objects or new worlds when we close our eyes, and we can make things change within them.

So far we have not referred to pictures as such, but only to the consequences of normal perception of objects in three-dimensional space. Pictures are objects in space and have a similar status to other objects – they are accurately perceived and can be appropriately handled. However, the pattern on the surface of the picture – the *pictorial image* – is almost always treated as a representation of something else, of some other space than the one it occupies. This is the traditional dual reality that pictures are said to possess. The question addressed earlier was where is this dual reality processed in the scheme of images proposed here? Clearly, a pictorial image can form a retinal and visual image, but this would result in its veridical perception as a flat textured surface. It was suggested that an additional level is required to account for the allusory nature of the pictorial image – the *graphical image*. At the graphical image stage the contents of the pictorial image are treated in terms of the surfaces they represent rather than what they are. Thus, the arrangement of lines might create the allusion to a space they do not occupy, to an allusory three-dimensionality. The familiarity of the surfaces and objects alluded to will be dependent upon access to the mental image level, as was the case for the perception of objects in space. This access to the mental image – to memory – is even more evident when dealing with the most specifically pictorial images, written script.

I have suggested that the model outlined here can be applied to the production of pictures. Indeed, the dotted lines ascending from the visual and mental image levels to the pictorial image indicate ways in which marks made on the picture plane can be influenced by those processes. However, a bolder claim is made: the development of artistic styles is also reflected in the sequencing of the model. Proceeding in the reverse direction to perception (starting from the mental image), different ways of alluding to three-dimensional space can be associated with the imaging levels described. Of course, all styles of pictorial representation engage all the levels of imaging in the model, because they all involve perception. None the less, it is suggested that greater emphasis has been implicitly placed on particular levels at various periods in the history of art.

Let us consider, as an initial example, the cave paintings of Southern France and Northern Spain. These remarkable relics are to be found in deep recesses of the caves, which are often difficult to reach. Accordingly, they must have been painted by torchlight. The subjects were mostly animals, like bison and horses, and they were usually depicted in outline; if the body of the animal represented was painted it was probably from mouth-spraying the pigment inside an outlined area. The purposes the paintings served remains a matter of speculation, but the function must have been of considerable significance because the paintings were produced over a period of thousands of years. In the context of the present discussion what is of greater relevance is the viewpoint from which the animals were represented – they are almost all depicted in profile.

The issue here is very similar to that raised when discussing Magritte's *Perfidy of Images* (see Figure 1.4). The stereotypical view (in which the asymmetrical axis of the object is minimally foreshortened) is the most informative (or least ambiguous) pictorial image of that object. The asymmetrical or major axes of the animals depicted on the cave walls were also minimally foreshortened. The animals themselves were unlikely to have been seen in this way in the natural environment: when hunting they would have been seen from all viewpoints – approaching and receding as well as in all intermediate bearings with respect to the hunter. However, it is obvious that the cave artists were not painting what they saw. They did not paint from life or even from death! The access to the vaults in which the paintings are found are usually so confined that a large dead beast could not have been manoeuvred into them. Therefore, the artists were painting from memory – in my terms, they were representing their mental images of the animals. This does not itself answer the question regarding profile depiction, but it is a step towards an answer. If the manner in which the mental image of the animals is coded in memory corresponds to the stereotypical view (the profile) then this could account for the mode of representation adopted. It has been argued that the pictorial image of an object is most informative when its major axes are not foreshortened; it could similarly be argued that such economy is operating in the mental coding and storage of visually-derived information about objects in the environment.

Another related speculation can also be advanced. Perhaps at the genesis of cave painting many viewpoints were depicted, corresponding more closely to the visual images of animals encountered in the wild. Thereafter, certain pictorial images of the animals could have proved more readily recognisable than others, namely profiles. The ready recognition of profile pictorial images could then have acted as a spur for generations of other artists to represent them in this way, so that their other social functions could be fulfilled. Even here, at the dawning of artistic representation, we find the counterpoint appearing between reflections of perception on the one hand and convention on the other. As soon as the artificial dimension of pictorial imaging becomes available to a culture it is no longer possible to ignore the influence of earlier pictorial images on the expression of later ones.

This point is evident when considering one of the next styles to emerge – early Egyptian art. The prevalent painting style involved stereotyped profiles of the head (usually with a frontally viewed eye) connected to frontal representations of the torso. It could be said that the minimal foreshortening principle was being applied to the major articulating parts of the body independently. However, the three-dimensional sculptures produced at the same time were in correspondence to the dimensions of the human form, and they are immediately recognisable by us today. Thus, the abstraction of shape (two-dimensional representation) from form (three-dimensional structure) followed conventional rules that were not deemed so necessary for the modelling of form.

The conventional rules that are brought to bear on painting styles can reflect the influences of former pictorial imagery as well as the prevailing social and religious values (as in Byzantine religious iconography). There are also likely to be universal features of the visual image that are incorporated into the conventions. Two such are those of interposition and height-in-the-field. When two objects are at different distances but have almost the same direction with respect to an observer, then the nearer object will obscure parts of the more distant one. Interposition is embodied in all representational styles, and this aspect of the visual image is transferred to the pictorial image, thereby alluding to the separation of the objects represented. On a flat surface objects that are farther away appear to be higher than those that are nearer. Accordingly, height in the picture plane is used as an allusion to distance in most representational styles. For many medieval and Eastern paintings these provided the principal means of alluding to three-dimensional space.

In the late medieval period the visual image started to play an increasingly important role in determining the contents of the pictorial image. Artists were concerned with distilling aspects of their own perception, and capturing them in the pictorial image. The visual image (our immediate perceptual experience) corresponds closely to the three-dimensional layout of space. Therefore, objects (like people) of the same size but at different distances from us look the same size. Objects do not appear to fluctuate in size or shape when they move towards or away from us. This aspect of perceptual constancy is reflected in many medieval paintings: people are represented in the pictorial image as about the same size despite the fact that some occlude (and would be nearer) others, and some are pictured higher in the plane (and would be farther away) than others. The problems arose when different features of the perceived world had to be integrated in the pictorial image. These problems did not arise so much for the people portrayed as they did for the ground and landscape in which they were portrayed. It is the inconsistencies of the represented architectures and grounds that are taken as the hallmark of pre-Renaissance painting, and this attests to the impossibility of capturing the visual image on a picture plane.

It is suggested therefore that stone-age artists represented their mental images of significant objects in their environment. There might also have been some conventional influences from the observation of other pictorial images. Later styles of painting, like Egyptian, can be thought of as blending aspects of the mental and visual image – what they stored mentally and what they saw. By the late medieval period artists were relying much more on their vision of objects in space when producing their pictorial images, and so can be thought of as trying to represent the visual image level of perceptual processing. Thus, styles of representational painting can be considered as emphasising imaging processes that progress from the more central levels towards the more peripheral.

This trend is followed dramatically at the next stage of artistic style – the emergence of linear perspective in the Renaissance. Linear perspective harnessed Euclid's laws of optics into a set of rules for scaling dimensions in the pictorial image. In order to comply with these rules artists had to disregard their visual images and use a range of artificial aids to facilitate scaling the contents of the pictorial image. It has often been remarked that perspective artists were representing the retinal image, but this analysis betrays the misunderstanding of the retinal image inveighed against earlier in this chapter. Moreover, the nature of image formation in the eye was not even dimly appreciated at the time (in the early-15th century). Theories of vision were then generally formulated in terms of light emission from the eye – light was projected from the eye to meet objects and then returned to the eye with some image of the objects. Linear perspective consists of interrupting Euclid's visual cone, encompassing all the rays leaving and entering the eye, artificially in front of the eye. Both Alberti and Leonardo likened a painting in perspective to viewing a scene through a glass window from a particular point (with one eye) and marking the position of contours on the glass. Interrupting the path of light from a scene in front of the eye is equivalent to its projection on a screen behind the eye. That is, Alberti's window is projectively equivalent to the theoretical abstraction of the optical image. It is with the misjudgement of hindsight that perspective has been equated with the retinal image. This misjudgement has had many unfortunate manifestations. For example, it has encouraged the pictorial metaphor in the early analysis of vision, which has resulted in the consideration of vision as a process of picture analysis. In addition, it has led commentators on art to think of perspective projections as simulacra of the space they represent. A pictorial image in linear perspective is often considered to be a more faithful representation of the scene depicted than any alternative style.

The optical image is a conceptual convenience when analysing vision; it is an abstraction that does not correspond to any stage in normal vision. Linear perspective is a procedural convenience for creating an allusion to three-dimensional space in a pictorial image. There is an infinite number of perspective views that could be made of the same three-dimensional scene. For instance, the scene could be photographed from the same position, but the characteristics of the photographic images will depend upon the cameras and lenses used, the varieties of which are vast. Moreover, the scene would be recognisable from all the photographic images, even when looking at them with two eyes and making no attempts to find the appropriate centres of projection. These are amongst the reasons, detailed in Chapter Two, for treating pictorial images in linear perspective with less awe than might be customary in analyses of artistic representation.

Subsequent developments in art, up to the late-19th century, generally accepted the perspective rules for representing space, and styles were distinguished largely on the basis of their subject matter. Styles in the late-19th century, like neo-Impressionism, were influenced by contemporary scientific studies of vision. For example, various phenomena associated with colour vision were incorporated into some painterly procedures. Most particularly, the differences between colour mixing of lights (which is called additive) and pigments (subtractive) were appreciated by scientists, and it was argued that more faithful renditions of natural (light-reflecting) scenes would be produced by making pigments act like light in their combination. This proved possible if small spots of pigment were applied to the canvas in pure colours, so that the colour combination could occur in the eye rather than on the palette. Seurat and his colleagues put this into practice with their pointilliste paintings, which were thought to be more life-like than those produced with traditional methods of mixing pigments on the palette prior to applying them to the canvas. They could be thought of as attempting to produce a pattern of retinal stimulation that was more closely akin to that occurring in the natural environment.

The neo-Impressionists initiated a trend that has become more prevalent in the present century – the influence of visual science on visual art. Often the influence is less direct than in the case of Seurat's style, but there is a similarity in the underlying ethos of both. Twentieth century visual art and visual science have been driven by considerations of two-dimensional stimuli. In visual science almost all phenomena studied are those produced on a two-dimensional surface. That is, pictorial images (often of extreme simplicity) provide the stimuli for scientific investigations of vision, rather than objects in three-dimensional space. Similarly visual art now considers the pictorial image – the picture plane – as the appropriate subject matter for its enquiry. Rather than being a reflection of some allusory space the flat picture plane, and the marks made on it, are of intrinsic interest. Thus, varieties of geometrical abstraction emphasise the interplay of shapes, devoid of external reference, or the unreality of the allusory space is emphasised via surreal images that defy the projective rules of perspective. The style selected for detailed scrutiny in Chapter Four was op art. There it was argued that the paintings are reflecting aspects of processing at the graphical image level. That is, the perceptual aberrations that arise when we look at geometrically periodic pictorial images are due to processes operating at the graphical image level.

Visual art and visual science, which have pursued separate courses for so long, can now be thought of as converging on similar concerns – analyses at the graphical image level. While it is laudable for visual art to examine the artificial nature of its own enterprise, it is a less beneficial goal for visual science. Most modern visual science is necessarily directed at understanding the graphical image level of processing, because the stimuli are pictorial images. This might be a reasonable approach to the study of part of human vision, since humans alone produce pictorial images. It would not, however, lead to any wider appreciation of the way we, and other biological organisms, respond to objects in space. The analysis of the graphical image will provide insights into the allusory nature of pictorial stimuli. It might be an illusion to think that it will illuminate our understanding of vision generally.

Bibliography

General

Blatt, S. J. (1984). *Continuity and change in art. The development of modes of representation.* Hillsdale, N.J.: Lawrence Erlbaum Associates Inc. Sydney Blatt considers that development in artistic representation follows the course of individual cognitive development, which in turn is influenced by social and cultural factors. He advances this thesis in terms of the major changes that took place with the emergence of linear perspective and then conceptual art. "We can only understand our universe through the cognitive structures that are part of our cultural heritage and are available to us within our current cultural context."

Deregowski, J. B. (1989). Real space and represented space: Cross-cultural perspectives. *Behavioral and Brain Sciences, 12,* 51–119. Jan Deregowski starts from the assumption that "pictorial space is not a convention but a derivative of real space". He suggests that there are two types of representational picture: one leads to recognition of the three-dimensional object without any impression of three-dimensional space; the other evokes an impression of space as well as yielding object recognition. These ideas are applied to cross-cultural studies on picture perception, and he concludes that the same perceptual task can be performed using a variety of skills, which will differ between cultures. There are also 26 critical commentaries on the paper, together with a response to them by Deregowski. In defence of his approach he remarks: "If one were to wait for a proper theory of picture perception before embarking on cross-cultural work, then one would have to wait forever."

Honour, H. & Fleming, J. (1982). *A world history of art.* London: Macmillan. A prize-winning history of painting, sculpture and architecture which is impressive in its scope. Its treatment of the art of the East is its particular strength. There are five parts: foundations of art; art and world religions; sacred and secular art; the making of the modern world; and 20th century art.

Janson, H. W. (1970). *A history of art. A survey of the visual arts from the dawn of history to the present day.* New revised and enlarged edition. London: Thames & Hudson. A survey of art from the stone age to the skyscraper. Janson commences: "When did man start creating works of art? What prompted him to do so? What did these earliest works look like? Every history of art must begin with these questions – and with the admission that we cannot answer them." The book is divided into sections concerned with: the ancient world (from prehistory to Byzantium); the middle ages (from Islamic to Gothic art); the Renaissance (from late Gothic to Northern Baroque); and the modern world (from neo-classicism to this century). Architecture and sculpture are considered alongside painting, and illustrated time charts are included for each section.

Additional

Arnheim, R. (1966). *Towards a psychology of art. Collected essays.* Berkeley: University of California Press. Arnheim has written elsewhere: "When art historians and critics deal with art objects as visual images they rely inescapably on psychology." Arnheim's psychology draws upon Gestalt studies of perception which proposed organising processes that structure either visual images or pictorial representations. His position is clearly stated in this collection of essays, which are grouped under the headings: the sense of sight; the visible world; symbols; generalities; plus a postscript to teachers and artists.

Crozier, W. R. & Chapman, A. J. (Eds.) (1984). *Cognitive processes in the perception of art.* Amsterdam: North-Holland. The edited proceedings of a conference. Of particular interest are chapters by Pratt, on a theoretical framework for thinking about depiction, and by Willats, on getting the drawing to look right as well as to be right.

Deregowski, J. B. (1984). *Distortion in art: The eye and the mind.* London: Routledge & Kegan Paul. Deregowski here examines art forms in which systematic distortions are introduced. He introduces his distinction between epitomic and eidolic pictorial images; objects represented can be recognised in each but only the latter evokes an impression of depth. He also discusses the typical (profile and frontal) views of objects that have been represented since the stone age. He concludes: "Complex pictures all rely in some manner and to some extent on perceptual experience, but the extent to which they do so varies."

Freeman, N. H. & Cox, M. V. (Eds.) (1985). *Visual order. The nature and development of pictorial representation.* Cambridge: Cambridge University Press. This is a very useful collection of essays. Those by Costall, on how meaning covers the traces, by Pratt, on traditional artistic practices, by Hagen, on the absence of developmental trends in art, and by Willatts, on drawing systems, are particularly recommended.

Gombrich, E. H. (1972). *The story of art.* Twelfth edition enlarged and revised. London: Phaidon. A very readable history of art. The treatment of prehistoric art is rather cursory and the book's strength lies in the period from the Renaissance to the late 19th century.

Gombrich, E. H. (1982). *The image and the eye. Further studies in the psychology of pictorial representation.* Oxford: Phaidon. This collection of essays concentrates on the perception of images rather than patterns. An image is taken to be an imitation in some sense, and it is distinguished from a word, which is symbolic and conventional. The contrast between word and image, or between convention and realism, is the subject of Gombrich's final essay, and he sits firmly on the side of realism. Of the many other essays, those on moment and movement in art, mirror and map, and theories of pictorial representation, are of especial interest.

Goodman, N. (1969). *Languages of art. An approach to a theory of symbols.* London: Oxford University Press. Nelson Goodman focused debate on the nature of representation with this book, by arguing for the arbitrariness of the symbols used. "The most literal portrait and the most prosaic passage are as much symbols, and as 'highly symbolic', as the most fanciful and figurative."

Graziosi, P. (1960). *Palaeolithic art.* London: Faber & Faber. A comprehensive and well-illustrated survey of European stone age carving, painting and sculpture.

Stillings, N. A., Feinstein, M. H., Garfield, J. L., Rissland, E. L., Rosenbaum, D. A., Weisler, S. E., & Baker-Ward, L. (1987). *Cognitive science. An introduction.* London: The MIT Press. Cognitive science is considered to integrate psychology, artificial intelligence, linguistics, philosophy and neuroscience in their approaches to information processing and knowledge acquisition. These involve stages of representation and formal rules for the transformation from one level to another. This is a textbook describing the cognitive approach. It discusses cognitive categories and prototypes (most typical members of a category) and it concludes with a chapter examining computational approaches to vision.

APPENDIX 1: HIGH-CONTRAST PHOTOGRAPHIC TECHNIQUES

The possibilities of manipulating photographic images were created the moment William Henry Fox Talbot invented the negative process in the 19th century. Any negative that can be reproduced can also be manipulated. In general terms, we still use the system Talbot devised for reproducing images. Light reflected from objects in the environment is focused by the lenses of a camera onto a surface (the film) comprised of silver salts that are transformed by it. The transformation is not evident until the film has been processed; before this stage it is called a latent image. The processing of the film consists of two essential phases – development and fixing. Development involves reducing the silver salts to metallic silver, so that those parts of the film previously exposed to light will change to black. This negative image is then fixed with a solution that removes from the film the silver salts that were not exposed to light. If this was not done the film would turn uniformly black when exposed to light. The fixed film requires to be washed thoroughly in order to remove all traces of fixative from the film, as these could discolour and degrade the surface otherwise. The processes of development and fixing are normally carried out in complete darkness, but once the negative has been fixed it can be exposed to light without chemical changes taking place. The film only requires drying to be in a form for further use. The end result of this processing is a negative – an image in which all the contrasts in the original scene are reversed. The light areas in the scene will be black and the dark areas will be transparent in the negative.

In order to restore the image to the original contrasts of the scene, the process is repeated once more, except this time the negative is used to transmit or to block light. The negative of a negative is a positive, and this is the name given to the end result of this process, which is called printing. Printing can be carried out in a number of ways and on a number of surfaces. For example, a negative can be enlarged optically and then printed, or it can be printed at the same size by placing it in contact with another light sensitive surface. Enlarging and contact printing can be used with either film or photographic paper. The positive film will consist of areas varying in transparency, whereas the paper will provide variations in whiteness. It is, of course, photographic papers that we are most accustomed to seeing.

The early photographers required a good working knowledge of chemistry in order to practise their art. Paradoxically, as the chemistry associated with films, papers and processing has become increasingly sophisticated, our need to understand it has declined. If we purchase the appropriate materials and use them in the manner directed, then we need know little of their constituents or their modes of operation. Suffice it to say that these two essential steps of developing and fixing have also been extended by modern techniques. The most important additional stage that is almost always used occurs between the development and fixing of the image. Developers now contain a number of chemicals which act upon the exposed and unexposed silver salts in different ways; the solution is alkaline and it is advisable to remove the developer solution from the film or paper before it is fixed. This can be achieved simply by washing in water, but more controllable results are possible with a weak acidic solution that is called, logically, a stop bath. Thus, the developed film or paper is stopped before fixing. Traditionally the fixing solution used was hypo (sodium thiosulphite), but now alternatives are used which act more rapidly. Moreover, the fixing solution usually contains a hardener to protect the fixed emulsion – the light sensitive coating on the film or paper base – from damage and degeneration.

The same basic procedures are followed for processing roll or sheet film or for printing on paper. Specialised developers and fixers can be used for each, but the sequence is essentially similar. The roll film that is exposed in the camera is typically panchromatic; that is, it is sensitive to light covering the whole visible spectrum. Accordingly, it must be processed in complete darkness, and the developing tanks that are readily available make this task straightforward. Lith film and most black-and-white enlarging papers, on the other hand, are orthochromatic – they are insensitive to red light and so can be processed under a red darkroom safelight. This makes the whole sequence of events both easier to control and more interesting, as it is possible to determine what to do and when to do it on the basis of vision rather than time. That is, the processing can be controlled by what we see happening, and it can be terminated or extended on that basis.

Lith Techniques

Film has the light sensitive silver salts suspended in gelatin and coated on some stable and transparent base. The sensitivity of the film to light varies according to the size and distribution of the silver halide crystals in the gelatin. Film emulsion with large crystals will be sensitive to lower intensities of illumination, or will be able to respond more quickly, than emulsion with smaller crystals. The factors of crystal size and their distribution in the emulsion determine the speed of the film. Fast films have large crystals and slow films have small ones. This in turn influences the granularity or sharpness of the captured image. The compromise usually demanded by using fast film is the granularity of the image – although this may only be a problem if the image needs enlarging considerably. The speed of a film is defined by the ISO, ASA or DIN rating: fast films have high ratings whereas slow films have low ones.

Lith film produces such sharp images because the crystals suspended in the emulsion are so small. Their ASA rating is less than 10, so they are very slow films. In fact, they are rarely used as roll film in the conventional way – for taking photographs with a camera. Rather, they are used for copying art work or illustrations that are themselves black and white. For such copying the camera requires a rigid support in order to prevent any movement during the relatively long exposures necessary.

The lith techniques discussed here use sheet rather than roll film. Sheet film is generally available in sizes from 5 × 4 to 10 × 8 inches (12.7 × 10.2 to 25.4 × 20.3cm, respectively), and it is sold in boxes of 50 or 100 sheets. This high-contrast film will produce images that are composed of black and white (transparent) only, with no intermediate greys. If tones do appear in the lith image it is because of the stippled areas that have small spots of black and white in close proximity.

The principles of processing lith film are similar to those mentioned above, but some of the materials are different. Rather than using a single developing solution, two are used. They are called A and B, and they are kept separately until they are needed for processing. The constituents for A and B can be

obtained in powder form or as liquid. Both of these are concentrated more strongly than is required for processing, and so are diluted for use. Once mixed the A and B developing solutions have a limited life: as their strength declines, because of reducing the silver salts, they require longer for development. They can be used for about an hour, or until the development time has extended to about 50 per cent longer than that needed with the fresh solutions.

Processed 35mm negatives can easily be reduced to high-contrast images on lith film. The essential items of equipment required in the darkroom are an enlarger, lith film, solutions A and B, stop bath, fixer, three developing dishes, tongs and a safelight. A lightbox is the next item of importance. It is not essential to start with, but for any of the more detailed manipulations it becomes hard to manage without one.

Equal volumes of A and B are measured and mixed in a developing dish; stop bath and fixing solution are poured into the other two dishes. The negative is enlarged to the size appropriate to the dimensions of the sheet film, and focused. The lith film can simply be placed on the baseboard of the enlarger with the emulsion uppermost and exposed to the negative, by removing the red filter before the lens. (The emulsion side of the film is lighter in colour than the backing.) The duration of exposure would have been determined by a test strip. The film is then placed in the developing solution and agitated gently for about 2.5 to 3 minutes. These times are approximate, and are given only as guidelines; because what is happening can be seen then vision can be the guide. It is easy to learn what constitutes a developed image in this way, but it should be borne in mind that our vision is at its poorest in red light. A general rule of thumb is to watch the film until it looks completely developed and then leave it in the developer a little longer, until it looks slightly overdeveloped. When it is eventually examined in normal light it will appear sharply defined, and the black areas will block out any light. Lith film is remarkably tolerant – it produces acceptable results over a wide range of exposure and development conditions.

The developed film is then transferred to the stop bath and agitated gently for at least 10 seconds. Some authorities recommend using a water wash for stopping development instead of an acid stop bath, because the latter tends to produce small pinholes in the black emulsion. The film looks black and milky white at this stage. When it is transferred to the fixer the milkiness gradually disappears, and those parts of the film become transparent. The time taken to clear the film gives an index of the strength of the fixing solution: the longer it takes the weaker the solution. The film should be fixed for at least three times the duration required to clear the film. The film can now be exposed to normal light without affecting the emulsion and it can be washed and dried. There are many elegant ways of doing both these, but washing the film carefully under the tap and hanging it up to dry with paper clips proves quite adequate.

Once the film has dried it can be checked against a light or over a lightbox for the presence of any pinholes or dust marks in the black areas. Because of the high acutance of lith film (the sharpness of the image of any object in contact with the emulsion), any small particles of dust or fabric will show up in the processed image. It is for this reason that extreme cleanliness is required in the darkroom when working with lith film. The dustmarks and pinholes can be readily blocked out by applying photographic opaque paint with a brush to the offending areas. Photographic opaque is a viscous liquid that can be diluted with water for ease of application. A variety of brush sizes is useful, so that the size appropriate for the area to be blocked out can be used. A very fine brush will be needed for the regions in which very delicate textures require opaque paint. Since the black emulsion of the film is fully opaque there are no problems of matching tones with lith film. Moreover, if the opaque is inappropriately applied the film can be washed again: because the paint is water soluble it will all be removed without damage to the film. Since the film is likely to be used in further manipulations, it is advisable to apply the opaque paint to the non-emulsion side of the film. This can be determined by inspecting the film at an angle to the light – the black emulsion is matt and the other side is shiny. Contact printing is normally done emulsion-to-emulsion, so applying the paint to the emulsion side would prevent even contact between the exposed and unexposed films, and so the sharpness of the lines would be degraded.

The opposite modification to filling in unwanted light areas with opaquing paint is the removal of unwanted black emulsion from the film. The simplest way of doing this is to scrape away the emulsion with a sharp scalpel or scraper. This tends to score the acetate base, too, and the scrape marks can show up on contact printing the film. These marks can easily be blocked out at the next stage with opaque. Indeed, an alternative method of removing the unwanted parts of the image is to contact print the film onto another sheet of lith film, making the unwanted parts transparent and then they can be removed by applying opaque paint.

It does not take long to learn the techniques associated with lith film, and to modify them to individual requirements. Only the most basic darkroom equipment is necessary, but it is helpful to have some type of lightbox for checking the film and for combining films in the ways to be outlined below.

The distinction between a full-tone photograph and its lith image can be seen in Figures A1.1 and A1.2. Only the high contrasts of the landscape are reproduced in A1.1, with the details of the bridge and woods being lost in the conversion. Depending on the degree of exposure and development, desired features, like the structure of the bridge, can be accentuated. On the other hand, large parts of the full-tone image that are not desired can be excluded by cropping the enlargement, as in A1.2. In this case the image has been manipulated, too, by retaining only the most distinctive features of the face, making the lith image more puzzling perceptually: where is the left eye and what has happened to the left side of the face? These effects were achieved by underexposing the original lith enlargement and then contact printing it onto another sheet of lith film. Lith images are ideally suited for enhancing the ambiguity in pictorial images, and this will be a constant theme in the pictures presented here.

In the case of both these first two photographs, the starting point was a continuous tone, black-and-white negative. The same general procedures can be followed with either colour positives or negatives. Figure A1.3 was derived from a colour slide. The initial conversion to lith film did not have sufficient contrast, and so further contact prints onto lith film were made to obtain the picture, during which processes the unwanted details of the surroundings were also removed. Figure A1.4 was derived from a colour negative. The degree of the initial exposure was varied, being less for the upper version, and the development was also stopped sooner. The tone-like stippling effect can be seen in the most distant windmill, and there is a stronger impression of depth

A1.1 *General Wade's bridge, Aberfeldy.* Continuous-tone photograph and a lith image derived from it.

A1.2 Continous-tone photograph and a lith image of a detail derived from it.

in the upper photograph than in the starker, lower one. It is clear that one of the many advantages of using lith film is the facility with which images can be manipulated (see Figure A1.5) and combined (Figure A1.6).

Another use to which negatives can be put is to sandwich them with a positive in order to produce a line image. If the registration is exact then little light will be transmitted to the unexposed film in contact with the sandwiched sheets. Therefore there is usually a slight displacement of the negative to the positive, or the two are placed with their emulsions apart rather than together: the thickness of the two transparent bases is sufficient to allow an appreciable amount of light through at the boundaries between light and shade. This light transmission can be accentuated by inclining the sandwiched film and the unexposed film (kept in fixed contact) to some light source, and rotating them so that the light will fall on the unexposed film all round the contrast boundaries. Figure A1.7 is a relatively straightforward line image produced in this way. The subject in Figure A1.8 is the head of a girl wearing a

A1.3 *Pisa.*

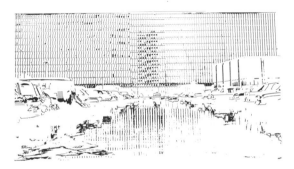

A1.6 *Sydney Harbour Bridge.*

A1.4 *Windmills.*

A1.7 *Ming Wing, Monash University.*

A1.5 *Mother and child.*

A1.8 Superimposition and rotation of line images.

hooded sweater; the turbulence of the wind has tossed the hair around in front of the head. Two line images were made from the same positive and negative and they were then superimposed, slightly out of register. The impression of motion and turbulence is enhanced by the rotation of one line image with respect to the other.

Another technique that can be used with lith film is called bas relief. It tends to be applied to full-tone negatives and positives of objects in low relief illuminated from the side. The technique has many features in common with that for producing a line image. A negative is placed in contact with a positive and displaced a little to produce a clear edge effect. In applying this technique with lith film it is best to have an underexposed positive and a normally exposed negative (see Figure A1.9).

The Sabattier Effect and Solarisation

When Armand Sabatier discovered, in 1862, the effect that now bears his name, he provided a process that has given both enduring fascination and boundless frustration to the darkroom enthusiast. The fascination is in the intricate and subtle effects that can be produced by this technique. The frustration is in discovering a method that will yield them. Sabatier found that a normally exposed print can be changed quite radically by re-exposing it to diffuse white light (fogging) during development. He called the effect pseudo-solarisation, but it is now termed the Sabattier effect. It is frequently referred to as solarisation although this is, strictly speaking, inappropriate. Solarisation is the partial reversal of an image due to gross overexposure (by 1000 times or more), and it is difficult to achieve with modern materials. It is the difficulty in achieving solarisation in this sense that has helped fog the distinction between it and the Sabattier effect. Indeed many writers treat the two synonymously, and I will follow the same practice for descriptive convenience. However, the technique involved is that of normal exposure and then fogging part way through development.

The techniques recommended to this end are many and various. All writers are at pains to stress the difficulty of achieving consistent results, and the need for individual experimentation to find the appropriate method. I can only echo these strictures, and describe the methods that I have found successful. The procedures for film and paper are similar, but their differences are sufficient to warrant discussing them separately.

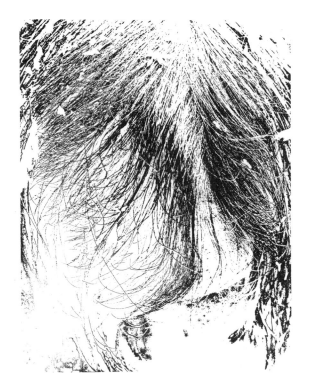

A1.9 Bas relief of a girl's head viewed from above.

Film

The graphically alluring feature of the Sabattier effect is the fine white outline which is formed at all the contrast boundaries in the original image. These are called Mackie lines, and they can be seen in Figures A1.10 and A1.11. In order to derive Mackie lines a negative (or positive) with high contrasts is required. I usually convert a negative – either a full-tone black-and-white or a colour negative – to lith film, enlarging to 5 × 4 inches or half-plate size. This conversion will give the sharp contrasts that are necessary.

The essential feature of the Sabattier effect is the fogging of an image followed by further development. Surrounding this essence are a host of variables of which the following are a few: the contrast of the negative, the duration of the initial exposure, the stage of development for the fogging exposure, the duration of the fogging exposure, whether to remove the film from the developer and wash it before fogging, the strength of the developing solution (or solutions, if different ones are used for the first and

A1.10 *Boat yard, Arbroath.*

A1.11 *Clown.*

second developments), and whether to stop the development with water or stop bath. Obviously, it can get very complicated, but it need not.

The following procedures will, hopefully, provide a simple basis for those who might wish to experiment with and enjoy the fascination of the Sabattier effect. Anyone trying the process must be prepared for the frustrations, too, as even with a workable method repeatability is not assured. If a 50 per cent success rate is achieved that is remarkably high.

Starting with a positive or negative on sheet lith film, this can be contact printed onto another sheet using an exposure that would normally give a good two-tone image. Immerse the exposed film in the fresh developing solution and agitate it gently and briefly. Place the developing dish on the baseboard of the enlarger, beneath the light (with its red filter in place so that the film is not affected). Do not agitate or disturb any further – the film should remain still and evenly immersed for the rest of the process. About two-thirds of the way through development, fog the film with white light for half the duration of the initial exposure, and with the same aperture setting on the enlarger. In the normal development of lith film the image forms gradually, and then, after about two minutes of development, the darkening areas go a much more intense black.

The fogging exposure for the Sabattier effect should be started just prior to this deepening of the blackened areas. Experience will soon facilitate determining when this is about to occur. The film will look little affected by the fogging initially, and then the light areas will begin to darken. As they do so the Mackie lines will become apparent. The lines are due to the deposit of bromide ions from the first development which retards the development at the borders after the second, fogging exposure. The reason for not agitating the film during the first development is to allow the accumulation of the bromide at the borders. The Mackie lines may be quite broad initially, but they will become thinner with increasing second development. Indeed, they will disappear altogether if the second development is not stopped. As soon as the image is seen to have the appropriate Sabattier effect it can be transferred quickly to the stop bath and then fixed. It is worth repeating that while we can watch what is happening, under the red safelight, our vision is not at its best in such illumination. Consequently, an image might appear to be suitably dark from the second exposure, but be found to be underdeveloped when viewed in white light. Thus, it is worth allowing the second development to proceed for slightly longer than looks appropriate.

These are the basic steps involved in producing the Sabattier effect on film. Since the processing is on lith film, the end result will consist of the originally developed black areas, the Mackie lines, and the original light areas that have darkened. The extent of this latter darkening will depend on the fogging exposure duration and the length of the second development. If it is not opaque when viewed over a lightbox it can be made so by the application of photographic opaque.

As with all photographic manipulations, it is wise to start with test strips that will indicate the optimal initial and fogging exposures. These can then be employed, and a personally satisfying strategy will emerge with practice.

The Sabattier effect applied to lith film is ideal for producing outline effects. That is, the Mackie lines are the sole features of the original image that are reproduced. The great advantage of such solarised film is its reproducibility, since this enables the combination of solarised images with other unsolarised components, as will be shown below.

The Mackie lines yield a border effect that is similar to the line image from a sandwiched positive and negative. The main difference is that it is more difficult to obtain an even border effect with sandwiching than with the Sabattier effect, and this is more particularly so when there are many small areas of black in the initial film. The manner in which fine stippled regions appear with the two techniques is also different. The line image yields a fine black outline on a transparent base, whereas the Sabattier effect gives a white outline on an otherwise blackened film. Figure A1.12 shows the effects of producing a line image (the upper picture, after it has been contact printed once more to give a black base) from a sandwiched positive and negative, together with the results of solarising the same negative (lower left) and positive (lower right). The outline of the hair is more complete with the solarised images, but it is virtually lost in the line image. The latter retains more of the very fine detailed stippling, as in the shadowing on the forehead and cheek. The difference between the solarised negative and positive might not seem too marked here, but there can be definite pictorial advantages in using one or the other. Here it is in the fine strands of hair where the difference is most noticeable: solarising the negative leaves them as white bands, but they are flanked by more delicate white bands in the solarised positive. This is because the white strands in the developing negative were too narrow to allow the formation of Mackie lines within them, whereas the fine black strands in the developing positive formed Mackie lines on either side.

The Sabattier effect can be applied more than once to the same image, making it increasingly abstract with each solarisation. Figure A1.13 is an example of this. Another variation is to combine images in the ways described earlier, and then solarise them. This was done with Figures A1.14 and A1.15. In A1.14, a single stockinged leg was doubled and combined on lith film before it was solarised. The width of the Mackie lines in the final print can be influenced by the size of the film (and image) used for solarisation. In this case the images were processed on 2.25 × 2.25 inch (6 × 6cm) pieces of film, which can make the Mackie lines more dominant when the film is enlarged. The combinations in Figure A1.15 are rather more complex. A single torso is the basis for the four paired images. The factor distinguishing them is the degree of overlap of the outlines. The four combinations were made independently and then arranged symmetrically. The final composite was solarised to produce these rather puzzling shapes.

Figure A1.16 is a picture of a lone beachcomber,

A1.12 A line image, from sandwiching a positive and negative, is shown above, together with the solarised images from a negative (lower left) and a positive (lower right).

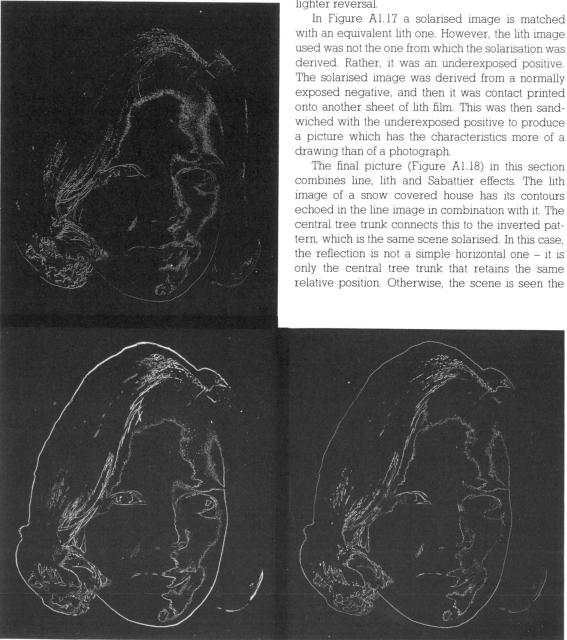

pensively pursuing the water line. The subject is represented twice, enclosed within herself, and the ripples of the water provide the texture that lends itself so well to solarisation. The subject matter is here better represented in the form of the solarised film, with a sombre black background, than in its lighter reversal.

In Figure A1.17 a solarised image is matched with an equivalent lith one. However, the lith image used was not the one from which the solarisation was derived. Rather, it was an underexposed positive. The solarised image was derived from a normally exposed negative, and then it was contact printed onto another sheet of lith film. This was then sandwiched with the underexposed positive to produce a picture which has the characteristics more of a drawing than of a photograph.

The final picture (Figure A1.18) in this section combines line, lith and Sabattier effects. The lith image of a snow covered house has its contours echoed in the line image in combination with it. The central tree trunk connects this to the inverted pattern, which is the same scene solarised. In this case, the reflection is not a simple horizontal one – it is only the central tree trunk that retains the same relative position. Otherwise, the scene is seen the

A1.13 Multiple solarisations.

A1.14 *Stockings.*

same way irrespective of the side from which it is viewed.

Paper

While solarising film emphasises the Mackie lines, producing a fine drawn-like image, applying the same processes to paper can yield a wider tonal range. However, the solarised print is a one-off production. It can be re-photographed carefully on continuous-tone film, but it is difficult to retain the subtlety of the original image. Within the context of high-contrast photography this need not be such a problem, as the aim of solarising prints is also to emphasise the Mackie lines, and these can readily be reproduced. There is an alternative to re-photographing the solarised print that is also more convenient. The print itself can be used as a negative, and it can be contact printed like film. In order to do this, it is essential to contact print the papers emulsion-to-emulsion, and close contact must be maintained between the two papers. The paper negative can also be used to print onto lith film. Therefore, a desirable solarised print can be reproduced in a number of ways, although the reproductions rarely have the sparkle of the original.

As with applying the Sabattier effect to film, there are many different techniques possible when using paper. The variables are much the same, and the method I will recommend is essentially similar to that used for film. One major difference concerns the strength of the developing solution used. Film requires fresh developer. However, with paper the reversal of contrast can occur very quickly with fresh, or full strength developer. Moreover, the Mackie lines soon disappear, too, and the paper will blacken all over. For this reason it is advisable to use either very dilute (about one-tenth the normal dilution) or "spent" developer for solarising prints.

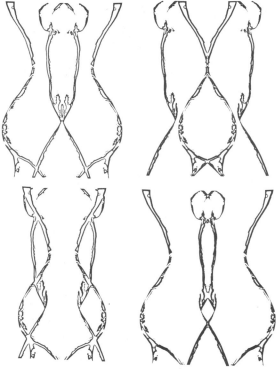

A1.15 *Bodies.*

A1.16 *Beachcomber.*

A1.17 *Boat, Crail.*

These slow the whole process of contrast reversal down, thereby adding to the control that can be applied. My preference is for using spent developer, that is, developer that has been used for normal printing; it can be stored for a long time and used repeatedly.

The first stage is to select or produce a suitably contrasty negative (or positive). A good strategy is to enlarge a negative onto lith film to give the sharp contrasts that are helpful in solarisation. Often, if the film is slightly underexposed it will provide a good starting image, particularly if it has been enlarged to 5 × 4 inches (12.7 × 10.2cm) or half-plate (4.65 × 6.5 inches or 12.1 × 16.5cm). The film is contact printed with a high-contrast paper, using an initial exposure that would produce an acceptable image under normal development. The paper is placed in the developing dish with the dilute or spent developer,

A1.18 (Facing page)
Night and day.

A1.19 *Familiarities.*

There is an alternative method for solarising prints, and it has many advantages for the beginner. Again, spent or very dilute developer is used so that the various chemical effects work at a more controllable rate. With this method, sometimes called gentle solarisation, the print is developed normally to its desired contrast. At that stage it is exposed to a weak fogging light for as long as is required to produce the Sabattier effect. I have found that directing an angle-poise lamp upwards to the ceiling produces a suitably weak light source – then only the light reflected from the ceiling and walls falls on the print. It is also possible to continue gentle agitation throughout this second exposure. One obvious advantage of this method is that you can watch what is happening under white light rather than the poorer safelight.

The wider tonal range in solarised prints is illustrated in the next three figures, which have been given partial rather than complete contrast reversal. Thus, in Figure A1.19 the silvery sheen that covers the highlights of the faces gives the photograph a surreal appearance. Note, too, how the denser shadows have been reversed more completely, giving the white Mackie lines at their borders. Similar surreal effects are seen in Figure A1.20. The Mackie lines emphasise the lattice work of the Tay Bridge's construction, and the lighter and more distant central spans appear to be floating in air rather than water. It is not surprising that one of the greatest exponents of solarising prints was the surrealist artist and photographer, Man Ray. The combination of partial solarisation and the white Mackie lines in the same image gives it the appearance of unreality. These effects can best be achieved with prints rather than with lith film, although the Sabattier process can be applied to faster films, too.

The degree of reversal varies according to the contrast in the negative used. The high contrasts will yield Mackie lines and the lower ones take on the silvery and insubstantial appearance. The contrasts in Figure A1.21 are relatively uniform, so that the geometrical layout of the tables and benches remains the dominant theme of the composition. The rippling water in the upper part of the photograph provides a good subject for solarisation due to the multiple contrasts in the reflections. However, the process does tend to flatten the appearance of the whole scene, by removing some of the contrast gradients that we normally associate with three-

and agitated briefly. The developing dish is placed on the baseboard of the enlarger, and the paper is left undisturbed from this point onwards. Because the paper, particularly if it is resin-coated, will tend to curl and lie near the surface of the developing solution, it will need to be kept evenly immersed to ensure an even second exposure. A simple method of accomplishing this is to have spare pairs of tongs that can be placed on the edges of the print to keep it evenly submerged and still. The fogging exposure is given between one-half and two-thirds of the way through normal development. The fogging exposure can be relatively longer than in the case of film – the same duration or even double that used for the first exposure. Again the effect of the fogging will take some time to appear, and with the weak developer its progress can be observed under the red safelight. Mackie lines will form where there have been sharp contrasts, and the process can be terminated when the image is in the desired state, by transferring the print quickly to the stop bath.

A1.20 *Girders.*

A1.21 *Benchmarks.*

dimensional scenes. Figure A1.22 shows the sides of stone cottages in a Fife fishing village. The steps, stone walls, the gutter and road all provide textures that have been emphasised by the Sabattier process. The figure of the running girl provides some pictorial contrast between the peace and tranquility of the village life and the activity of the people who inhabit it.

The influence of solarisation on photographic images not only yields the surreal appearance of the subjects, but it also makes them more abstract. The degree of abstraction achieved depends in large measure on the character of the photographic image used. For example, the two pictures in Figure A1.23 might look like objects from outer space – but they are actually much closer to earth, being hydraulic-

A1.22 *Cottages, Crail.*

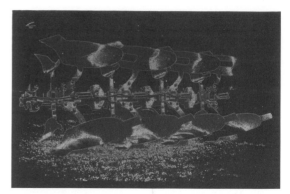

A1.23 *Ploughs.*

ally operated ploughs. The two solarisations are presented to illustrate the difference between using a negative and a positive film image for contact printing with the paper. They also show how suitable textures like grass can be for reproducing delicate and densely packed Mackie lines.

The final photographs have used the solarised papers as negatives for further contact printing. The solarised print was sandwiched with another sheet of unexposed paper, and they were kept in firm contact, between two sheets of plate glass, for the exposure to white light. Thus, the solarised print can be treated like a conventional film negative for use in contact printing. In fact it is often a good idea to keep the original solarised print as a master negative, and to work from the contact prints. The contact printing from a paper negative must be carried out

emulsion-to-emulsion, because of the thickness of the paper backing. Otherwise, a blurred image will be produced, with a loss of all the fine detail in the original solarised print. Contact printing with film is also recommended to be emulsion-to-emulsion, but it is not so critical since the acetate base for film is much thinner than the paper base. Moreover, it is often necessary to contact print film with the emulsion uppermost, when combining images, and this is an obvious advantage of working with solarised film rather than paper. Figure A1.24 represents a crowd watching a Punch and Judy show. The attention of all the spectators is directed to the puppets – apart from the diminutive and disconsolate figure near the centre. The original photograph was taken with colour negative film, and it was enlarged onto half-plate lith film. The positive was contact printed on paper and solarised. The solarised print was used as a paper negative to produce the upper picture. A second image was produced from the same lith positive. This time the paper was differentially solarised by fogging the central area, around the girl, far more than any of the other parts. The solarised print was then used as a paper negative to produce the lower picture. The outer parts now appear as conventional (high-contrast) positives, whereas the

small girl is outlined by the black Mackie lines, and she is framed by the backs of the other spectators.

Solarising paper prints can act as a good introduction to the delights of the Sabattier effect, and it can give images with a wider variety of tones than is possible with lith film. When using spent or dilute developer the technique might also be more easily controlled for paper than film. However, for the purposes to which solarised images have been employed in this book, film provides a far more flexible and manipulable source of line images. Not only can the Mackie lines be emphasised to the full, but film images can also be combined more easily than can images on paper.

A1.24 *Dam Square, Amsterdam.*

Bibliography

General

Burchfield, J. (1981). *Darkroom art*. New York: American Photographic Book Publishing. A clearly-written guide to processing and manipulating black-and-white film. It deals with image reduction and intensification, photograms, the Sabattier effect, multiple images, high-contrast techniques, posterisation and toning.

Gaunt, L. (1982). *Film and paper processing*. Sevenoaks, Kent: Focal Press. A good introduction to the nature of film, how light operates on it, and how the latent image is expressed by the processes of chemical development and printing. It describes the materials and equipment needed for both colour and black-and-white processing and printing.

Langford, M. (1981). *The book of special effects photography*. London: Ebury Press. This book is concerned specifically with ways of modifying the photographic image by means of camera accessories, lighting and studio effects, special purpose films, and darkroom manipulations. The basics of photography are presented together with many colour and black-and-white illustrations.

Additional

Croy, O. R. (1977). *Camera trickery*. Translated by W. D. Emanuel. London: Focal Press. Croy has written several books on photographic manipulations. This one describes how to produce a variety of distortions, separations and combinations when processing film.

Freeman, M. (1982). *The complete guide to photography techniques and materials*. Oxford: Phaidon. This book gives a detailed account of the camera, light and film, the darkroom, and uses of photography. It deals with colour as well as black-and-white photography.

Haas, R. (1985). *Special effects in photography*. London: J. M. Dent. Contrary to its title this book has relatively little to do with darkroom manipulations, but concerns comparatively straight and studied photographs. The discussion of Hockney's photo composites is of interest.

Holter, P. (1972). *Photography without a camera*. London: Studio Vista. Many ways of making and modifying images directly on to film or paper are described.

Schofield, J. (Ed.) (1981). *The darkroom book*. London: Spring Books. An elementary guide to photographic processing and image manipulation. The colour illustrations of equipment and procedures are helpful, and a glossary of photographic terms is appended.

Tait, J. (1977). *Beyond photography*. London: Focal Press. This book introduces techniques of silk screen printing, lithography, toning and multiple imaging to extend the photographic image. Illustrations using all these procedures are shown.

Walker, S. & Rainwater, C. (1974). *Solarization*. New York: American Photographic Book Publishing Co. A book devoted to solarising prints, presenting many of the authors' own pictures. The description of gentle solarisation is very useful. The authors also describe methods for producing texture screen effects, repeated images and colour toning.

APPENDIX 2: THE COMBINATION OF GRAPHICS WITH PHOTOGRAPHY

Traditionally graphic arts were considered to be drawing and engraving – that is, the forms of representation that did not involve colour. Nowadays the term is used more broadly, but it still includes drawing and printmaking: typography, illustration and design would also be included under this rubric. The graphics with which we will be primarily concerned are the drawings that involve simple but repetitive features – geometrical designs of straight or curved lines that might be abstract or representational. It is the geometrical regularity that lends itself so readily to combination with photographic images. A variety of such designs, and the directions on how to draw them will be given in the first section of this Appendix.

It is not essential to use your own drawn designs as a basis for photo–graphic imagery. You can use some of the many textures that surround us, by photographing them and then converting the negatives to lith film. A second alternative is to purchase texture screens from your photographic suppliers. Both of these approaches will be described below.

Once you have either a graphic design or a derived texture on lith film, then it is possible to multiply or modify it using the techniques detailed in

Appendix One. Designs can be combined in many ways, and they can also be solarised at any of the intermediate stages. Examples of these manipulations will also be given in this Appendix.

Drawn Designs

The graphical elements suitable for photo–graphic imagery echo the characteristics of the lith film used in its combination. That is, the designs are two-tone black and white, and they contain sharply defined contours that occur with regularity throughout the pattern. The essential items for producing such drawings are: a flat surface on which a large (e.g., 24×24 inch or 60×60cm) sheet of graph paper can be fixed firmly, and a good quality, transparent drawing paper (this can be purchased in large rolls); a straight-edge, compass and protractor (all as large as possible); a scalpel or scraper; and either special drawing pens or good quality black felt pens. The drawing paper is placed over the graph paper and firmly fixed in position. The lines of the graph paper will be visible through the paper, and the two should not move with respect to each other until the design is completed. The simplest designs to make, and often the ones that can be used to best photo–graphic effect, are those consisting of straight line elements. To produce a pattern, like Figure A2.1, the edges of each line are first drawn with a fine pen (as on the left). A convenient separation on

A2.1 Outline and blocked grid.

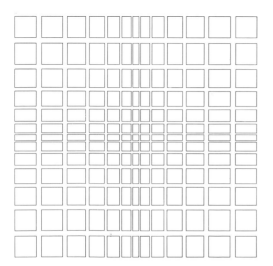

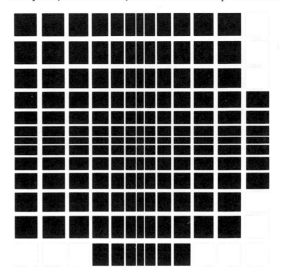

A2.2 Checkerboard with cells of varying size.

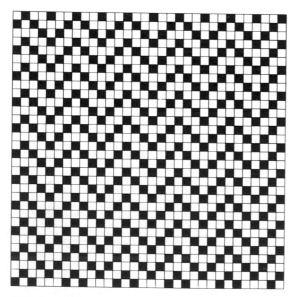

A2.3 A regular line grid with systematic displacements of the blocked cells.

the underlying graph paper can be used as a guide. Once this has been completed for the whole sheet, then the spaces between the lines can be blocked in using a thicker pen (as on the right). Extreme care must be taken at the edges of the lines to avoid marking the open spaces, but if an error is made it can be corrected by scraping away the unwanted ink from the paper with a scalpel. In this respect the same techniques are used for removing emulsion from lith film and unwanted ink from a drawing.

It is important to draw the line patterns carefully because any unevenness can show up when the design is used in combination with itself or in other patterns. The larger the initial drawing the greater will be the evenness of the design when it is reduced in size photographically. In Figure A2.1 the outline squares and rectangles were drawn with separations and sizes increasing from the centre outwards, and then it was blocked in. When the original design is completed it will not look uniformly black and white. In some parts the ink will be thicker than in others, so that the black areas look a bit patchy. The unevenness of the contrast will be removed when the pattern is photographed using high-contrast film.

Photographing the design involves using lith roll or line film in the camera, a copy stand to support the camera, and side lights to illuminate the design evenly. The photography can be done personally or by a photographic laboratory. The latter is often preferable since there will be specialised equipment for this purpose, and it is relatively inexpensive. There is another advantage of using a professional photographic service: the design can be photographed on sheet film, so that the fine details will be more faithfully recorded. Once there is a large master negative it can be contact printed on film to give positives for further combination.

If you wish to do the photography yourself, the following method should prove adequate. You can use your usual camera, but it will need to be loaded with lith roll film. The camera will need to be fixed to a rigid copy stand, or on a solid tripod. The drawn pattern is placed over a piece of white card on a flat surface. It can be kept flat with a large piece of plate glass. As a less precise alternative, the white card and drawing can be pinned to a flat vertical surface at a suitable height for the camera tripod, and illuminated evenly from the sides. The ASA rating of lith film is not usually given but it is less than 10. Therefore exposures of several seconds are necessary to get a sharply defined image. The precise exposure will depend upon the distance of the camera from the drawing and the intensity of illumination. For these reasons it is best to take exposures at different durations, and then select the appropriate negative later. If the tripod method is used then a cable release should prevent any movement of the camera when the shutter is opened and closed. The exposed lith film is processed using the same stages as described in Appendix One for sheet film, but the roll film can be more conveniently handled in a developing tank. Once you have a sharp negative of the design it can be enlarged to a size that will be convenient for further combinations and manipulations.

Other simple geometrical patterns that can be produced with a pen and ruler are shown in Figures A2.2 and A2.3. The two figures present variations on a regular checkerboard pattern. In A2.2 the dimensions of the separations have been varied to give the central framing effect. Although all the lines in the design are straight, the corners of this frame appear curved unless they are observed directly. Figure A2.3 is a more regular pattern in outline terms, being a regular grid. However, the squares have been blocked in to make a zigzag pattern which distorts the vertical and horizontal lines markedly: the horizontals seem to be wavy whereas the verticals splay out in different directions. Another family of figures can be drawn with the aid of a compass, preferably one with a large extension (see Figure A2.4).

Some of the most pleasing designs can be drawn with a template rather than a straight-edge or compass. For example, if some curve is drawn on a piece of card it can be made into a template by cutting along the curved line with a pair of scissors. Figure A2.5 displays a radiation of a representational form.

It takes a little practice to develop the graphical skills required for such designs, but the rewards of mastering them make it worthwhile. It is then possible to create unique images from graphics designed specifically for certain photo images.

Naturally Occurring Textures

It is not necessary to use a pen to produce patterns that have geometrical regularity, as we are surrounded by them. The following illustrations are a few of the textures I have photographed, either on

A2.4 *Eccentric circles.*

A2.5 *Ribbon profiles.*

A2.6 Grasses.

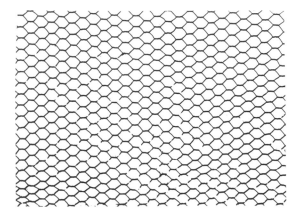

A2.7 Chicken wire.

full-tone black-and-white film or on colour film, and then converted to lith film. The first (Figure A2.6) is a photograph of grasses taken in a botanical garden. The randomness of their orientations and the regularity of their sizes and shapes makes this a good texture. Regularity of shape and density of contours are general characteristics to look for in textures that are to be used in combination with other photo–graphic images. The texture is usually the background of the photo–graphic image, and so it should not have dominant features which compete with the other pictorial image it carries. The sea-shore also provides many textures that can be captured by the camera.

Many man-made (or more properly machine-made) objects contain regular geometrical components. Figure A2.7 is a picture of fencing wire and in Figure A2.8 we see part of a modern skyscraper soaring upwards.

It will be evident that I have only scratched the surface of the environmental textures that can be photographed. As soon as you are aware of the textural possibilities of your surroundings you may view them in quite a different guise. Searching for appropriate patterns will sharpen your perception for other aspects of your environment that can provide good subjects for photographs generally.

Texture Screens

It is possible to pursue the photo–graphic image without recourse to either pen or derived pattern by purchasing texture screens from photographic suppliers. These are available as either 35mm or 2.25 × 2.25 inch (6 × 6cm) screens that are recommended for use in contact with the negative in the enlarger. A variety of patterns has been reproduced in this manner. Because they are intended for use with full-tone negatives the screens are not in high contrast. They can be so converted by contact printing or enlarging them onto lith film. The texture screens that are most appropriate for photo–graphic imagery are the regular geometrical ones, like the grid line (a pattern of parallel lines) and the centric (concentric circles).

While the texture screens provide a convenient introduction to photo–graphic imagery, they do not offer the challenge that is provided by drawing or deriving the design most suited to the image with which it is to be combined.

Another way of obtaining textures that does not

require drawing of the type described above is to let something else do the drawing for you. There are various toys on the market that can yield geometrical designs. Some of them give very detailed and regular patterns if they are used with great care. Once the patterns have been produced, preferably with black ink on white paper, they can be photographed on lith film for use in subsequent darkroom manipulations. The particular instrument that I like is called an harmonograph, and I have constructed one that is rather more sturdy than the variants available as toys. The harmonograph consists of a base that moves with respect to a stationary pen in contact with the paper on it. The following two designs were made with it. Figure A2.9 shows a very fine line pattern that is almost regular. In fact, it is rarely possible to reproduce the same design as the mechanical variables associated with the device are so complex. For the same reason, it is very difficult to produce a symmetrical pattern like a circular one. The path of the pen can be made quite complex to trace patterns like that in Figure A2.10. Such patterns often give a compelling impression of depth and three-dimensionality. Interesting as this pattern is in its own right, it is not ideally suited to photographic imagery because of its complexity. It is often the simpler repetitive designs that prove most generally useful in combination with photographic images.

Graphics and High-contrast Techniques

Once you have designs on film they can be modified and multiplied in many ways. Any geometrical pattern on film can be superimposed on itself or on other patterns to produce moiré fringes – the interference bands due to the interaction of the two designs. The simplest moiré interference fringes arise from the overlay of gratings, such that one is at a small angle to the other. The fringes are the denser parallel bands that bisect the angle between the two component gratings. The moiré fringes are often so dominant that it is difficult to see the patterns from which they were composed. The symmetrical moiré fringes in Figure A2.11 were produced from patterns of concentric squares and circles. They can be arranged to be black or white, depending on the use of positives or negatives in the final print.

Moiré patterns will only be produced if there is a high degree of geometrical regularity in the two designs, and when they are not displaced by too

A2.8 Skyscraper.

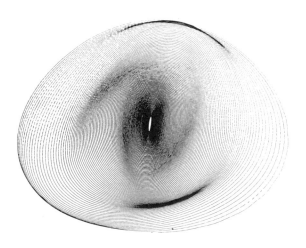

A2.9 *Harmonograph 1.*

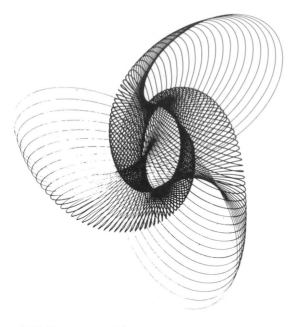

A2.10 *Harmonograph 2.*

great an angle with respect to one another. For instance, if the two gratings were superimposed at right angles they would produce a grid rather than a moiré pattern. Designs can also be transformed by repeating the patterning and introducing some systematic shift in their relative positions. Superimposing the wire fencing pattern shown in A2.7 on itself in different displacements gave the two patterns shown in Figure A2.12.

Perhaps one of the most general uses that combinations on film can be put to is in multiplying the original drawn design to give it more spatial detail. The following two figures have been derived from simpler graphic designs. In each one the original drawing is given together with the final combined image. In the case of Figure A2.13 a zigzag pattern was drawn and then photographed. Four positives were made from the lith negative, and these were registered in reflection and rotation to produce the final, more symmetrical, pattern. Another way of combining designs is to contact print the negatives

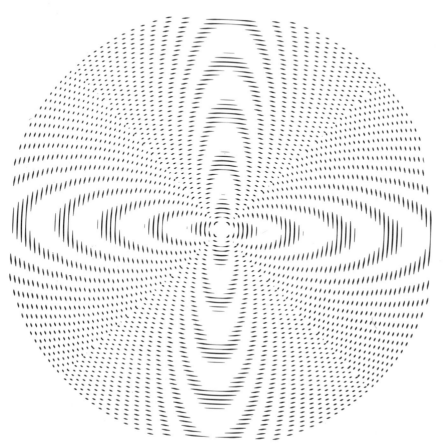

A2.11 Moiré fringes formed from circles and squares.

A2.12 Superimposed
wire patterns.

A2.13 *Chevrons.*

onto paper, with due regard to whether the emulsion should be up or down to ensure that the design is in the appropriate orientation for matching. The four prints can be cut along their adjoining edges with a scalpel and then pasted together on a piece of solid card after they have been registered. The combined image can be rephotographed on lith film for further use. One advantage of such multiplication is that often the visual vibrancy of the graphic designs is greatly increased. Sometimes the outcome from such graphical manipulations and combinations can be quite surprising. With Figure A2.14 the drawn design was not particularly interesting on its own,

and it was not drawn with the intention of producing the "binocular" image that it could yield. This was discovered by trying out various arrangements of the positives together, because they could give a symmetrical pattern about any of the four corners. Once this possibility was appreciated then the composite design could be used more successfully than could the original pattern on its own.

Solarising Designs and Textures

Designs, either drawn or derived, on lith film can be further transformed by applying the Sabattier effect. When drawn designs are so treated they become

A2.15 Solarised design.

A2.14 *Centralise.*

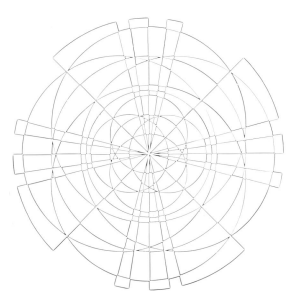

A2.16 *Crosses.*

outlines. In one sense, this returns them to a state rather like that in which they were initially in drawing – the outlines before the blocking in was carried out. Thus, for example, the Mackie lines in Figure A2.15 trace the initially drawn lines of a spiral zigzag pattern. It can be quite tricky solarising regular geometrical designs because any unevenness in the Mackie lines can show up very clearly in the final image. However, once the designs have been solarised they can be contact printed on lith film and then combined with other designs or photographic images. Figure A2.16 is comprised of overlapping circles and radiating lines. In the original drawing all the lines were continuous, but because of the displacement of the Mackie lines to the light side of the first development, the outlines are slightly displaced as can be seen on careful inspection.

Whereas a solarised drawing retains close visual contact with the design from which it was derived, natural textures can be transformed into abstract patterns by applying the same process. Figure A2.17 is a solarisation of a natural texture, namely stones on a beach.

Photo–graphics

The combination of graphic designs with photographic images is straightforward, once both have been rendered on lith film. The two or more elements are treated as equivalent film-based images, which can be modified in the ways described in Appendix One. For example, Figure A2.18 is what I refer to as a photo–graphic image. Its graphic qualities are obvious: the pattern is made up of interlaced white circles which form black crosses where they overlap. In some areas fewer circles are intertwined than in others, making darker and lighter regions throughout the picture. But where is the

photo image and how is it incorporated into the design? It is actually embedded in this interplay of lighter and darker regions. You probably cannot see it immediately, but it will become visible if you view the picture from a distance, or if you blur the picture

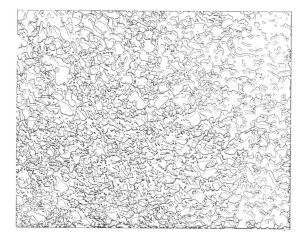

A2.17 *Solarised stones.*

A2.18 *Rebecca.*

A2.19 Original black-and-white photograph.

A2.20 Original drawn design.

by moving it about or by defocusing your eyes. Then the smiling face of a girl with windblown hair will be seen! This image of a face seems far removed from any conventional photograph, but the techniques involved are simple, although there are quite a few stages in the process. Surprisingly enough, all that is needed to produce this, is a single photograph and a single design. The stages through which they pass will be summarised here.

There are, therefore, two essential ingredients for photo–graphic imagery – a photo and a design. The photo can be in full-tone black and white or in

A2.21 Lith positive of Figure A2.19.

A2.22 Lith negative of Figure A2.19.

colour and it can be on positive or negative film. The design can be drawn or derived photographically from some naturally occurring texture. The photo used in constructing Figure A2.18 was a full-tone black-and-white picture of a girl (Figure A2.19). There is little in the background (the sky) to inter-fere with the details of the windblown hair, and only the subject is represented. There is a wide tonal range with some strongly contrasting areas, particu-larly between the hair and the skin. The photo was taken with a simple 35mm camera under normal daylight conditions.

A2.23 Combination of positive face and design.

A2.24 Combination of negative face and design.

The design is a drawing of a geometrically repetitive sequence of interlaced circles (Figure A2.20). It has sharply defined lines and consists of black and white alone. It was initially drawn on a much larger scale in black ink on paper: all the circles were described in outline, using a compass, and then the black areas were blocked in. The contrast is accentuated when the design is photographed on lith film. The drawing can be the most time consuming part of the total process. However, it

A2.25 Sandwiching the
negatives of Figures
A2.23 and A2.24.

will probably be found that the greatest satisfaction derives from the marriage of some photo image with graphics that have been designed for that alone.

The first stage in the transformation involves removing all the grey tones in the photo by processing the negative on lith film to make a positive, as is shown in Figure A2.21. Obviously most of the detail is lost in this rendering to high contrast, but, according to the degree of exposure and development, the essence of the subject can be retained. A negative can also be made from the lith positive by printing in contact (Figure A2.22). At each of these stages details can be added or removed either by scraping away emulsion from the film or by applying photographic opaque paint to block out areas. The graphic design can also be contact printed on to lith film to give a negative.

It is now possible to combine the graphic design with the photo image. One simple method is to sandwich and contact print the two positives together (Figure A2.23), and then the two negatives (Figure A2.24). This results in two components, each with large opaque areas; if they are contact printed on to more lith film then the black areas become transparent. There are now two images on film, each containing transparent and patterned regions, but in different parts – the figure for one and the background for the other. They can be combined by sandwiching the components to give a composite image in which there is both a figure and a background (Figure A2.25).

This composite is not too successful visually, because the image of the face seems lost amongst the mass of intertwining circles. A rather more subtle combination can be made by superimposing a transparency of the original graphic design over a transparency of Figure A2.23, yielding the photo–graphic image with which we started (Figure A2.18). I found this picture far more satisfying because it can work at several levels. Firstly, and most immediately, the graphic elements and their interplay lend a unity to the picture. Secondly, the discontinuities in the pattern become evident. Finally, and more subtly, the discontinuities become organised into the image of the face with which we started. This image is hovering at the limits of recognition, but it can be rendered more readily visible by viewing it from a little further away, by blurring or defocusing the image, or by moving it about in a jittery way. The final picture is at one and the same time an abstract geometrical design and a recognisable pictorial image, whose fleeting presence lends a certain visual tension to the picture. It is this fine balance between the clarity of the graphic elements

A2.26 Solarisation of Figure A2.21.

A2.27 Solarisation of Figure A2.18.

and the insubstantial visibility of the image that makes the photo–graphic approach so intriguing.

The modification of the image need not end here, although this was the stage at which I was pleased with the pictorial image, and enlarged it into a limited edition print. Further manipulation is possi-

ble by harnessing the somewhat fickle photographic phenomenon of Sabattier, which yielded Figure A2.26. Accordingly, this presents another way in which graphical qualities can be introduced in photo images. The technique can be applied to film from any of the previous stages. For example, the solar-

A2.28 Combination of high-contrast photo–graphic image with a solarised background.

A2.29 Combination of a solarised photo–graphic image with a high-contrast background.

isation of the original photo–graphic image is shown in Figure A2.27. The facial image is not so readily visible in this picture as there is too much uniformity throughout the pattern. However, the possibilities are greatly increased when film from an inter-

mediate stage is rendered in line form by the Sabattier process, and then combined with other high-contrast components. Two examples of this are shown here (Figures A2.28 and A2.29).

The modification of the image can go even

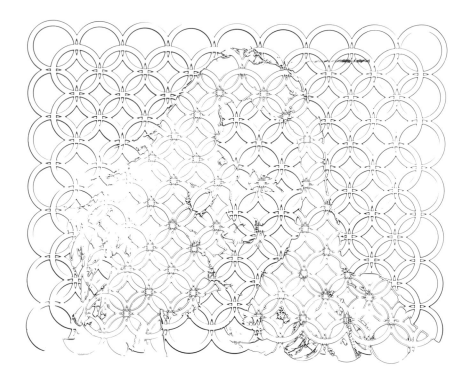

A2.30 Solarisation of Figure A2.29.

further still, as the solarised combinations can themselves be solarised. Figure A2.30 was derived from Figure A2.29. Where the black-and-white, high-contrast areas meet in A2.29 a single Mackie line is formed. However, a thin black line on the developing film will form a pair of fine Mackie lines either side of it following the fogging procedure, as can be seen in the central region of Figure A2.30. While the line effects that are produced are very delicate, the image of the face tends to be lost, or it is only visible because of its familiarity from the previous pictures.

All the processes that have been described above have been carried out on film. Reducing a full-tone negative to lith film is often thought of as a simplifying process, but it is clear that very subtle effects can be obtained using high-contrast materials. It is only when some satisfactory pictorial image has been produced that it is normally printed on paper, and it usually looks much better when it is enlarged. The end result is, of course, critically dependent on both the photo and graphic images you start with and the ways in which they are altered. As with all image manipulation techniques, whatever the medium, the problems are not determined solely by what you can do, but rather when you should stop. My own interests are not primarily in the techniques of photo–graphics; they are more concerned with using them to tap the subtleties and complexities of our vision. The photo–graphic images pose perceptual paradoxes by being two different things at the same time. Usually we are aware of one aspect initially and then gain the visual appreciation of the other facet by more protracted observation.

Bibliography

General

Seeley, J. (1980). *High contrast*. New York: Van Nostrand Reinhold. This excellent and imaginative book by an artist, printmaker and photographer describes the range of black-and-white high-contrast applications and their combination with some graphic techniques. The basic darkroom procedures are introduced and then the following manipulative methods are described: lithograms; texture screens; Sabattier; and other line image techniques. The final section is concerned with photomontage – combining a sequence of manipulated high-contrast images. Throughout, the illustrations are an example of clarity, and many of Seeley's own ingenious photo–graphic designs are reproduced; of particular interest are pictures from *The Stripe Portfolio*.

Stone, J. (Ed.) (1979). *Darkroom dynamics. A guide to creative darkroom techniques*. London: Newnes Technical Books. A collection of chapters by photographers specialising in areas of image manipulation. Those most closely related to this study are by Craig on the Sabattier effect, by Laytin on infra-red film, by Ranalli on photograms, by Seeley on high-contrast techniques, and by Dutton on photomontage.

Additional

Albarn, K., Smith, J. M., Steele, S., & Walker, D. (1974). *The language of pattern*. London: Thames & Hudson. This book is primarily about the interplay between visual aesthetics and geometry. The authors are designers who have explored the intricacies of Islamic interlaced patterns. They describe and illustrate how patterns of this type can be built up and broken down.

Gillon, E. V. (1969). *Geometric design and ornament*. New York: Dover. A book of several hundred black-and-white designs, both in outline and blocked in. There is no text.

Horemis, S. (1970). *Optical and geometrical patterns and designs*. New York: Dover. Over 90 designs by the artist Spyros Horemis are shown, some of which are in colour. The text is very brief because "words about art and design stand a little incidental to the works they talk about".

Hornung, C. P. (1976). *Background patterns, textures and tints*. New York: Dover. A collection of good quality designs from regular gratings, dots and squares to random textures. There is no text.

Lancaster, J. (1973). *Introducing op art*. London: Batsford. Op art is initially related to mathematics, music, psychology and abstract art. A series of projects involving simple pattern elements is followed by a cursory analysis of vision. Finally op is placed in the broader context of art history.

Magnus, G. H. (1986). *Graphic techniques for designers and illustrators*. New York: Barron's Educational. An introductory guide to the materials and methods of graphic design. The most relevant sections are those concerned with drawing techniques and the use of overlay screens.

Ouchi, H. (1977). *Japanese optical and geometrical art*. New York: Dover. A large collection of black-and-white op art patterns, without any commentary. There is little (other than the title) to suggest any differences between Eastern and Western approaches to this genre.

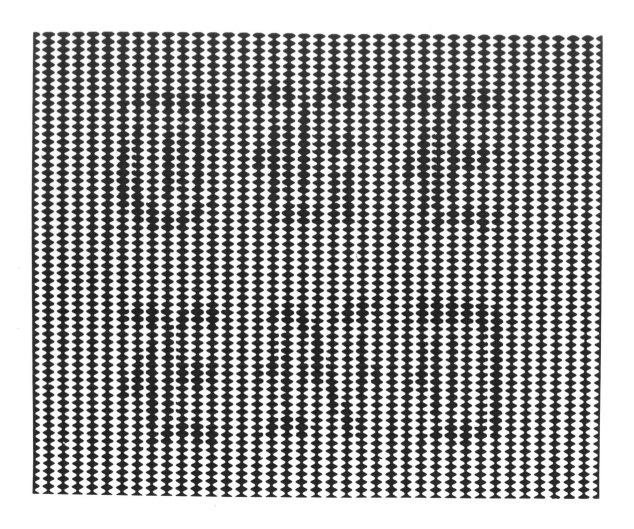

AUTHOR INDEX

SUBJECT INDEX

Entries in italics refer to illustrations.